Principles that Shape English Teacher Education

Principles that Shape English Teacher Education

Pedagogy for Innovation and Change

Edited by
Jessica R. Gallo, Christopher M. Parsons,
and Heidi L. Hallman

ROWMAN & LITTLEFIELD
Lanham • Boulder • New York • London

Published by Rowman & Littlefield
An imprint of The Rowman & Littlefield Publishing Group, Inc.
4501 Forbes Boulevard, Suite 200, Lanham, Maryland 20706
www.rowman.com

86-90 Paul Street, London EC2A 4NE

Copyright © 2024 by Jessica R. Gallo, Christopher M. Parsons, and Heidi L. Hallman

All rights reserved. No part of this book may be reproduced in any form or by any electronic or mechanical means, including information storage and retrieval systems, without written permission from the publisher, except by a reviewer who may quote passages in a review.

British Library Cataloguing in Publication Information Available

Library of Congress Cataloging-in-Publication Data

Names: Gallo, Jessica R., editor. | Parsons, Christopher (Christopher M.), editor. | Hallman, Heidi L., 1976- editor.
Title: Principles that shape English teacher education: pedagogy for innovation and change / edited by Jessica R. Gallo, Christopher Parsons and Heidi L. Hallman.
Description: Lanham, Maryland: Rowman & Littlefield, [2024] | Includes bibliographical references and index. | Summary: "This book examines practices that illustrate the principles that guide English educators' teaching of the English Language Arts Methods course. By including both theory and practice, this book attends to current realities and potential futures of the field"—Provided by publisher.
Identifiers: LCCN 2023041417 (print) | LCCN 2023041418 (ebook) | ISBN 9781475868975 (cloth) | ISBN 9781475868982 (paperback) | ISBN 9781475868999 (ebook)
Subjects: LCSH: English teachers—Training of. | English language—Study and teaching.
Classification: LCC PE1066.P75 2024 (print) | LCC PE1066 (ebook) | DDC 428.0071—dc23/eng/20231019
LC record available at https://lccn.loc.gov/2023041417
LC ebook record available at https://lccn.loc.gov/2023041418

Principles that Shape English Teacher Education Pedagogy for Innovation and Change

Contents

Acknowledgments ix

Introduction: Within and Beyond Our Beliefs as
English Teacher Educators 1
Christopher M. Parsons and Jessica R. Gallo

1. Revisiting Reflection with Dialogic Partners in Methods Courses 11
   Amber Jensen

2. Designed for Dissonance: Embracing Teacher Candidate Field
   Experiences as Dissonant Spaces 25
   Christopher M. Parsons

3. Uniting Preservice Teachers and Pedagogical Thinking 37
   Melanie Shoffner

4. An Argument about Argument Writing: Taking a Stance on
   the Five-Paragraph Essay 49
   Mike Metz

5. The English Classroom as a Contested Space: Fostering Critical
   Dialogue and Antiracist English Language Arts Practices 61
   Hilary Lochte and Kristen Pastore-Capuana

6. Planning Units to Work Within and Subvert the System by
   Critically Viewing Canonical Texts through Literature Circles 75
   Julie Bell

7. Using Text Sets and Mini-Lessons to Develop Sense of Authority
   as Teachers of Reading 87
   Allison Wynhoff Olsen and William J. Fassbender

8	English Pedagogy through Critical Lenses: Empowering English Teachers as Agents of Change *Katharine Covino*	101
9	Figuring Out the Path Forward Together: The Power of Collaborative Reflection and Problem-Posing in Field-Based English Language Arts Teacher Education *Michelle Fowler-Amato*	115
10	Using the NCTE SPA Program Review as a Catalyst for Change: Moving Beyond the Methods Course *Lara Searcy*	127
11	The Impact of Policies that Promote the Science of Reading on English Teacher Preparation *William Kerns*	137
12	NCTE/ELATE Beliefs Meet Economic Realities: The Struggle to Prepare Students Facing Financial Challenges *Jeremy Glazer and Emily Wender*	149
13	Pre- and Corequisite Content Knowledge and Pedagogy Development: Antiracist Future English Teachers *Christian Z. Goering and Holly Sheppard Riesco*	161
14	Beyond the Book: Expanding Critical Connective Literacies between Students and Authors on Social Media *Nora Peterman and Connor K. Warner*	173
15	Debating the Discourse of *Professionalism* with Preservice English Teachers *Heidi L. Hallman*	185
Index		199
About the Authors		205

Acknowledgments

The editors and authors of this book are deeply indebted to the consistent conversations and work of the ELATE Commission for Methods Teaching and Learning. The Methods Commission membership—both past and present—has been a source of inspiration, from the echoing ballrooms of conference meetings to the Zoom sessions of the pandemic. So, while the contents of this book will be of interest to everyone who cares how English teachers are prepared, we hope the Methods Commission finds this book to be a familiar space, a mini-conference meet-up you can hold in your hand.

Introduction

Within and Beyond Our Beliefs as English Teacher Educators

Christopher M. Parsons and Jessica R. Gallo

This edited collection focuses on the ways English teacher educators design Methods of Teaching English courses and field experiences. Within, experienced methods and field instructors lay out the frameworks, practices, theories, and research that guide their instruction. These approaches certainly exist within broader programs of English teacher education (e.g., English content coursework, other teacher education courses, external licensure, and testing requirements); however, methods courses and field experiences form the ideological and practical core for the preparation of new English teachers.

As such, this book might serve as a starting place for a new methods or field instructor. It might help a more experienced instructor think through or refresh their own established practices. It might raise questions for researchers seeking to learn more about how beginning English teachers train and develop. Regardless, we hope the deep experience and careful thought contained in these chapters are both useful and inspirational—one part "what could I do tomorrow?" and one part "why am I doing this at all?"

Each chapter has roots, inspiration, and/or a point of contrast from a common source. In May 2020, the English Language Arts Teacher Educators (ELATE) Commission on Methods Teaching and Learning published a Position Statement, "Beliefs about Methods Courses and Field Experiences in English Education." The Beliefs Statement, deeply revised from an original 2005 version, was first released on the National Council of Teachers of English website (https://ncte.org/statement/methodsinee/) and later reprinted with a handful of supporting assignments in the January 2021 issue of the journal *English Education*. Readers can find the text of the Beliefs Statement at the end of this introduction. While six members of the Commission served as Statement authors, the entire Commission collaborated, offering feedback and critique over email and in conference center ballrooms.

It was a delightful challenge to put words to some of our most closely held beliefs about our work as methods and field instructors, and each chapter in this book is authored by a member of the Methods Commission. One premise of using the Beliefs Statement as an orienting touchpoint is the acknowledgment that it is important to know what we are about as English teacher educators—and that we do not do this work alone. All times in teacher education have probably appeared fraught, but especially in a volatile landscape of teacher burnout and shortages, of divisive concepts laws and teacher bounties, of recent learning disruptions and long-standing inequities, a statement of belief seemed timely.

But, shared beliefs about how to design methods courses and field experiences, like any educational practices, must be provisional. Many of the chapters in this book push against and beyond the ideas outlined in the Beliefs Statement. For good reason. Jargon like "best practice" and "high-impact practice" have entered the educational discourse as shorthand for a top-down, uncritical approach to teacher education: "It is a well-acknowledged best practice to do X"—so you better do it. One of the great limitations of belief and position statements can be that impulse toward universality regardless of variation, and each of the authors in this collection comes from a different (sometimes vastly so) context for English teacher education.

Even the idea of "belief" itself in a professional community is rarely fixed or united. The word "belief" should raise the question "whose beliefs?" and a consideration of who is and is not involved in the conversation. Even the shared beliefs that are present are constantly shifting. As a Commission member noted in a meeting, once we write down a belief, we have almost already moved past it, a sort of Heisenberg uncertainty principle for measuring shared ideas about English teacher education. This uncertainty of belief is, for one, temporal: by the time we write, revise, and publish something, the conversation has moved along. But the uncertainty is also process-based: once one writes something down in print, it offers us a fixed target on which to sharpen or to generate our own ideas.

Thus, our work is to hold onto something that resists being pinned to one place, or document, or time. The Beliefs Statement captures a moment, and even as we look to it for guidance and support to advocate for what we hold dear in our work as English educators, we see the spaces that allow for new directions and new practices.

While we embrace the inclination to push against the permanence of the Beliefs Statement, we also acknowledge the important role that such a document plays in our professional lives. There are many aspects of our work as English educators that we return to repeatedly, despite the changes to the educational landscape, not because these are the only closely held beliefs, but because the Beliefs Statement represents an element of unity across our varied contexts.

For many English educators, the work we do as scholars can feel isolating. Those of us in small teacher education programs might be the only voice for English education at an institution. English educators who are primarily field-based can feel disconnected from professional networks as we work everywhere and nowhere all at once. And many of us feel the pressure of budget constraints and increased calls to seek external funding in a field that typically has little access to state and national grants.

In these cases and many others, a document like the Beliefs Statement can provide much-needed support as we advocate for our programs and practices to a wide range of stakeholders. We lean on the Beliefs Statement as a collective document written by experts when we need the support of a group to advocate for our approaches. In the Beliefs Statement, we find inspiration and validation from our English education colleagues when we feel as though we are going it alone. And we point to the Beliefs Statement as a public statement of the importance of our work and evidence of practices that decades of research has shown to be effective in our particular field.

For all its possible constraints as we grow and change as a field, the Beliefs Statement can provide the stability we need when so much of our work faces scrutiny from within and without.

The Beliefs Statement is not only a collection of practices and ideals for teaching the ELA methods course and its connected fieldwork. It is a call to action, a statement of our collective desire to always consider where we have come from, whose shoulders we stand on, and where we are going next as a field. It is a document designed for advocacy so that we may call on experts who have tread these paths before us even as we work to forge new pathways for our own expertise. It is an invitation, a set of practices and principles that support new scholars in the field and provide opportunities for innovation and creativity.

Beyond providing guidance about how to approach our teaching of methods courses and field experiences, the chapters in this book are designed to raise questions about how we collaborate with and advocate for the people within our ecosystem. What is our role as English educators in supporting cooperating teachers, often uncompensated partners in teacher education? How do we account for the time and space we believe are central to developing excellent teachers while also acknowledging the financial burden these principles place on prospective teachers? How do we reckon with the racist and violent history of linguistic and literary traditions in ELA, many of which still predominate in school policy and practice, and prepare our prospective teachers to envision and enact liberatory practices? And what can we do as

English educators to sustain prospective teachers as they do the hard work of creating change in school systems and states that resist efforts toward justice?

The chapters in this volume capture practices and principles that begin to answer many of these challenging questions. In chapter 1, Amber Jensen shares findings from a three-year study of preservice teachers' dialogic learning logs to show that peer conversations can be an important source of support for preservice teachers' developing agency, identity, and reflection. Because the ecosystem of English teacher education is inherently complex, teacher candidates can sometimes feel a disconnect between the theoretical world of their English education programs and the practical world of their field experiences. In chapter 2, Christopher M. Parsons proposes we foreground that dissonance to prepare future teachers to be both critical and thoughtful.

Next, the book moves into a series of chapters that showcase assignments from methods courses. Chapter 3, by Melanie Shoffner, describes one English educator's approach to developing preservice teachers' pedagogical content knowledge through a series of assignments centered on young adult literature. In chapter 4, Mike Metz describes how he helps his teacher candidates critically examine the structure and purpose of the traditional five-paragraph essay. Chapter 5, by Hilary Lochte and Kristen Pastore-Capuana, describes an extensive course redesign with the goals of centering antiracist and antibias pedagogies in their Methods of Teaching Language course. Through descriptions of several course assignments, Lochte and Pastore-Capuana share strategies for increasing linguistic and cultural relevance for preservice teachers.

Discussion and use of texts are featured in the next series of chapters. Chapter 6, by Julie Bell, describes how teacher candidates have the opportunity to explore diverse texts through discussion with their colleagues. The chapter addresses the rationale, implementation, and successes/challenges of unit planning around literature circle texts in an ELA methods course. Chapter 7, by Allison Wynhoff Olsen and William J. Fassbender, focuses on a signature assignment in an undergraduate Teaching Reading and Literature course. This chapter details the assignment approach and uses preservice teacher-created text sets to illustrate how preservice teachers embrace the place-based and social justice content from previous courses and learn to incorporate it within a reading context. Finally, Katharine Covino's chapter 8 prompts readers to consider how methods of coursework should be designed to support teacher candidates in becoming critical, agentic, active, ethical, reflective, and socially just educators. Through engaging in discussion of literature, this chapter asks readers to consider the way methods courses can do this work.

Bridging in-class assignments with field experiences has always been a component of methods coursework. Chapter 9, by Michelle Fowler-Amato, explores the design of an online field experience tied to the Teaching Composition, Grades 6–12 course. In this course, preservice teachers were invited to partner with their methods instructor's first-year writing students. In chapter 10, Lara Searcy takes a view of a Methods course from a broad perspective, exploring how the Specialized Program Assessment (SPA) accreditation process can prompt innovative program change. More than just accreditation, the SPA process has the potential to prompt methods instructors to reconsider curricular choices and structures.

The next series of chapters continues to pursue the theme of a broad view of methods coursework. Chapter 11, by William Kerns, examines the impact of debates around the science of reading for the preparation of English teachers and offers guidance to programs and methods courses preparing teachers in states where the science of reading-based policies hold sway. The following chapter 12, by Jeremy Glazer and Emily Wender, pushes English teacher educators to consider teacher candidate financial constraints in enacting the tenets of the Beliefs Statement—and offers recommendations for doing so.

Chapter 13, by Christian Z. Goering and Holly Sheppard Riesco, shares strategies for methods courses and English teacher education programs to engage candidates in the antiracism and antibias threads from the *2021 NCTE Standards for Initial Preparation of English Language Arts Teachers, Grades 7–12*. The following chapter 14, by Nora Peterman and Connor K. Warner, explores the promise of teacher candidates' interaction with young adult (YA) literature authors' social media presence as a way to benefit from author interaction and expand ideas about the reading of, and interaction with, different types of text. The concluding chapter 15, by Heidi L. Hallman, uses historically shifting models of teacher professionalism to frame teacher candidate perspectives on their emergence as professionals in the field and to make recommendations about how methods courses can facilitate their reflections about professionalism.

We believe that there is something for every English educator contained in these pages, from those of us preparing to teach our first English Methods course to those of us whose work has shaped the field for years. As editors, we look forward to the continuing conversations about how the Beliefs Statement and the practices in this book can provide inspiration, advocacy, and collaboration for preparing prospective English teachers.

BELIEFS ABOUT METHODS COURSES AND FIELD EXPERIENCES IN ENGLISH EDUCATION

Originally developed in July 2005, this statement, formerly known as What Do We Know and Believe about the Roles of Methods Courses and Field Experiences in English Education? *was updated in April 2020 by members of the ELATE Commission on Methods Teaching and Learning.*

OVERVIEW

Methods courses within English language arts teacher education programs focus on the representation and teaching of English language arts content. Because of their focus on pedagogy, Methods courses often include a concurrent field experience. This Beliefs Statement presents key recommendations that guide the theoretical and practical purposes of Methods courses and their related field experiences in preparing teacher candidates to teach ELA at the secondary (U.S. grades 9–12) and middle (U.S. grades 6–8) school levels. While there is no "best" way to teach a Methods course, it is important to understand how context, content, disposition of the instructor, the course's situation within a program, the demands of local schools, state requirements, student characteristics, and other factors affect instructors and students (Smagorinsky and Whiting, 1995; Pasternak et al., 2018).

This Beliefs Statement focuses narrowly on the Methods of Teaching English course(s) and concomitant field experiences. Importantly, English Methods courses exist within, and must react to, a dynamic English teacher education ecosystem with influences from without (e.g., changing national and state accreditation standards) and within (e.g., candidates' other courses in a specific teacher education program). Programs must help candidates make explicit connections between courses in English Methods, English content area, and the education major, as well as develop concepts of teaching and learning, content knowledge, content pedagogy, knowledge about learners and learning, and professional knowledge and skills. All to say, Methods courses cannot (and should not) do it all; however, they necessarily adapt to the programs in which they are delivered.

This Beliefs Statement articulates core recommendations for Methods courses and concomitant field experiences. These core recommendations represent what we know and believe based on research in the fields of English education and teacher education. Pasternak et al.'s (2018) study of English teacher education programs across the United States breaks new ground in our knowledge of Methods courses. They found that five "focal areas" (156) shape English teacher education programs today. These areas include (1) field experiences, (2) preparation for racial, cultural, and linguistic diversity, (3) new technologies, (4) content area literacy, and (5) K-12 content standards and assessments. These new areas of emphasis function as focal points within programs, thereby urging programs to innovate around them. With this research in mind, the goal of the Beliefs Statement is to be usefully general; that is, the core recommendations articulate principles and practices for designing excellent Methods courses (e.g., field experiences should be scaffolded based on candidate development) without insisting on a specific manner of delivery (e.g., a "rounds" model vs. extended time in one classroom).

Dimension 1: Methods Coursework

English language arts Methods coursework plays an integral role in shaping both the landscape of our field and the professional lives of prospective English teachers. Coursework must support teacher candidates in developing a deep understanding of not only *what* to teach in English language arts curricula but also *how* to approach our work as English language arts teachers in our classrooms and as part of an engaged professional community. Further, English language arts Methods coursework must empower candidates to be teachers who work for social transformation because "preparing English teachers is part of the larger effort to imagine and create a more just and democratic society" (Alsup et al., 2006, p. 285). Current and foundational research in the field supports the following recommendations for teaching English language arts Methods courses.

Core Recommendations

- Methods coursework should examine the broad, evolving landscape of the field of English education. Coursework should provide candidates with opportunities to understand the historical, social, political, global, and economic influences that shape our work as English teachers.
- Methods coursework should explore the nature of teaching and learning. Instructors can do this, in part, by supporting teacher candidates to understand that teaching and learning are social practices that impact and are impacted by the communities in which they are situated.
- Methods coursework should emphasize the diversity of literacies, texts, and learners that constitute our field and our work as English language arts teachers. To do this, coursework must support teacher candidates in attending to the cultural backgrounds of students and choosing texts and learning opportunities that nurture students' unique literacies.
- Methods coursework should prepare candidates to become engaged and effective teachers who can plan, implement, assess, and articulate rationales for pedagogical choices.
- Methods coursework should foster candidates' professional identity development. Coursework should be designed to support teacher candidates in becoming critical, agentic, active, ethical, reflective, and socially just educators.

Dimension 2: Field Experiences

We define field experiences as any work required of English teacher candidates by their preparation programs that take place outside of the college or university classroom. Common examples of field experiences are structured observation of a master teacher, facilitation of students' small group work, or enactment of a full lesson plan. English language arts Methods courses often have field experiences associated with them, but not all field experiences are connected to Methods courses. Field experiences are necessarily idiosyncratic (Zeichner and Conklin, 2008; Pasternak et al., 2018). For example, programs might prioritize a "rounds" model or extended time in one classroom. Ultimately, programs establish partnerships with local schools, communities, and families and design clinically rich field placement opportunities for candidates based on factors such as program structure and philosophy, local school contexts, and placement availability; however, current and foundational research in the field supports the following recommendations for Methods-based field experiences.

Core Recommendations

- Field experiences should begin as early as possible in the program and should be designed in a manner that candidates take on increasing responsibility as they gain pedagogical expertise and experience in the field. Traditionally, field experiences begin with active observation and culminate in the full assumption of teaching duties during the student teaching semester(s).
- Field experiences must prepare English teacher candidates for many and diverse contexts and with awareness of the richness and variety of the profession as a whole; therefore, field experiences should connect candidates to the widest available variety of students, teachers, schools, and communities (e.g., middle and high school, more and less visible community diversity). That said, field placements should, ideally, also offer field experience in a context resonant with likely first teaching jobs.
- Field experiences require that cooperating teachers function in many roles: they model effective teaching; they instruct candidates in the planning, delivery, and assessment of English language arts curricula; they evaluate candidates' developing pedagogical skill and professional dispositions; they mentor candidates into the professional community of English teachers. It is crucial to recruit, professionally develop, and compensate excellent cooperating teachers.
- Field experiences require that field instructors observe, cocreate knowledge with, and assess candidates. Field instructors should create opportunities for structured conversation and reflection that connect candidates' college or university coursework with their field experiences.
- English teacher education programs should structure opportunities for candidates to reflect on, unpack, and learn from their field experiences. Examples

of such opportunities are field experience seminars, guided debriefing sessions with field instructors and/or cooperating teachers, and/or professional learning community meetings.

NCTE STATEMENTS INFORMING THIS DOCUMENT

Conference on English Education. 2005. *What do we know and believe about the roles of methods courses and field experiences in English education?* Accessed November 17, 2018. http://www2.ncte.org/statement/roleofmethodsinee/

National Council of Teachers of English/Council for the Accreditation for Educator Preparation. 2012. *NCTE/NCATE Standards for Initial Preparation of Teachers of Secondary English Language Arts, Grades 7–12.* Accessed July 19, 2019. http://www.ncte.org/cee/caep.

National Council of Teachers of English/International Reading Association. 1996. *Standards for the English language arts.* National Council of Teachers of English; International Reading Association. Accessed July 3, 2019.

RESEARCH SUPPORTING THIS STATEMENT

Alsup, J., Emig, J., Pradl, G., Tremmel, R., and Yagelski, R. (2006). The state of English education and a vision for its future: A call to arms. *English Education* 38 (4), 278–94.

Anagnostopoulos, D., Smith, E., and Basmadjian, K.G. (2007). Bridging the university-school divide: Horizontal expertise and the "two-worlds pitfall." *Journal of Teacher Education* 58 (2), 138–52.

Bain, R. B. and Moje, E. B. (2012). Mapping the teacher education terrain for novices. *Phi Delta Kappan, 93*(5), 62–5.

Beach, R., Appleman, D., Fecho, B., and Simon, R. (2016). *Teaching literature to adolescents* (3rd ed.). Routledge.

Brass, J. and Webb, A. (Eds.). (2015). *Reclaiming English language arts methods courses: Critical issues and challenges for teacher educators in top-down times.* Routledge.

Cercone, J. (2015). Communities of practice: Bridging the gap between methods courses and secondary schools. In J. Brass and A. Webb (Eds.), *Reclaiming English language arts methods courses: Critical issues and challenges for teacher educators in top-down times* (pp. 109–22). Routledge.

Goldhaber, D., Krieg, J. M., and Theobald, R. (2017). Does the match matter? Exploring whether student teaching experiences affect teacher effectiveness. *American Educational Research Journal, 54*(2), 325–59.

Grossman, P., Ronfeldt, M., and Cohen, J. (2011). The power of setting: The role of field experience in learning to teach. In K. Harris, S. Graham, T. Urdan, A. Bus, S. Major, and H. L. Swanson (Eds.), *American Psychological Association (APA) educational psychology handbook, Vol. 3: Applications to teaching and learning* (pp. 311–34). American Psychological Association.

Morgan, D. N. and Pytash, K. E. (2014). Preparing preservice teachers to become teachers of writing: A 20-year review of the research literature. *English Education, 47*(1), 6–37.

Roskelly, H. (2005). Still bridges to build: English education's pragmatic agenda. *English Education, 37*(4), 288–95.

Paris, D. and Alim, S. (2017). *Culturally sustaining pedagogies: Teaching and learning for justice in a changing world.* Teachers College Press.

Pasternak, D. L., Caughlan, S., Hallman, H. L., Renzi, L., and Rush, L. S. (2018). *Secondary English teacher education in the United States.* Bloomsbury Academic.

Ronfeldt, M. (2015). Field placement schools and instructional effectiveness. *Journal of Teacher Education, 66*(4), 304–20.

Ronfeldt, M., Brockman, S. L., and Campbell, H. L. (2018). Does cooperating teachers' instructional effectiveness improve preservice teachers' future performance? *Educational Researcher, 47*(7), 405–18.

Smagorinsky, P., Rhym, D., and Moore, C. P. (2013). Competing centers of gravity: A beginning English teacher's socialization process within conflictual settings. *English Education, 45*(2), 147–82.

Smagorinsky, P. and Whiting, M. E. (1995). *How English teachers get taught: Methods of teaching the methods class.* National Council of Teachers of English.

Zancanella, D. and Alsup, J. (2010). English education program assessment: Creating standards and guidelines to advance English teacher preparation. *English Education, 43*(1), 65–71.

Zeichner, K. and Conklin, H. (2008). Teacher education programs as sites for teacher preparation. In M. Cochran-Smith, S. Feiman-Nesmer, D. J. McIntyre and K. E. Demers (Eds.), *Handbook of research on teacher education* (3rd ed., pp. 269–89). Routledge.

STATEMENT AUTHORS

Jessica R. Gallo, University of Nevada, Reno
Heidi L. Hallman, University of Kansas
Christopher M. Parsons, Keene State College
Kristen Pastore-Capuana, Buffalo State College
Sue Ringler Pet, Independent Scholar
Lara Searcy, Northeastern State University

Chapter 1

Revisiting Reflection with Dialogic Partners in Methods Courses

Amber Jensen

Because developing reflective practitioners is a goal of English teacher educators, reflection activities feature prominently in methods courses and field experiences. Scholars note that reflection helps teachers develop professional identities, negotiate tensions, and foster ongoing learning (Korthagen and Vasalos, 2006; Smagorinsky et al., 2015). Reflection assignments prompted by English educators might invite preservice teachers to draw on course readings as they navigate teaching decisions or develop teaching philosophies, for example. Mentor teachers and university supervisors engage with preservice teachers in formal and informal reflective conversations about teaching practice throughout field experiences.

Typically, the act of reflection for preservice teachers is elicited as an assignment by a supervisory figure who is the sole audience and respondent. Effective teachers, by contrast, reflect regularly in conversation with colleagues in professional communities (Gallagher and Kittle, 2018). The challenge in teacher education, then, is to create opportunities for preservice teachers to engage in reflective practice that puts them in dialogue with other preservice teachers, who, while also novices, are their most proximate peers.

This chapter considers the role of dialogic reflection in accomplishing two major tenets of the ELA methods course described in the NCTE Statement *Beliefs about Methods Courses and Field Experiences in English Education* (Gallo et al., 2020). First, how might dialogic reflection *support teacher candidates in developing deep understandings of how to approach [their] work as English language art teachers in [their] classrooms?* And second, what dialogic reflective practices help preservice teachers participate *as part of an engaged professional community?*

To answer these questions, the author and a research team of graduate students conducted a three-year study on thirty-nine undergraduate preservice

English teachers across three academic cohorts of ELA methods classes at a private university in the western United States. Findings show that revising reflection assignments to engage preservice teachers in reflective dialogue with each other activated their professional identities, helped them critically reflect upon various approaches to teaching ELA, and gave them practice engaging in a professional community. Developing habits of reflection and collaboration will elevate preservice teachers' ability to connect coursework with teaching practice, in turn shaping decisions they make as professionals.

THEORETICAL FRAMEWORK

Dialogism and Reflection

The practice of dialogic reflection among preservice teachers exists at the intersection of the two foundational frameworks after which it is named: dialogic theory and reflective practice. Dialogism recognizes the importance of multiple voices and experiences in socially constructed and culturally shared meaning-making (Bakhtin, 1994; Fecho et al., 2010). Caughlan and Juzwik (2014) defined dialogism in English classrooms as "learning talk that promotes the interaction of various voices in grappling with the concepts and the genre of the discipline over time" (p. 85).

In the ELA methods course and field experiences, preservice teachers draw from their diverse experiences, multiple identities, developing beliefs about teaching and English, and actions (or inactions) in both university and secondary classrooms to consider ideas about teaching. As preservice teachers learn about, observe, and enact teaching, they may be in dialogue with themselves about these ideas across their identities and positionalities. They may also be in dialogue with others (mentor teachers, university professors, teacher colleagues, each other) as they make meaning of their experiences.

Over the past thirty years, various models of reflective practice have taken hold in teacher learning (Schön, 1987; Shulman, 1987). Pairing experiential learning with critical analysis is at the heart of field experiences; by doing, reflecting, and planning, prospective teachers begin to think as agentive professionals. Reflection is a practice sometimes enacted individually, in pairs, or with mentors. However in teacher education, reflection is often activated by course assignments such as teaching journals or lesson reflections written for supervisors or for professional certification.

Dialogism and reflection are symbiotic practices that serve teachers: dialogic interactions foster a range of perspectives and positionalities, and reflection offers frameworks for making sense of teaching and learning experiences. Zeichner and Liston's (1996) critical reflection model is particularly useful in conjunction with dialogic theory. To enact critical reflection, practitioners must identify and critique the ways their own and others' sociocultural histories, identities, and contexts shape their beliefs, experiences, and actions. Without acknowledging systems of power and hierarchies, as Zeichner and Liston argue, teachers will not be able to fully understand the multivalent dynamics at play within schools and among teachers, learners, and communities.

Dialogic reflection between at least two preservice teachers, then, engages them beyond their own limited context and experiences as they determine who they are as professionals, what they believe about teaching English, and how they might engage with a wider professional field. If dialogic interaction surfaces a range of viewpoints on course readings, field experiences, prior learning, and other factors relevant to developing a teacher's identity and teaching beliefs, it can become a powerful way to critical reflection.

Identity Discourses and Identity Development

Reflection and dialogism are useful tools in making sense of the identity shifts preservice teachers experience as they occupy space in both universities and secondary schools. Hallman (2015) borrowed the term "shape-shifter" (Gee, 2004) to highlight how millennial teachers, in particular, negotiate their teacher identities through changing contexts, expectations, and beliefs.

Preservice teachers also have to balance contradictory demands placed upon them by institutions, mentors, colleagues, students, administration, parents, public perception, and academic tradition. Smagorinsky et al. (2013) noted that these "competing centers of gravity" pull at preservice teachers in ways that demand they make sense of their beliefs, values, and identities as teachers within multiple worlds.

Alsup (2019) coined the term "balancing discourse" to signify how teachers make sense of the identity complications and contradictions they experience. Balancing discourses "reflect contradictions between local and global concerns, practice and theory, and authority and vulnerability" (p. 102). Externalizing the discourses wherein preservice teachers make sense of the tensions inherent in themselves, their teaching and learning contexts, and their ideas about their students and about teaching English, is essential to teachers' identity development.

DIALOGIC LEARNING LOG: THE ASSIGNMENT

The dialogical learning log (DLL) (Falter, 2019; Alford and Jensen, 2021) emerged as a way to help preservice teachers critically consider their emergent teaching identities alongside the shifting nature of the fields of education and literacy. English educators have used the DLL assignment at various stages—during ELA methods courses, practicum, and student teaching—to develop preservice teachers' reflection through collaboration in a professional community. In ongoing reflective discussions throughout the semester (or longer), two or more students draw on and synthesize learning from university coursework, field experiences, and other relevant "centers of gravity" as a way to develop and challenge their beliefs and identities.

At least weekly, students dialogue with each other through their choice of written, audio, and/or visual modes. Their logs become discursive spaces for students to reflect on, challenge, and extend course readings, class discussions, field experiences, and their developing teaching philosophies and identities. Details about the expectations and procedures of the DLL the author has used in her undergraduate ELA methods courses for the past three years are included in excerpts from the assignment sheet (figure 1.1).

Dialogic Learning Log

Dialogic Learning Logs (DLLs) are designed for you and a partner to dialogue about your learning and evolution as teachers in a way that will be meaningful to you both now and into your early careers.

Your Task   Compose your dialogues in any genre of your choosing. Consider how teachers in the field communicate about teaching and learning.

Participate in an ongoing conversation for at least **10 of 14 weeks** in the semester. Partners will alternate weekly who posts first and who posts second.
- **Partner A should initiate the week's conversation**, including reflections about the week's readings, as well as about any relevant other course activities, including field experiences.
- **Partner B should respond to the post**, adding insights gained from class discussion and their own field experiences and class activities.

Be sure you are *in dialogue* with each other rather than posting two parallel but unconnected responses. Logs should draw upon the following:
- Course readings
- Field experiences (interactions, teaching, planning)
- Professional communities and conversations
- Class activities and discussions

The dialogic learning log is open-ended. You are encouraged to bring diverse approaches to the table. If you need inspiration, try reflecting on the following:
- Points you agree or disagree with and why
- Connections to prior readings, images, videos, audio files, etc.
- Personal experience as a student or from working with students
- Questions arising from readings or coursework
- Quotations (with citations) and explanations of why that quotation is meaningful, troubling, inspiring, thought-provoking to you
- Applications you see to your future life as a teacher

Figure 1.1   **Dialogical Log Assignment Sheet (excerpt).**

METHODOLOGY

Across three cohorts of undergraduate English teaching majors and minors enrolled in the ELA methods course, a total of twenty dialogic partnerships participated in the DLL assignment. Groups of two or three were determined by the methods course instructor (this chapter's author) with input from the students. Although students chose the medium through which they communicated, the majority opted to correspond using a shared Google document—only two of the pairs, both in the fall 2020 cohort, used video (FlipGrid and Marco Polo) for their DLLs.

An initial round of coding DLL transcripts for types and purposes of reflection led to the selection of three sets of partners—one from each cohort—as case studies. These groups were chosen because the modes of their reflections and the diversity of their teaching placements highlight the range of ways students engaged with each other through this assignment.

Across the three partnerships, the research team examined how participants' engagement in dialogic reflection intersected with their professional identity development and/or their critical understanding of teaching English. The DLL transcripts for each of the case studies were coded based on the following three recommendations from the NCTE *Methods Beliefs Statement*:

1. Methods coursework . . . should be designed to support teacher candidates in becoming critical, agentic, active, ethical, reflective, and socially just educators (Gallo et al., 2020).
2. Field experiences should . . . create opportunities for structured conversation and reflection that connects candidates' college or university coursework with their field experiences (Gallo et al., 2020).
3. Methods coursework should . . . [support] teacher candidates to understand that teaching and learning are social practices that impact and are impacted by the communities in which they are situated (Gallo et al., 2020).

Finally, to understand how the preservice teachers themselves perceived the DLL with regard to their identity development, reflective practice, and emerging beliefs about teaching and learning, the research team used the same three *Beliefs Statement* recommendations to code participants' mid-semester reflections, written in response to the following mid-semester reflection prompt:

In a **one- to two-page mid-semester reflection letter**, you will:

1. Document your progress and describe the process you have used as partners to reflect on your learning and teaching practice this semester.

2. Discuss what you have gained/learned from your dialogical logs about (a) English teaching in theory and practice, (b) yourself as a learner and a teacher, (c) working with a partner, and (d) collaborative writing.
3. Explain your plan moving forward for the rest of the semester with your DLL.

Selected responses from the preservice teachers' mid-point reflection letters, as well as excerpts from DLLs of the three case studies, suggest ways forward for prompting dialogic reflection through the DLL as a methods course assignment.

Enacting the ELA Methods Course *Beliefs Statement*: In Students' Own Words

Becoming Critical, Agentic, Active, Ethical, Reflective, and Socially Just Educators

Two preservice teachers, Kristen and Maile,[1] wrote back and forth in a shared Google Doc during the fall semester of 2019. Although their communications were private, they also experimented with writing in a public-facing genre they might use as teachers: Instagram posts. They referenced each other, members of their cohort, their mentor teachers, their professor, and even the scholars whose work they read in their methods course by made-up Instagram handles (e.g., @mailecruz). Both teachers' practicums were in middle school English classrooms in the same district, formerly quiet agricultural neighborhoods transitioning to suburban commuter communities. Both schools have a primarily white (80 percent) population, with a growing (15 percent) number of Latinx students.

An exchange between Maile and Kristen toward the end of the semester depicts two kinds of reflection the DLL activated for them: Kristen's post reflected on a field experience lesson she taught, while Maile's response extended her thinking about readings and discussion from their methods course. In both cases, the preservice teachers grappled with their conceptions of what it means to be a teacher who enacts the values of student-centered instruction, social justice, and teacher activism they bring into their teaching practices. Their reflection acknowledges where their practices do not yet match their values, as well as what they hope to become and do as they develop as teachers. Their dialogic space activated critical views into the ethics and values that underscore who they are as teachers and professionals.

In her post, Kristen realized that her practicum lesson consisted mostly of teacher-led, whole-group activities rather than interactions with and between individual students. "I'd gone the whole morning without having a conversation with an individual student," she wrote. Even though she had been implementing "the pre-reading strategies we've talked about in 378" (a reading methods class in her teacher education program), she realized in practice a disconnect between her values as a teacher—to help the individual student—and the way she had taught her lesson that day—by standing in front of the group.

Kristen also identified a disconnect between her values as a teacher in her use of differentiation. She remembered it as a concept from her methods courses, admitting that while the idea "still seems an abstract concept to me," she recognized the principle as a way to teach that shows individual learners that she knows "their learning preferences, their strengths and weaknesses" and that she "will help them succeed." Finally, she made a connection to a situation Maile had raised in her previous log: not knowing how to engage a new student, Marco, in her class who spoke very little English.

While Kristen's posts identified the challenge of differentiating individual students' learning needs during a teaching moment, Maile's response engaged a discussion from their methods class relating to the identities and related learning needs students may have. Maile considered her role as a teacher in direct interface with students; she also engaged with the narratives about students that exist beyond the classroom: "I want to take being aware and informed further," she wrote. "I want to work to change the narrative. I want to be able to talk about privilege and circumstance in my classroom. I know that will be one of the first steps in changing the narrative."

Here, Maile's sense of who she was as a teacher included the topics she planned to bring into her instruction, but also her sense of herself as an ethical and activist educator: "I want to think about how these factors play into [my students'] lives and literacies. I am so happy to be more aware and more informed than I was yesterday. I know that I will be a better teacher for knowing."

Kristen's sense of who she was as a teacher really shows up in the mid-semester evaluation which reinforces how the DLL experience likewise activated a teacher identity rooted in agency, critical reflection, and ethical decision-making. She wrote:

> I've learned that I need time to prepare my thoughts before I participate and also time to solidify my thoughts after a learning experience. I am a pretty trusting, believing person, and it's easy for me to just adopt the beliefs of whoever is teaching me. But I've learned through evaluating my experiences in this class that I don't always agree with certain things. I do have my own opinions and values, and I need to take time to see how each new idea fits within my personal framework (constructivism, anyone??) For example, my [mentor teacher] told me all of her ideas about homework, grades, reading logs, etc. I just nodded and agreed with

her at the time; but when I took the time to write about it later in my DLL, I realized that I don't completely agree with her ideas. I'll ride with them for the time being while I am in her classroom; but I'll probably change things up eventually.

Creating a space for preservice teachers to critically evaluate their own developing beliefs and to find trust in themselves as professionals is one intended outcome of the DLL assignment.

Connecting Candidates' College or University Coursework with Field Experiences

Emily, Veronica, and Naomi were three preservice teachers who composed letters each week during the fall 2020 semester in a shared Google Doc, using the comment feature to respond to each other. This approach created parallel threads of dialogue alongside the initial partner's reflection. They addressed their letters using variations of the group nickname, "Sisterhood of the Teaching Pants." Their field placements reflected primarily white (75–83 percent) and economically advantaged communities: Emily taught at a high school in the same suburban district as Naomi's middle school whereas Veronica taught at the transitional neighborhood school where Kristen had been the year prior.

Throughout this group's DLL, they made connections across the readings from their methods course, concepts learned in prior courses in the English teaching program, and their respective field experience observations and teaching decisions. In response to one of Naomi's logs, Emily and Veronica acknowledged the teaching tensions that come up when a mentor teacher's pedagogical approach does not align with the principles learned in university teacher preparation.

When Naomi shared a practice from her mentor teacher's classroom—using a program called "No Red Ink" to teach and test students on grammar—Emily flagged this as contradictory to what they had learned together in a previous grammar methods course: "This goes against all my gut feelings from [their university professor's] class and emphasis on teaching grammar in context." Later, Veronica picked up on this same thread, noting their professor "would be so proud" at Naomi's decision to subvert her mentor teacher's normal grammar lesson by first asking students to apply the concept to their own writing.

Because all three partners in this dialogical group had taken classes together in their teacher preparation program, they had a shared background and a shared commitment to certain teaching principles that were not always reinforced or applied evenly in the field. They used each other to identify and navigate the conflicts between values and practices they witnessed across university and secondary classroom spaces.

The teachers used the dialogical spaces to problem solve together: knowing her dialogical group would understand why the "No Red Ink" practice did not sit well with her, Naomi asked for their advice on how to align her teaching with the pedagogical values they shared. "How would you suggest I encourage them to use grammar more in their writing?" she inquired. Emily's response offered a possible way: "Do they do any sort of writer's notebook/ daily writing activity?" Though Naomi did not yet feel she had the agency to include writer's notebooks in her teaching placement, she did suggest that perhaps that would be possible when she took on more responsibility as a student teacher.

Problem solving together became an important outcome of the DLL practice: identifying challenges, naming values, and problem solving to understand possibilities for enacting different principles across a range of contexts. Emily and Veronica's participation in the dialogue helped situate them as critical thinkers and helped them become aware of the kinds of divides they may see throughout their own teaching experiences across contexts. Naomi was able to reach out for validation and to calibrate her experience in the field with the principles she had learned through her methods courses. In this way, the DLL fostered reflection on important connections—and disconnections—across teaching experiences and university methods coursework.

Charlotte, another preservice teacher from the fall 2019 cohort of the study, noticed a similar pattern as she reflected on the way her DLL interactions enabled her to see and solve problems between theory and practice in a mid-semester reflection. She said:

> The past few weeks I've realized how exhausting it can be to live the dual identities of student/learner and teacher (even though I'm not teaching all the time yet). I've been compartmentalizing my student self so far this semester so that I can get everything done, and I need to start being more proactive in doing the tangible aspects of planning and getting what's in my head on paper. Some of that does come out in my DLL posts and conversations with Sara. It's honestly really nice to have someone else to be accountable to. Specifically, someone who is learning and growing alongside you and isn't responsible for your grade. Working on the DLL with Sara helps me get a slightly different perspective on the things we learn in class as we talk about what parts stood out and how we are fitting them into our personal ideologies. And a decent opportunity to be vulnerable about hopes and worries.

Navigating contradictions and tensions is inherent in moving from theoretical to practical; what the "Sisterhood of the Teaching Pants" group and Charlotte made clear, however, was that the DLL created a space for accountability, new perspectives, and vulnerability about navigating change. This seems an important precursor to other kinds of professional communities teachers may find themselves in throughout their careers: checking in with peers who have similar values and goals can be a true support to both developing and seasoned teacher professionals.

Understanding Teaching and Learning as Social Practices

In their DLL during the fall 2021 semester, preservice teachers Hannah, James, and Mara used a shared Google Doc to respond to each other's reflections in the body of the document itself using different colors for each participant. Unlike the previous groups, this group's log featured long blocks of text with occasional engagement back and forth in a different color. James and Mara were placed at two rival high schools in the same school district; James's school is the most racially and socioeconomically diverse of any of the schools sampled in this study (50 percent white, 40 percent Latinx), whereas Mara's draws from a more affluent side of town with less racial diversity (65 percent white, 20 percent Latinx). Hannah's junior high school draws from a mix of neighborhoods with racial and socioeconomic demographics close to that of James's school.

Although all three were placed in field experience schools within just a few miles of each other, their DLL reflections were often situated in identifying and making sense of the social practices and communities that shaped their unique teaching experiences. Though their university program gave them a common background, their reactions to the particularities of their school placements offered them a way to talk about their developing teacher identities and how they would be able to enact the teaching practices they value.

Understanding their new role as teachers within a learning community seemed to be on the forefront of their minds after their first visits to their placement schools. Hannah wrote,

> I often find myself having to tell myself that I am not an eighth grader student, I am an adult soon to be teacher and that is my role in the classroom . . . finding the balance and presenting myself as a confident adult with a defined role to students is kind of challenging to me.

Unlike in the prior example, where the dialogical partners drew on common backgrounds, James offered Hannah some strategies he brought with him into the classroom from a different social context: improv comedy. He noted that developing a teacher identity and relationships of trust with students can be informed by the same kinds of questions that improv comedians have to think about: "(1) Who are you in relationship to others around you? (2) What are your goals moving forward and how are others' goals going to impact yours? (3) Where are you and what are the rules you need to keep in order to retain the reality of that space?"

By making connections across different contexts—including contexts beyond the university and field experience classrooms—James provided a new perspective on Hannah's identity dilemma. Even though he, too, admitted to feeling the discomfort of the identity transition in his field experience ("becoming an adult," as he said), he was able to offer insight into understanding the situated and social nature of identity within teaching and learning.

Simone, a preservice teacher in the fall 2019 cohort, made similar observations about the way she navigated the new social rules of taking on a teacher identity within a learning community. In her mid-semester reflection, she wrote:

> The dialogical learning logs have helped me learn about myself as a learner and a teacher. I really do like doing extra research, experimenting, and taking more time than is required on assignments. But, usually I don't do that because I am afraid of being wrong, or getting "docked" points, or running out of time. I love the freedom of this space. I have done extra research to answer my group's questions or to find answers to my own questions. I wouldn't have done that otherwise (well . . . I probably wouldn't have even known that I had those questions if it weren't for the time I have taken after class to decompress and write). I love the community of the process—it is fun to build on the ideas of my group and explore things together.

With so much shifting about the identities and communities as preservice teachers navigate during their final semesters of their teacher education program, there can be a freedom, as Simone noted, in being able to check in with peers who are in the same transition. Notably, she pointed to the DLL assignment itself as the motivator behind engaging with her group's questions and finding answers to hers—questions she may not have even known she had "if it weren't for the time [she had] taken after class to decompress and write."

RECLAIMING THE "CENTER OF GRAVITY"

In the process of becoming a teacher, there is much to be unsettled about: shape-shifting identities, competing centers of gravity, and multiple worlds. There are constantly changing expectations around professional expectations, disciplinary knowledge, and teaching practices, made more complicated by intervening cultural and political agendas. Yet despite the discomfort, tension, and contradictions about becoming a teacher, participants reflecting on the DLL assignment echoed a similar refrain as Naomi, who said:

I like that I feel heard. I like that someone has a deeper understanding of my experience who is also in my same boat. It's different than just chatting with friends before/after class. Instead, I have extra support both for my teaching and my life. It feels really good.

Dialogic reflection creates a space for preservice teachers to navigate a complicated transition together with peers who can offer support, understanding, experience, and empathy. They become a safety net for each other in a way that, at least according to Naomi, "feels really good." Alsup (2019) suggests that the goal for millennial preservice teachers is not reconciliation of the tensions and contradictions they occupy, but instead, "a balance of the ideological, professional, and emotional contradictions that make up their psyches" (p. 105). It seems that creating communities and spaces for authentic, ongoing, dialogical reflection becomes a way for preservice teachers to negotiate that balance together.

NOTE

1. All names and references to participants and schools are pseudonyms.

REFERENCES

Alford, K., & Jensen, A. (2021). Cultivating dialogic reflection to foster and sustain preservice teachers' professional identities. *Teaching/Writing: The Journal of Writing Teacher Education*, *10*(1), 1–8.

Alsup, J. (2019). Using discourse to create a teacher identity. In J. Alsup (Ed.), *Millennial Teacher Identity Discourses* (1st ed., pp. 101–12). Routledge. Accessed August 5, 2022. https://doi.org/10.4324/9781351036542-6.

Bahktin, M. M. (1994). *The dialogic imagination: Four essays* (C. Emerson & M. Holquist, Trans.). University of Texas Press.

Caughlan, S., & Juzwik, M. M. (2014). Working through dialogically organized instruction through video-based response and revision. In J. Brass & A. Webb (Eds.), *Reclaiming English language arts methods courses* (pp. 83–96). Routledge.

Falter, M. (2019). Learning from others through writing: Exploring dialogic writing practices in English education methods courses [Conference presentation]. ELATE 2019 Summer Conference, Fayetteville, AR, United States.

Fecho, B., Collier, N. D., Friese, E. E. G., & Wilson, A. A. (2010). Critical conversations: Tensions and opportunities of the dialogical classroom. *English Education*, *42*(4), 427–47.

Gallagher, K., & Kittle, P. (2018). *180 Days: Two teachers and the quest to engage and empower adolescents.* Heinemann.

Gallo, J., Hallman, H. L., Parsons, C., Pastore-Capuana, K., Pet, S. R., & Searcy, L. (2020). Beliefs about methods courses and field experiences in English Education. Accessed March 24, 2021. https://ncte.org/statement/methodsinee/.

Gee, J. P. (2004). *Situated language and learning: A critique of rraditional schooling.* Routledge.

Hallman, H. L. (2015). Teacher as "shape-shifter": Exploring the intersection of new times and the teaching of English language arts. *Changing English, 22*(3), 282–293. Accessed August 5, 2022. https://doi.org/10.1080/1358684X.2015.1053789.

Korthagen, F., & Vasalos, A. (2006). Levels in reflection: Core reflection as a means to enhance professional growth. *Teachers and Teaching, 11*(1), 47–71. https://doi.org/10.1080/1354060042000337093.

Schön, D.A. 1987. *Educating the reflective practitioner.* Jossey-Bass.

Shulman, L. S. (1987). Knowledge and teaching: Foundations of the new reform. *Harvard Educational Review, 57*(1), 1–23. Accessed April 1, 2018. https://doi-org.unr.idm.oclc.org/10.17763/haer.57.1.j463w79r56455411.

Smagorinsky, P., Rhym, D., & Moore, C. P. (2013). Competing centers of gravity: A beginning English teacher's socialization process within conflictual Settings. *English Education, 45*(2), 147–83.

Smagorinsky, P., Shelton, S. A., & Moore, C. (2015). The role of reflection in developing eupraxis in learning to teach English. *Pedagogies: An International Journal, 10*(4), 285–308. Accessed June 12, 2015. https://doi.org/10.1080/1554480X.2015.1067146.

Zeichner, K. M., and Liston, D. P. (1996). *Reflective teaching: An Introduction.* Routledge.

Chapter 2

Designed for Dissonance
Embracing Teacher Candidate Field Experiences as Dissonant Spaces

Christopher M. Parsons

One tenet of the National Council of Teachers of English (NCTE) position statement, *Beliefs about Methods Courses and Field Experiences in English Education* (Gallo et al., 2020), is that "Programs establish partnerships with local schools, communities, and families and design clinically rich field placement opportunities for candidates based on factors such as program structure and philosophy, local school contexts, and placement availability." Easier said than done. A cursory close read makes evident the potential clashes in frameworks, interests, and operations of the named partnership groups: English education programs, local schools (and teachers), communities, and families.

And, of course, those groups are heterogenous in themselves. Consider, even *within* "English education programs," the program coordinators, field placement officers, field instructors, educator preparation units, teacher candidates, and college faculty who make up a "program." A goal, effectively preparing beginning English teachers, unites; however, the hows of that goal vary.

This chapter argues for a theoretical and practical embrace of English teacher candidate clinical field experiences as dissonant spaces. That is, English education programs should not vaguely "navigate" dissonance (or prioritize its prevention)—they should *design* candidate clinical experiences around dissonance itself. A dissonance design saves English education programs from attempting the near-impossible goal of homogenizing field experience partners with often definitionally varying considerations. Under a dissonance model, all partners must only agree with two premises: first, that beginning English teachers benefit from thoughtful, thorough preparation, and, second, that disjunctions between partners are not dealbreakers for the partnership.

What's more, a dissonance design in English teacher candidate field experiences takes advantage of jarring but essential moments when attention and reflection are demanded, preparing English teacher candidates for the unpredictable future educational ecologies of their first (and second and third) jobs. From the perspective of a sustainable career, teacher candidates are better served by structured, authentic engagements with dissonance than they are by a misleadingly seamless unity of perspectives among field placement partners.

This chapter makes four linked assertions about clinical field experiences for English teacher candidates:

(a) The school-based partnerships needed for teacher candidate field placements are exceptionally complex, both in terms of the sheer number of partners and the variability within partners.
(b) The dominant model of English education programs' field experience frameworks has often been one of theoretical and practical alignment between program and field partners.
(c) English education programs should shift focus from an alignment framework to a dissonance-based framework for field experience partnerships.
(d) While dissonance-based frameworks allow for (and even encourage) contrasting theoretical, practical, and ideological approaches, open communication about—and reflection on—these moments of dissonance are a non-negotiable mandate for every partner.

COMPLEX ECOLOGIES OF FIELD EXPERIENCE PARTNERS IN ENGLISH EDUCATION

The notion that field experiences encompass clashing perspectives is well-established. Smagorinsky et al. (2013) refer to them as "competing centers of gravity . . . [that] pull beginning teachers toward particular conceptions of teaching, often in ways that are difficult to resolve" (p. 148). Generally, the two most prominent "centers" are what Feiman-Nemser and Buchmann (1985) call the "two-worlds pitfall": the university/college-based teacher education program and the school-based field placement site—with concomitant binaries like theoretical/practical and real-world/ideal-world (Smagorinsky et al., 2013; Whitney et al., 2013; Orzulak et al., 2014).

Even "theory" and "practice" as binary points are shifty ones when it comes to field placement partners. Consider "theory." Brass (2015) persuasively argues the field of English education has taken a "turn," in the last thirty-five years, toward a "critical," "multidisciplinary," and "polymorphous discourse" (p. 10) around theory. A question for partnerships, then, becomes not just "theory or practice?" but also "which theory(ies)" and "which practices"?

While Brass (2015) embraces the ways "shifts have expanded the possibilities of teaching and teacher education" (p. 11), he is also clear-eyed about potential challenges for field partnerships and placements:

> Those seeking to bridge teacher education with contemporary scholarship now must embody multidisciplinary ways of knowing and learn several specialized languages to navigate the many frameworks that legitimate and structure language and literacy education . . . *Negotiating multiple discourses may be even more difficult for classroom teachers.* (p. 11, emphasis added)

Brass implies a challenging question: even if heterogeneous English education programs can muster theoretical and practical coherence, can/should partners like school principals, cooperating teachers, school boards, university Offices of Educator Preparation be expected to as well?

Even *outside* the partnership itself, public policy realities exert a force on partners—but not necessarily the same force. Brass (2015) observes, "The bigger challenge may be navigating educational policies that mostly contradict contemporary research, theory, and pedagogical models" (p. 12). For example, emerging state laws banning "divisive concepts" in classrooms (e.g., New Hampshire's 2021 *Right to Freedom from Discrimination in Public Workplaces and Education*) could influence each partner differently, from a cooperating teacher worried about being fired, to a teacher candidate planning a unit using antiracist pedagogy, to an English education program designing teacher candidate key assessments for an accreditation report. The specific effect of a given law on a given individual/partner is not uniform (e.g., Gigliello, 2022), but the effect of public policy on education is an inescapable aspect of the partnership.

Since the influence of education theory and policy on the "competing centers of gravity" in a partnership can seem vague due to the large scale, it is worth noting, too, the variation even within the partners for whom all this sound and fury is designed: the teacher candidates themselves.

Candidates may see their field placement work in any number of clashing ways. Perhaps they want to get out of the ivory tower and engage with teachers and students on the ground—or perhaps they enjoy the university's ivied classrooms and bemoan their cooperating teachers' ignorance. Perhaps they are looking at these field experiences with a career exploration lens ("Do I even want to be a teacher?")—or perhaps they have wanted to teach since first grade (Parsons, 2019). Perhaps divisive concepts laws scare them—or perhaps fighting that battle is the reason they want to teach in the first place.

To summarize, partnership groups in field experience design may have competing interests and will almost certainly be composed of heterogeneous individuals within a group. In a sense, the analogy of "competing centers of gravity" (over)simplifies the reality of the "programs establish partnerships" section of the *Beliefs about Methods Courses and Field Experiences in English Education* position statement: the quantity of centers of gravity is larger—and each center also contains its own centers of gravity.

THE LURE OF ALIGNMENT IN FIELD PLACEMENT PARTNERSHIPS

In university-based teacher preparation, clinical field experiences are the sites where all these moments of potential competition between partners (or at least their effects) are most likely to become apparent. Pasternak et al.'s (2018) large-scale study of English teacher education flags field placements as liminal, crucial spaces: "Our data reveal that teacher educators consider the field experience as the main location to address the tension between teacher candidates' becoming aware of issues and being able to resolve those issues through their teaching practice" (p. 45). Despite this importance, researchers also note that little research has been done on effective field experiences in English education specifically and teacher education more broadly (Pasternak et al., 2018).

Given the complexity, the importance, and the uncertainty, it makes a certain amount of sense that the dominant, if not explicit, model for teacher candidate field placements has been one of alignment. That is, English education programs seek field placement partners whose notions of teaching, learning, and teacher development align with their own.

Despite this preference, alignment is also notoriously difficult to achieve. Pasternak et al.'s (2018) study bursts with examples of this alignment concern and the "tensions" it creates:

> Questionnaire and focus group respondents expressed difficulty with finding mentor teachers who *share the philosophy* of the teacher education program. Often, these *misaligned placements* reinforce for the teacher candidate practices not supported by the program as effective or those that do not address twenty-first-century literacy practices. (p. 56, emphasis added)

Or, consider: "As our respondents showed, *the philosophy of the teacher education program is misaligned* with the philosophy or teaching practices that are found in the schools where teacher candidates conduct their field experiences" (pp. 57–58, emphasis added).

The desire for alignment between partners in a field placement is an assumed preference. Whether that alignment is about a "mentor teacher," "school," or "placement," "philosophy," "practice," or "twenty-first-century literacy practice," the desire for alignment among partners is common sense, the water in which English teacher education programs swim. While this alignment ideology manifests in any number of ways, one might see it, for example, in the quotidian statements of English education programs: "A cooperating teacher who models good instruction is worth their weight in gold" or "I told our placement office to look for placements in School X because they get what we are trying to do."

Since aligned field placements are, almost by definition, hard to find, scholars and English teacher educators have proposed creative models in search of alignment. For example, Cercone (2015) and Cercone and Pastore-Capuana (2019) created "hubs" of like-minded teachers and methods courses where teacher candidates, both in field placement and out, join in communities of practice rooted in English education program beliefs. The goal is to "bridge the gap in methods by providing pre-service teachers with on-going access to networks and communities of practice that value, support, and encourage the approaches to ELA instruction they are studying" (Cercone, 2015, p. 113).

Alignment is alluring. The vision of English education program, methods course faculty, field instructor, cooperating teacher, teacher candidate, school site, school community, and any other partner all pulling in the same direction has understandably driven English teacher education programs. After all, if programs do not believe they are correct in the theory and practice advocated in, for example, their Methods of Teaching English curricula and field experience guidelines, then what are they doing in the first place?

But, an alignment-based model has shortcomings. Some reasons are prosaic: How can an English education program's field placement apparatus locate enough aligned placements? How can cooperating teachers engage in the professional development to excel in aligned teacher candidate mentorship? Some reasons are more conceptual: Is it hubristic to design a model where partners align with programs—rarely vice versa? While English teacher educators offer crucial expertise, are programs structurally suited to hear enough "outside" perspectives about how English teachers should be trained?

Most centrally, though, alignment-based models may not do enough to imagine the uncontrollable: the teacher candidate's first (and second and third) job as an English teacher. Research shows that contextual similarity between student teaching field placement and the first job is the most meaningful factor in first-year teacher success (Goldhaber et al., 2017). It seems important to ask, then, whether alignment-based teacher preparation models might prove less useful if/when a candidate's first job does not much resemble their field experience. Instead, might a field experience with explicit, reflected-upon disunities between English education program and field site better equip candidates for the inevitable gulfs between that program and sustainable work in the field?

To be clear, this chapter does *not* suggest that English teacher educators should purposefully avoid alignment between the English education program and its field experience partners. Teacher candidates benefit, of course, from observing exemplary cooperating teachers, perhaps especially when the qualities that define a particular "exemplar" align with the programs. What this chapter *is* arguing, however, is that some level of dissonance between a program and its partners is inevitable. While programs have often sought to avoid dissonance or smooth it over, that impulse misses a crucial opportunity. Dissonances should not only be embraced—but fronted.

FIELD EXPERIENCES AND ENGLISH EDUCATION PROGRAMS: CONCEPTUALIZING DISSONANCE

This chapter recommends that English education programs design a dissonance-based model for field experience partnerships. Such a model systematically names, organizes, and discusses dissonances and regards them as a positive, productive element of an English teacher candidate's preparation. In the long term, explicitly grappling with dissonance is a more valuable tool than smoothly internalizing a given teaching practice. How many times have English teacher educators heard (and bemoaned) the tale of the thoroughly prepared new English teacher who takes that first job and either (a) simply reverts to the (perhaps less desirable) practices entrenched among the context of the school, or (b) becomes so disillusioned at the "bad" school versus the "good" preparation they have received that the candidate leaves (the school and/or the profession).

But what is dissonance? In terms of designing fieldwork experiences for English teacher candidates, dissonance is any disunity among partners in the recommended practices, and/or rationales for those practices, in the preparation of effective English teachers. Dissonance can be quotidian: for example, a placement school's format for learning objectives differing from the format a candidate learned in a program's English methods course. Dissonance can also be systemic: for example, a state legislature and board of education enacting a "divisive concepts" law banning antiracist instruction when teacher candidates in that state must show mastery of "antiracist/antibias instruction" on programmatic key assessments of the 2021 *NCTE Standards for the Initial Preparation of Teachers of ELA* (NCTE, 2021).

While alignment-based models often implicitly guide English education programs, English teachers recognize the opportunities of dwelling on the sticky wicket, the problematic, the dissonant. Lillge (2023), in considering frameworks for teachers' socially just instructional decisions, refers to "sticking points" in those decisions as "spaces of dissonance between and among frameworks . . . [which are] an opportunity to pause in determining our next best action for the greater good" (p. 49). Lillge argues that glossing over dissonance "results in a missed opportunity to realize and strengthen our commitment to educational equity and justice. We risk acquiescing to other frameworks that may well be misaligned with our stated goals" (p. 50).

When applied to English teacher candidate field experiences, a dissonance model forces a reflective "pause" when a teacher candidate encounters a disunity between their coursework and fieldwork. But what happens during this dissonance-initiated pause is crucial. Lillge (2023) focuses on the way "acquiescing" can lead a teacher to abandon important principles, and, applied to field experiences, this concession might look like a teacher candidate quietly going along with the status quo of a placement site. Dissonance offers space for new English teachers to be productively disruptive.

Crucially, though, a dissonance model in fieldwork also forces teacher candidates (and English education programs) to deeply consider, during the pause, the other voices that may be part of the disunity (e.g., a cooperating teacher, a schoolboard, a student). English teacher candidates who quickly label disagreement or variation from English education program practice as "bad" risk becoming more inflexible than principled. The dissonance "pause," though, allows for productive questions: What educational principle/practice is going on at this field site? What is its rationale? What are its affordances and limitations? How might it be revised? Where must one push back against it?

A dissonance model must be polyvocal, but, importantly, must hear these subjectivities without positioning English teacher preparation as infinitely subjective. English education programs should champion, without compromise, principles like educational equity and justice and linguistic approaches to grammar and language instruction. In doing so, though, the benefit of a dissonance model is twofold. First, teacher candidates are prepared for the inevitable resistance to these principles in an educational context that, as Brass (2015) shows, has not always taken the same "critical turn" as English education programs. Second, teacher candidates and their preparation programs, through deep listening, can maintain principles but avoid the hubris of assuming their way is the only way.

Designing for dissonance is not one specific structure but rather a design principle that any field placement design/progression must be flexible enough to know that many competing interests will be operating simultaneously. The *Beliefs about Methods Courses and Field Experiences in English Education* position statement notes as much: "English methods courses exist within, and must react to, a dynamic English teacher education ecosystem with influences from without . . . and within" (Gallo et al., 2020). Field placement designs should not attempt to quash the competition; rather, they should attempt to bring them out into the open, to reflect on them, and, to consider, in that particular moment, how they might productively live together for the benefit of training this English teacher and educating their students. When we don't design for dissonance, we prepare inflexible teachers, ones that break (rather than bend) in the first stiff wind—and schools are windy places these days.

ENGAGING DISSONANCE IN ENGLISH TEACHER CANDIDATE FIELD EXPERIENCES

This chapter focuses on centering the concept of dissonance as a model for English teacher education program field experiences; however, a dissonance model could go from concept to specific practice in any number of ways. For example, in a methods-based field experience, a methods instructor might ask teacher candidates to find examples from the field of the way core texts in actual classrooms do/do not align with the principles of text selection discussed in methods seminar. Or, in a student teaching experience, teacher candidates might write a weekly reflection journal in which they consider an effective practice they are using that seems to go against a concept they were taught in a university teacher education course. All to say, if English teacher educators are to meaningfully organize around dissonance, that shift must happen in theory *and* practice.

In that spirit of practical dissonance, this chapter concludes with a brief but illustrative example: grammar and language instruction in schools. The topic is noteworthy for the oft-observed dissonance between the linguistically informed grammar instruction advocated in English teacher education programs and the grammar worksheets and daily oral language correct-alls frequently observed in schools. But it is also noteworthy for the clear scorn some teacher educators express for those school-based practices; Baron (2011) asserts, "English teachers have typically side-stepped advances in linguistics, content instead with a *flat-earth view of grammar and usage* that has changed little since it emerged in the eighteenth century" (p. 279, emphasis added).

What happens when a student teacher equipped with supposed "round-earth" approaches to teaching grammar and language is asked to hand out the same noun worksheet as the rest of the seventh-grade English teachers? What about when they are asked to define a noun as a "person, place, or thing"? First off, a dissonance-based approach, rather than being surprised and scornful, expects and revels in the disunity. Second, though, the clear dissonance initiates a pedagogically reflective pause.

Table 2.1 shows an example of a reflective template that teacher candidates and field instructors might use to explore the dissonance. The first column, labeled Dissonant Practice, puts the candidate on the lookout for

Table 2.1 Reflective Template for Teacher Candidate/Program and Field Partner Dissonance

Dissonant Practice	English Education Program Approach		Field Placement Partner Approach	
	Approach Description	What are the benefits and drawbacks of this approach? What is its rationale?	Approach Description	What are the benefits and drawbacks of this approach? What is its rationale?
Based on your consideration of this dissonance, what will you do in your teaching practice during this field experience?				
Based on your consideration of this dissonance, how would your teaching practice look in your own English classroom?				

the cognitively challenging task of critically noticing a potential dissonance between what they learned in their college coursework and what they are seeing in their fieldwork. For example, they might write something like "grammar difference," or "worksheet and context," or "noun definition." The crucial skill, at this point, is to learn to notice—but not yet evaluate—a possible misalignment between the way they have been trained to teach English content and the way they are seeing it happen in field placement.

After the work of noticing, the teacher candidate moves to the sets of columns labeled English Education Program Approach and Field Placement Partner Approach. In each, the Approach Description box asks the candidate to offer deep description of what they have learned to do and what they are now seeing. In terms of the English education program, the candidate should be pushed back to class notes, pedagogical texts, and their own assignments. "How exactly was I taught to do this?" they should ask. For the Field Placement Partner Approach, the candidate should describe: What is on the worksheet? What is the exact wording of the "noun" definition? What do the examples look like? Is this the only planned lesson on nouns and other lexical items—or the beginning of a longer unit? How does my cooperating teacher talk about grammar and language?

It is possible that these deep descriptions might yield more similarity than expected; however, if the approaches seem, in fact, dissonant, the boxes labeled "What are the benefits and drawbacks of this approach? What is its rationale?" ask the candidate to consider the "why" for each approach. Responses will vary. Teacher candidates are often surprised, given the horror stories of grammar boredom, to see students run to the board for their turn to correct a semicolon in a sentence bursting with context-free errors. The key, here, is to reflect on each rationale genuinely: why is this practice happening and how might that be positive (or less so)?

Perhaps the dissonance begins to make more sense. Perhaps the candidate reflects that the time saved by the worksheet-based gloss on nouns has allowed for a more thorough literature circle unit or more time dedicated to source evaluation for research papers. Or perhaps the worksheet has a bit more depth than it first seems, asking students not simply to identify nouns but also to consider the function of proper nouns like Big Brother in their dystopian literature unit.

Or perhaps not. But considering (again) the rationale for the sorts of grammar and language instruction advocated by English education programs will, at least, offer the sort of applied use of those principles in first jobs where that application may seem dissonant. The new teacher might say, "Yes, this is a different approach, but here is why it is a useful one." Another possibility is that considering other, apparently dissonant rationales might reveal design challenges that a candidate could start to resolve with the support of the

English education program. For example, the delightful but languid pace of a unit on the use of phrases to nuance argumentative writing might be revised into quicker-paced, targeted mini-lessons.

Such a reflection on action, on the need to, eventually, make a specific instructional decision animates the final boxes of the template: "Based on your consideration of this dissonance, what will you do in your teaching practice during this field experience/how would your teaching practice look in your own English classroom?"

Field experiences offer one of the only occasions, in a teacher preparation program, when the compromise between putatively dissonant pedagogical practices can be explicitly tested. An action plan helps candidates decide, not only what to do under the specific realities of a field placement (i.e., a cooperating teacher or school maintains the final say on what can be taught), but also how the candidate might imagine their reconciliation of inevitable future dissonance in their own first, second, and third English classrooms.

THE IMPORTANCE AND EXHAUSTION OF DISSONANCE

On an everyday level, dissonance in English teacher education can be viscerally exhausting. And time-consuming. Many field instructors have begun rounds of student teacher debriefs with a little prayer to the god of "It's going great!" But engaging with dissonance in field placements can be energizing, too, both for teacher candidates and those who educate them. Sealed worlds, ones where all ideas align harmoniously, are efficient but can be cold—and they do not resemble many classrooms where teaching and learning happens. This chapter argues for dissonance in field placements because education is a dissonant ecosystem, and, to prepare English teachers for that ecosystem is to admit dissonance into their preparation program.

REFERENCES

Baron, D. (2011). Language and education: The more things change. In M. Adams and A. Curzan (Eds.), *Contours of English and English language studies* (pp. 278–97). University of Michigan Press.

Brass, J. (2015). Reconstituting teacher education: Literacy, critical theories, and English. In J. Brass and A. Webb (Eds.), *Reclaiming English language arts methods courses: Critical issues and challenges for teacher educators in top-down times* (pp. 1–21). Routledge.

Cercone, J. (2015). Communities of practice: Bridging the gap between methods courses and secondary schools. In J. Brass and A. Webb (Eds.), *Reclaiming English language arts methods courses: Critical issues and challenges for teacher educators in top-down times* (pp. 109–22). Routledge.

Cercone, J. and Pastore-Capuana, K. (2019). English education methods courses as sites of induction into English teacher communities of practice. In Hallman, H. L., Pastore-Capuana, K., and Pasternak, D. (Eds.), *Using tension as a resource: New visions in teaching the English language arts methods class* (pp. 105–16). Rowman & Littlefield.

Feiman-Nemser, S. and Buchmann, M. (1985). Pitfalls of experience in teacher preparation. *Teachers College Record, 87*(1), 53–65. Accessed August 5, 2022. https://doi.org/10.1177/016146818508700107.

Gallo, J., Hallman, H. L., Parsons, C., Pastore-Capuana, K., Pet, S. R., & Searcy, L. (2020). Beliefs about methods courses and field experiences in English education. Accessed November 17, 2018. https://ncte.org/statement/methodsinee/.

Gigliello, H. A. (2022). *Navigating controversial topics: A qualitative study of high school English teachers in the Live Free or Die state.* (Publication No. 29066953). [Doctoral dissertation, Plymouth State University]. ProQuest Dissertations & Theses Global.

Goldhaber, D., Krieg, J. M., & Theobald, R. (2017). Does the match matter? Exploring whether student teaching experiences affect teacher effectiveness. *American Educational Research Journal, 54*(2), 325–59.

Lillge, D. (2023). *Pursuing social justice in ELA: A framework for negotiating the challenges of teaching.* Routledge.

National Council of Teachers of English. (2021). *NCTE standards for the initial preparation of teachers of English language arts 7–12 (initial licensure).* National Council of Teachers of English. Accessed July 19, 2019. https://ncte.org/wp-content/uploads/2021/11/2021_NCTE_Standards.pdf.

Orzulak, M. J. M., Lillge, D. M., Engel, S. J., & Haviland, V. S. (2014). Contemplating trust in times of uncertainty: Uniting practice and interactional awareness to address ethical dilemmas in English teacher education. *English Education, 47*(1), 80–102.

Parsons, C. (2019). Teacher candidates' perspectives on tensions within the methods-based field experience. In Hallman, H. L., Pastore-Capuana, K., and Pasternak, D. (Eds.), *Using tension as a resource: New visions in teaching the English language arts methods class* (pp. 105–16). Rowman & Littlefield.

Pasternak, D. L., Caughlan, S., Hallman, H. L., Renzi, L., & Rush, L. S. (2018). *Secondary English teacher education in the United States.* Bloomsbury Academic.

Smagorinsky, P., Rhym, D., & Moore, C. P. (2013). Competing centers of gravity: A beginning English teacher's socialization process within conflictual settings. *English Education, 45*(2), 147–83.

Whitney, A. E., Olan, E. L., & Fredricksen, J. E. (2013). Experience over all: Preservice teachers and the prizing of the practical. *English Education, 45*(2), 184–200.

Chapter 3

Uniting Preservice Teachers and Pedagogical Thinking

Melanie Shoffner

The NCTE *Beliefs about Methods Courses and Field Experiences in English Education* statement (Gallo et al., 2020) asserts the importance of educational coursework that develops preservice teachers' (PSTs) pedagogical understanding of English language arts (ELA). The exploration and application of pedagogy underscores that content knowledge alone is not enough for teachers of English. Rather, English teachers' knowledge of ELA content must be combined with their ability to teach that content to specific adolescent populations.

Shulman (1986) identified this integrated understanding of content, instruction, and learner as pedagogical content knowledge (PCK). By developing PCK, teachers develop

> an understanding of what makes the learning of specific topics easy or difficult [and] the conceptions and preconceptions that students of different ages and backgrounds bring with them to the learning of those most frequently taught topics and lessons . . . teachers need knowledge of the strategies most likely to be fruitful in reorganizing the understanding of learners. (pp. 9–10)

Grounding curricular and instructional choices in understanding content, adolescent learning, and pedagogy may seem self-evident to experienced teachers but it is understandably difficult for PSTs. As students of education, they are still developing the knowledge, skills, and dispositions needed to become the "critical, agentic, active, ethical, reflective, and socially just educators" (Gallo et al., 2020, Dimension 1, Recommendation 5) needed in today's ELA classrooms.

ELA methods courses, then, are not focused solely on teaching PSTs how to select classroom texts or write lesson plans. They are also developing

PSTs' understandings of how and why to choose challenging texts and create meaningful lessons for their adolescent learners. In doing so, PSTs are engaging the PCK English teachers need to "plan, implement, assess, and articulate rationales for [their] pedagogical choices" (Gallo et al., 2020, Dimension 1, Recommendation 4).

The development of PCK is not an automatic outcome of methods courses, however. Van Driel and Berry (2010) point to the "complex interplay" (p. 659) of subject matter knowledge, understanding of student learning, and teaching experience (among other factors) in developing PSTs' PCK. To engage with that complexity, methods courses must integrate PSTs' content knowledge and educational beliefs "in combination with providing them with opportunities to gain teaching experience, and in particular, to reflect on these experiences" (p. 659).

This chapter focuses on a teacher educator's efforts to support PSTs' consideration and articulation of their pedagogical thinking in an ELA methods class. By examining and applying their understandings of curriculum and instruction, PSTs are working to develop the PCK needed to teach ELA content. At the same time, they are also exploring the processes, reasonings, and goals that shape the teaching of English.

MIDDLE SCHOOL ENGLISH LANGUAGE ARTS METHODS

ELA Teaching Methods for Middle School is offered in both fall and spring semesters at a mid-sized university in the South recently reclassified as an R2 institution. The course is required for secondary PSTs in both the undergraduate Bachelor of Science (BS) program and the graduate MAT program that—as stressed in the *Beliefs Statement*—work to "develop concepts of teaching and learning, content knowledge, content pedagogy, knowledge about learners and learning, and professional knowledge and skills" (Gallo et al., 2020, Overview, para. 2). Course enrollment typically ranges from six to fourteen students, with the majority of students identifying as white women.

During the methods course, PSTs are placed in local schools for a sixty-hour middle-grades practicum. The schools are located in both rural and urban areas, with predominantly white student populations. The exception is the city school system in which students represent seventy-four different countries of birth (e.g., Honduras, Iraq, Ethiopia) and fifty-seven different languages (e.g., Spanish, Kurdish, Russian).

The middle school methods course is grounded in concepts of constructivism (Richardson, 1997), communities of practice (Wenger, 2008), PCK (Shulman, 1986), and reflection (Zeichner and Liston, 2013). As such, PSTs frequently engage in collaborative work, small group and whole class discussion, and informal and formal reflection. In different iterations of the course, for example, PSTs have worked in pairs to lead the discussion on a specific topic, peer-reviewed lesson plans, written rationales for teaching a chosen text, and completed exit tickets reflecting on individual learning.

Throughout the semester, PSTs draft different instructional elements in class, both individually and collaboratively. Because this classwork is formative in nature, PSTs are under no pressure to submit a polished or even accurate product. Instead, they are able to develop their PCK by trying out ideas and applying developing skills without fear of failure while working with or receiving input from their peers as well as feedback from the professor.

After discussions addressing adolescent development and care in the classroom, for example, PSTs might work in pairs to create an activity for an eighth-grade class that supports community building. The pairs then share the activity with the whole class, prompting consideration of how the activity does or does not align with the concepts previously discussed. As an exit ticket, each PST then identifies one thing learned about the classroom community, one question that remains, and one way to enact what they have learned in future instruction.

WORKING WITH YOUNG ADULT LITERATURE

A repeated element of the methods course is the inclusion of young adult (YA) literature. Each semester, PSTs read one or more YA novels as a class, in literature circles, or individually, dependent on course enrollment. PSTs then work with these novels, individually and collaboratively, to examine course concepts (such as student engagement, writing instruction, and multimodality) and construct instructional materials suited to adolescent learning. In doing so, they are able to apply their pedagogical thinking in relation to teaching middle-grades ELA, supporting the development of their PCK.

For example, PSTs might work in small groups to outline a lesson on language that utilizes a chapter from the YA novel in one class and, in the next, revise the lesson to address different state ELA standards. In another class, following a review of Bloom's Taxonomy, PSTs might individually formulate discussion questions to engage adolescent learners in meaningful discussion of characters' motivations, followed by a peer-editing session to refine the questions. Lastly, as a class, PSTs might brainstorm texts that connect to the novel in some way before working in pairs to create a text set with a common element.

The YA novels are intentionally chosen to bring diverse authors, genres, and topics into the methods course that both engage and challenge adolescent readers. By disrupting (Ebarvia et al., 2020) the traditional literary canon, these books offer the mirrors, windows, and sliding glass doors (Bishop, 1990) that adolescents need while "emphasiz[ing] the diversity of literacies, texts, and learners" (Gallo et al., 2020, Dimension 1, Recommendation 3) found in the ELA classroom.

In keeping with these objectives, YA selections have included—among many others—*A Monster Calls* (Ness, 2013), *Listen, Slowly* (Lai, 2015), *Wolf Hollow* (Wolk, 2016), *Long Way Down* (Reynolds, 2017), *Marcus Vega Doesn't Speak Spanish* (Cartaya, 2018), *Pet* (Emezi, 2019), *New Kid* (Craft, 2019), *Freedom Summer for Young People* (Watson and Stefoff, 2020), *Show Me a Sign* (LeZotte, 2020), *Other Words for Home* (Warga, 2021), *Amari and the Night Brothers* (Alston, 2021), and *King and the Dragonflies* (Callendar, 2020).

Working with a designated YA novel throughout the semester engages PSTs' textual understanding and pedagogical thinking; the integrated application of both supports their development of PCK. Additionally, PSTs are drafting different pedagogical components throughout the semester that, collectively, inform teachers' creation of instructional units. However, while a unit plan is a typical assignment in methods courses, PSTs do not develop a standalone unit plan.

Instead, they complete various assignments in connection to their YA novel that engage their pedagogical thinking. While the specific details of these assignments change with each iteration of the course, the objective remains the same: to draw on the pedagogical content, knowledge, and skills—that is, the PCK—needed to plan a unit of study for middle-grades ELA. The following sections share composite descriptions of these different assignments, with excerpts of PSTs' work to illustrate their pedagogical engagement.

YOUNG ADULT RATIONALE

One assignment PSTs complete early in the semester is a written rationale for their YA novel. Following their reading of the novel, PSTs apply their understanding of curriculum and adolescents to consider the text's potential for adolescent engagement, ELA learning, interdisciplinary connections, possible pushback, and educational equity. The rationale centers on the question, "What does this text offer to my adolescent learners?"

As noted above, PSTs are concurrently completing a middle-grades practicum. By considering how their novel connects (or not) to adolescents in their practicum classroom, PSTs are utilizing the pedagogical thinking needed for teachers to "[attend] to the cultural backgrounds of students and [choose] texts and learning opportunities that nurture students' unique literacies" (Gallo et al., 2020, Dimension 1, Recommendation 4). In doing so, they are considering how to select novels for all students to see "themselves and others in powerful renditions... that offer counternarratives to what our schools have historically taught us" (Germán, 2021, p. 35).

PSTs first considered how their novel might engage students. One PST saw the potential engagement of the verse format in *Other Words for Home* (Warga, 2021) since it

> would be appealing visually to students because of its 'shortness'... presentation and formatting of texts, especially for adolescent readers, is important. The ratio between the white space [margins] and the black space [text] can make students feel more inclined to pick up a book.

Another offered that seventh graders would likely connect to *New Kid* (Craft, 2019) "because the protagonist is also in seventh grade and navigating the social landscape of middle school."

PSTs also examined their novel's support for students' learning of specific skills. In advocating for sixth graders to read *Amari and the Night Brothers* (Alston, 2021), a PST explained that the author's clear plot and intentional patterns supported younger readers' ability to "practice pattern spotting and predict future events" within a relatively long novel. Another PST argued for *Freedom Summer* (Watson and Stefoff, 2020) as a means for eighth graders to examine the development of a theme, in this case, community building, since people

> learn and work together to bring attention to injustice within the United States towards Black Americans (which is injustice to everyone). The community had guidelines, boundaries, expectations, and even significant disagreements at times... students can make [connections] between this community and their own communities whether that is family, sports teams, clubs, church, or potentially even friend groups.

Some PSTs focused on specific connections with the Virginia Standards of Learning (Commonwealth of Virginia Board of Education, 2017). One linked students' learning of the eighth-grade standards for nonfiction to their reading of *Freedom Summer* (Watson and Stefoff, 2020) "because it has obvious and frequent examples of headings, subheadings, pictures, captions, title pages." Another PST pointed to the support offered by *Amari and the Night Brothers* (Alston, 2021) for meeting the sixth-grade reading standards for narrative structure elements, cause and effect, character development, perspective, diction and imagery, and figurative language.

PSTs identified a range of issues addressed in their YA novels that might cause students, parents, administrators, and community members to push against these novels in the classroom—an increasingly salient problem, unfortunately: issues of class and race in *New Kid* (Craft, 2021) and racism and violence in *Freedom Summer* (Watson and Stefoff, 2020). One PST pointed to the likelihood of facing resistance with *Amari and the Night Brothers* (Alston, 2021) because the novel includes "socioeconomic status, families dealing with loss and neglect, racism, questionable morals, and exclusion based on one's identity."

Acknowledging potential issues, PSTs also explained the need to bring their novels into the classroom. One PST stressed the importance of *Other Words for Home* (Warga, 2021) as its ability to help students "gain empathy and counter negative stereotypes the media has spewed for years about immigrants and people of color." Another PST pointed to the power of students' seeing difference as normal in *Pet* (Emezi, 2019): "The beautiful thing about this novel is that it has such a diverse cast of characters, but it's never used as a focal point, it's just normal."

While this assignment does not require PSTs to create instructional materials, it does engage PSTs with the elements that support the development of PCK. In writing their rationale, PSTs must apply understandings of text (i.e., subject matter), middle-grades adolescents (i.e., student learning), and classroom instruction (i.e., ELA), the integration of which reveals their pedagogical thinking.

VISUAL THINKING

In a second assignment, PSTs use the medium of their choice (e.g., Canva, collage, original artwork) to create a visual text conveying a key theme, question, or issue from their YA novel. They are asked to think of this visual as something in their future classroom to capture students' attention and encourage them to read the novel. Different iterations of this assignment have placed different parameters on the created visual. In one semester, the assignment might allow no alphabetic text; in another, only the novel's title and author are allowed; in another, any alphabetic text is allowed as long as it is taken directly from the novel.

This assignment requires PSTs to "comprehend, create, respond to, and engage with diverse texts" (Shoffner et al., 2017, Dimension 1, para 1), in keeping with the variety of literacies and texts that constitute secondary ELA. In creating a visual text based on their comprehension of a YA novel, PSTs are engaging the cognitive, aesthetic, and analytical processes that make up visual literacy (Walsh-Moorman, 2018).

At the same time, PSTs are utilizing skills inherent to PCK. In creating their visual, they are integrating understandings of the novel and adolescents; in working with these visuals, they are applying understandings of textual analysis and student learners. In completing this assignment, PSTs are answering the question, "How can visuals engage critical thinking?"

This question comes to the forefront when PSTs work with the created visuals in class. When the visuals have no alphabetic text, PSTs might do a gallery walk before working as a class to group the visuals by suggested theme. In doing so, PSTs must read the images as text, infer meaning from that text, and support their conclusions with textual evidence.

When the visuals use the novel's title and author, PSTs might work in literature circles to consider how reading the same novel results in different interpretations. Rather than agreeing or disagreeing with their peers' conclusions, PSTs compare their understandings of the novel, analyze the visuals' portrayal of those understandings, and discuss the intersections of textual and visual literacies.

When text from the novel is included, small groups of PSTs might evaluate the visuals through the lens of adolescent engagement. In doing so, PSTs consider students' reading of the images, understanding of the text, and connection to the YA novel.

CURRICULUM CONNECTIONS

A third assignment engages PSTs with the question, "How will I organize, connect, and challenge students' learning?" by having them develop three assignments that would be embedded within a four-week unit guided by the essential question (EQ), *What does it mean to be brave*? At times, PSTs choose the grade level for these assignments; at others, they work with the grade level of their middle-grades practicum.

The proposed unit must incorporate their individual YA novel in some way (e.g., the whole novel as an anchor text or literature circle choice; one or more chapters as part of a text set). Depending on other work during the semester, PSTs might contextualize this assignment by drafting an outline of the unit, providing a rationale for their choices, or explaining connections to the chosen grade level. A culminating reflection on their work is a required element of the assignment.

PSTs use a version of the provided chart (figure 3.1) to create the three assignments, since different options are offered each semester. Each assignment incorporates an additional text, an interdisciplinary connection, and the YA novel in some way. The following example is provided to PSTs as clarification: In class, seventh-grade students analyze a set of *images* drawn from *current events* that depict different brave people. They then compare these depictions to a brave character in their *YA novel*. Finally, they create a *visual text* for display in the classroom that illustrates their response to the EQ.

While PSTs do create lesson plans in the methods course, they do not develop them for these assignments. Instead, they make their pedagogical

Assignment	Additional text	Connection
EQ: What does it mean to be brave?		
persuasive writing	song	science
group work	image	math
visual text	poem	current events
language/grammar	nonfiction	sports / games

Figure 3.1   Curriculum Connections Chart.

thinking visible through explanations of how each assignment addresses the EQ, supports student learning of specific outcomes, incorporates additional texts, and connects to non-ELA subject matter. The integration of these elements utilizes PSTs' pedagogical understanding and, by extension, draws upon their developing PCK.

Working with *Pet* (Emezi 2017), one PST created an assignment in which eighth graders read a three-page excerpt from the nonfiction *Beyond Katrina: A Meditation on the Mississippi Gulf Coast* (Trethewey, 2012). As a class, students use their reading of the excerpt and the YA novel to consider how monuments do/do not commemorate events or acts of bravery. Students then individually research a historical monument that they believe represents an example of bravery. They finish by creating a short presentation to explain why this monument is significant.

While centering students' exploration of bravery, this assignment also connects students to larger societal and cultural issues through the additional text (*Beyond Katrina*) and the assignment's topic (monuments). In considering "the similarities and differences between monuments in our world" and those in *Pet*, students analyze fiction, nonfiction, and visual texts to make connections, draw conclusions, and support ideas.

Amari and the Night Brothers (Alston 2021) served as the anchor text for a PST's sixth-grade assignments. Drawing from their study of the novel, students work to create personal definitions of bravery. In one assignment, students act out examples of bravery—provided as images—from favorite sports and video games to review their understanding of role, audience, and purpose. In another, students watch a nature documentary on "brave" animals to identify logos, pathos, and ethos; they then apply these devices in a short writing to persuade readers to accept their definition of bravery.

These assignments situate the novel as an introduction to specific grade-level concepts and skills before using different texts and subjects to apply students' learning. They also center students' interests while developing these concepts and skills. As the PST explained, students benefit "if they are able to use their imagination to accomplish a task" and "become invested in lessons when they related to their interests."

One PST used *Other Words for Home* (Warga 2019) as a springboard for sixth-grade assignments focused on perspective. In one, students watch different news clips—such as refugees leaving their country, firefighters rescuing a child, and adolescents speaking out about climate change—before working in groups to identify different acts of bravery. In the second, students identify an issue of importance to them and create a short speech explaining its importance.

Bravery is addressed both overtly and covertly in these assignments. While students discuss different understandings of what it means to be brave in one, they are asked to *be* brave in the second in order to stand up in front of their classmates (much like the main character does in the school play). Throughout, the assignments "encourage them to think critically" and "show students that there are always multiple sides to a story."

Another PST created a seventh-grade assignment with connections to science and technology following students' completion of *New Kid* (Craft, 2019). Using their annotations from the graphic novel and a selection of poems, students create a "bravery cell," with different parts of the cell representing different traits of what it means to be brave. They then use online software to create a poster depicting their bravery cell to be displayed in the classroom. In this way, the assignment encourages students to think critically about their own views of bravery and what defines it. Rather than having texts that provide broad overviews or definitions of bravery, these texts prompt readers to think about bravery in various circumstances and build their personal ideas and opinions based on the information provided in the texts.

CONCLUSION

As the *Beliefs Statement* (Gallo et al., 2020) asserts, there is no right way to teach a methods course, given the varied and diverse factors that shape the educational context. There is also no way a methods course can successfully incorporate the entire compendium of content, pedagogy, and instruction needed for the teaching of secondary ELA. However, a methods course can—and must—meaningfully engage PSTs with the contextual, social, cultural, pedagogical, and personal elements that shape their pedagogical thinking and, in doing so, support the development of PSTs' PCK.

The methods course described in this chapter is offered not as an exemplar but as an example of one teacher educator's efforts to develop PSTs' pedagogical thinking rather than accept that PSTs are unlikely to develop PCK before entering the classroom (Van Driel and Berry, 2010). The assignments discussed here are designed to engage PSTs' developing PCK by requiring both understanding and application of subject matter, student, and pedagogy.

Through their work, then, PSTs have the opportunity to build the pedagogical thinking needed to plan and implement meaningful ELA instruction and develop "deep understandings about not only *what* to teach in English language arts curricula, but also *how* to approach [their] work as English language arts teachers" (Gallo et al., 2020, Dimension 1, para. 1).

REFERENCES

Alston, B. B. (2021). *Amari and the night brothers*. Balzer + Bray.
Bishop, R. S. (1990). Mirrors, windows, and sliding glass doors. *Perspectives: Choosing and Using Books for the Classroom, 6*(3) ix–xi.
Callendar, K. (2020). *King and the dragonflies*. Scholastic.
Cartaya, P. (2018). *Marcus Vega doesn't speak Spanish*. Puffin.
Commonwealth of Virginia Board of Education. (2017). *English standards of learning for Virginia public schools*. Virginia Department of Education.
Craft, J. (2019). *New kid*. Harper.
Ebarvia, T., Germán, L., Parker, K. N., and Torres, J. (2020). #DisruptTexts. *English Journal, 110*(1), 100–2.
Emezi, A. (2019). *Pet*. Make Me a World.
Gallo, J., Hallman, H. L., Parsons, C., Pastore-Capuana, K., Pet, S. R., and Searcy, L. (2020). *Beliefs about methods courses and field experiences in English education*. National Council of Teachers of English (NCTE). Accessed January 24, 2023. https://ncte.org/statement/methodsinee/.
Germán, L. E. (2021). *Textured teaching: A framework for culturally sustaining practices*. Heinemann.
Lai, T. (2015). *Listen, slowly*. Harper.
LeZotte, A. C. (2020). *Show me a sign*. Scholastic.
Ness, P. (2013). *A monster calls*. Candlewick Press.
Reynolds, J. (2017). *Long way down*. Atheneum.
Richardson, V. (1997). Constructivist teaching and teacher education: Theory and practice. In *Constructivist Teacher Education: Building a World of New Understandings* (pp. 3–14). The Falmer Press.
Shoffner, M., Alsup, J., Garcia, A., Haddix, M., Moore, M., Morrell, E., Schaafsma, D., and Zuidema, L. A. (2017). *What is English language arts teacher education?* National Council of Teachers of English (NCTE). Accessed August 5, 2022. http://www2.ncte.org/statement/whatiselateachereducation/.
Shulman, L. S. (1986). Those who understand: Knowledge growth in teaching. *Educational Researcher, 15*(2), 4–14.
Trethewey, N. (2012). *Beyond Katrina: A meditation on the Mississippi Gulf Coast*. University of Georgia Press.

Van Driel, J. H. and Berry, A. (2010). Pedagogical content knowledge. In *International Encyclopedia of Education* (pp. 656–61). Academic Press.
Walsh-Moorman, E. (2018). A playful approach to teaching visual literacy. *English Journal, 108*(1), 59–65.
Warga, J. (2021). *Others words for home.* Balzar + Bray.
Watson, B. and Stefoff, R. (2020). *Freedom summer for young people: The violent season that made Mississippi burn and made America a democracy.* Seven Stories Press.
Wenger, E. (2008). *Communities of practice: Learning, meaning, and identity.* Cambridge University Press.
Wolk, L. (2016). *Wolf hollow.* Dutton Books.
Zeichner, K. M., and Liston, D. P. (2013). *Reflective teaching: An introduction* (2nd ed.). Routledge.

Chapter 4

An Argument about Argument Writing
Taking a Stance on the Five-Paragraph Essay
Mike Metz

Ultimately, through debating writing formats and structures with my peers, understanding educator and expert perspectives on writing instruction, and writing my own piece of argumentative writing on the subject, I have concluded that I want my students to have the experience that I had: of being part of a classroom community in which writing is taught as the valuable and important way of interacting with the world that it is. I don't think the five-paragraph essay format can accomplish this, but I now know that there are so many practices that can.

–Emily, ELA teacher candidate, reflecting on writing assignment

One of the great challenges of teaching is the need to make consequential decisions in the spur of the moment with imperfect information. We can equip teachers to make decisions in the face of complexity by helping them develop guiding principles. The NCTE *Statement of Beliefs about Methods Courses and Field Experiences in English Education* (Gallo et al., 2020) highlights the importance of preparing teachers who, among other things, can "articulate rationales for pedagogical choices." This chapter describes an inquiry-based unit in an English Language Arts Methods class designed to help teacher candidates uncover key principles to guide their teaching. The unit uses instruction in argument writing as an anchor to ground teacher candidates' inquiry.

The inquiry-based writing unit culminates with teacher candidates composing a position paper on the use of the five-paragraph essay. As they prepare to write the position paper, teacher candidates explore the historical, social, and political purposes of schooling tied to this writing structure. They read research articles and opinion pieces promoting or disdaining the use of structured writing in 6–12 classrooms. They discuss and debate the value of structured writing, with some extolling it as the foundation of their own writing skill and others vilifying it as destroying any joy they found in writing.

This chapter describes the assignment, teacher candidates' responses to the assignment, and the theoretical grounding of the assignment in a critical inquiry approach. The layered nature of this assignment aligns with the recommendation of the *Beliefs Statement* that "coursework should be designed to support teacher candidates in becoming critical, agentic, active, ethical, reflective, and socially just educators" (Gallo et al., 2020). By helping teacher candidates reflect on their own experiences of schooling alongside current research, teacher candidates are empowered to disrupt historically concretized artifacts of schooling and encouraged to create transformative experiences for their future students. The assignment guides teacher candidates to develop and articulate principles that guide their pedagogical decision-making through the complexity of teaching.

WHY FOCUS ON THE FIVE-PARAGRAPH ESSAY?

The five-paragraph essay and other forms of structured writing remain a staple of ELA classrooms despite efforts to move writing teachers away from these reductive styles (Caplan and Johns, 2019; Warner, 2019). Because the five-paragraph essay is nearly ubiquitous, teacher candidates will need to contend with it regardless of their own writing philosophy. By having teacher candidates conduct a critical inquiry into its use, they move beyond binary arguments about whether the five-paragraph essay is *good* or *bad*, and instead consider what the five-paragraph essay teaches students to do and what it prevents them from doing.

Over several weeks, as the teacher candidates reflectively enact a writing process to craft their position papers, key ideas emerge from their exploration of writing instruction: They critique purposes for writing assignments, questioning assignments based on tradition rather than clear learning goals. They embrace the social nature of writing, the iterative process of drafting and revising, and the inclusion of flexible mini-lessons throughout the process of composition. They weigh the value of freedom and constraint as teaching tools connected to issues of social equity. They interrogate the arbitrary nature of writing conventions and poke holes in prescriptive approaches to language use.

Ultimately, as the teacher candidates finalize this assignment, they communicate a new awareness of how social norms influence schooling, and they express a desire to challenge those norms in the interest of student learning.

While there are varied types of five-paragraph essays, most follow this generic form: An introductory paragraph that includes a three-point thesis statement; three body paragraphs that expand on the three points from the introduction; a conclusion that restates the thesis and summarizes the three supporting points. Other forms of five-paragraph essays include differing degrees of detail, with some telling students what to write in each sentence (e.g., topic sentence, evidence sentence, explanation sentence, transition sentence), and others detailing what to write in each part of a sentence (e.g., transition, lead-in, quote). As a collective approach, these varied prescriptive forms make up *structured writing*, with the five-paragraph essay being the most common type.

Arguments in favor of structured writing promote it as a scaffold that helps students organize their ideas (Seo, 2007), or as a stepping stone to other forms of writing (Smith, 2006). Critiques of structured writing bemoan the way rigid form restricts student thinking (Thomas, 2016), stifles creativity (Kittle and Gallagher, 2021), stunts the development of argumentation and rhetoric (Elbow, 2012), and truncates the writing process (Hillocks, 2011). In the Methods course, students read articles and chapters by the authors cited above to learn how the teaching of argumentation is framed in educational literature.

As students investigate methods for teaching argument writing, they focus on the question, "What do you gain and what do you lose from asking students to write within the constraints of a five-paragraph structure?" Students come away from this assignment with nuanced views and clarified purposes for why they will approach the teaching of writing in particular ways. Rather than reductive and binary views that the five-paragraph essay is good or bad, that teachers should never use it or always use it, teacher candidates consider the form/structure of writing as one element that can be manipulated to support student writing growth.

EXPLORING ARGUMENT WRITING

In our educator preparation program, middle and secondary English education teacher candidates have the luxury of a three-semester methods sequence. In the second semester, they explore the teaching of writing. Teacher candidates craft three major writing assignments; a personal narrative, a citizen sociolinguistics usage guide, and a position paper on the five-paragraph essay. During each assignment they take on the dual roles of teacher and student to engage in the writing process while also metacognitively considering the pedagogical moves that support quality writing. For the final assignment, the position paper on the five-paragraph essay, teacher candidates conduct research, debate ideas, and share personal stories, while they recursively draft, conference, revise, share, and publish their pieces.

Teacher candidates begin the inquiry into teaching argument writing by exploring the idea of argumentation. As a class, they examine Toulmin's model of argumentation, identifying claims, warrants, backing, qualifiers, counterarguments, and rebuttals. Descriptions of Toulmin's model can be found across the internet. Teacher candidates compare various descriptions on YouTube, campus writing resources, and other sources they discover.

Next, they read the arguments for and against the five-paragraph essay listed in the previous section. They debate the merits of the arguments the authors provide and come to an understanding of how different authors understand the goals of schooling (e.g., being able to produce competent writing for a standardized test versus being able to make rhetorical choices to craft a nuanced and persuasive argument).

Teacher candidates explore what counts as evidence in different contexts, considering the role of anecdote and story as evidence in many arguments. To evaluate the role of narrative in argument, teacher candidates share their own stories of learning to write essays in middle and high school. They share these stories on a class discussion board and then have follow-up conversations in small groups about their experiences. They use their stories as evidence of how different approaches to the teaching of writing work for different students in different contexts. Excerpts from these written discussions are integrated below as examples of teacher candidates' thinking about their writing experiences.

EXPERIENCES OF STRUCTURED WRITING

As teacher candidates reflect on their own experiences of learning to write in school, many describe the pain of high school writing in descriptive detail. As one recent teacher candidate, Sophia, explained,

> It was kinda like the sensation you get when listening to an automated voice mail—robotic, straight forward, and uniform. I remember writing typical 5PE's about *Romeo and Juliet*, *TKAM*, you name it . . . Within an hour, it'd be done.

Other teacher candidates extended their high school writing experience to the present day. Brianna expressed an idea typical of students adjusting from high school to college.

> I found that I didn't know how to write a paper that deviated from the 5PE formatting. I knew I was pretty good at writing, but I also thought it was boring. I had no sense of the creative processes that lay behind manipulating words

into conveying the message that I desired to get across. I'd never experienced that before. I had to retrain my brain—and 4 years later, I'm *still* retraining my brain.

Each year there are a handful of teacher candidates who are new to the idea of the five-paragraph essay, not having encountered it in their own schooling experiences. Most of these students come from nontraditional schools where they are not burdened with high stakes standardized tests that include timed writing prompts. As one student explained,

> I encountered the five-paragraph essay format for the first time as a junior in college. The experience was similar to interacting with someone you have always inexplicably disliked from afar. Meaning, I can't say it was a welcome or enjoyable encounter.

Later this student went on to describe the experience of writing a five-paragraph essay for the first time,

> The task reminded me of the multitude of factory jobs my grandmother often described to me. You complete one simple action, then another, in a specific sequence, and then you end up with a final product completely identical to every other product produced this way. Except in this scenario, the action was writing, not manning an assembling line, and the final product was supposed to be an original and thoughtful essay, not a $5 shirt available for purchase on a sketchy website. To me, the activity seemed no different than a Mad Libs, except without any of the creativity and humor involved.

Teacher candidates quickly note the diversity of their classmates' stories, and also note the power of these stories in shaping arguments about what kind of writing instruction is effective. Teacher candidates acknowledge the powerful use of narrative structures within these descriptions of their experiences of learning to write. By pairing students' own stories with written resources about the five-paragraph essay, students come to appreciate the broad landscape of approaches to teaching argument writing.

EXAMINING ALTERNATIVES TO FIVE-PARAGRAPH ESSAYS

As teacher candidates identify limitations to the five-paragraph essay, a few key questions come up year after year. Teacher candidates who had been conditioned to use a five-paragraph format throughout their schooling often wonder what the alternatives could be. We discuss this through the concept of *organizing frames*. The organizing frame of the traditional five-paragraph essay resembles the following:

- Here is my claim . . . Three reasons support this claim . . . In conclusion, here's my claim.

Teacher candidates read about several alternative organizing frames from Barry Lane (2015):

- I used to think . . . Then this happened . . . Now I think . . .
- One way to look at it . . . Another way to look at it . . . My way to look at it . . .
- Most people think . . . They are wrong . . . Here's why . . .
- On the one hand . . . on the other hand . . . I agree that . . . this is not to say that . . .

Once teacher candidates allow themselves to think about alternative organizing frames, they play with them and invent their own. For example, this past semester a teacher candidate described this frame for her argument about five-paragraph essays:

- Here's the issue . . .
- Here's why you should care about the issue . . .
- Here are people's misconceptions about the issue . . .
- Here's how we can fix the issue . . .

This is a more sophisticated approach than the traditional five-paragraph format that asserts a clear thesis from the beginning, backs it up with three reasons, and then restates the thesis.

USING NARRATIVE IN ARGUMENT WRITING

Perhaps the most compelling limitation of the five-paragraph essay, and one that I offer to teacher candidates, is the way the five-paragraph essay, and the associated focus on predetermined thesis statements, strips the writing of narrative movement. As Newkirk (2014) argues, it is the narrative journey that makes *all* writing engaging to read and write. By stripping away the unfolding discovery of an argument, the five-paragraph essay becomes a chore for students to write and teachers to read.

Newkirk (2014) describes the narrative movement as the "itch and scratch" of good informational writing. As opposed to the traditional five-paragraph essay, these alternative structures set up a journey of thinking. They create and resolve tension as the author's argument unfolds. Sometimes an author reveals a chronological unfolding of ideas, as in the first structure (I used to think . . .), other times an author creates a conflict that begs for a solution (Most people think . . .). Through the position paper assignment, many teacher candidates try out an approach that takes the reader on a journey through their thought processes, illustrating how their awareness of structured writing developed and how they come to appreciate the use of form as a technique to compliment an argument, not to constrain it.

To give teacher candidates the freedom to experiment with form, the restrictions of traditional academic college essays are removed from this assignment. Teacher candidates are asked to articulate a clear stance and convincing argument but there are no restrictions on form or voice in their writing. By opening rhetorical choices for the teacher candidates, their writing blossoms. Each year, these assignments are the most enjoyable academic papers I get the opportunity to read. Many teacher candidates build on the writing techniques they practiced in their personal narratives and use them to engage the reader in their argument.

For example, one teacher candidate experimented with using a second-person, present-tense perspective as a way to draw the reader in. This point of view is shunned in traditional school-based argument writing, but here the teacher candidate is applauded for taking a risk.

It's the fourth period.

You shift in your seat, causing its legs to squeak as you ball your hands into fists and perch your elbows on the table to create a resting spot for your chin. Your English teacher's long, floral skirt makes a swishing noise as she surveys the room. You look up at the clock and let out a small breath, squeezing your eyes together for a moment to inspire focus.

Glancing back down to your desk, you see your outline for the five-paragraph essay that your teacher assigned. It's already filled out and completed, with ten minutes to spare at the end of class. Looking around the room, some of your peers are doing the same thing you are— watching the clock tick by now that you speedily filled in your ultra-specific outline.

About half of the other classmates are fiddling with their pens and not bothering to fill out the outline at all.

Your teacher bounces around the room to counsel these students and they give her the same response they did the first few times she asked how things were going, "I don't know what to put down."

She brainstorms with them, which honestly seems kind of pointless. They probably did know what to write, but that was the problem. They

> knew what words and sentences to put in the blank spaces of their outline, but they had no desire to go through the ritual. A couple of weeks prior, they wrote details for our last essay assignment on an identical handout, and in all honesty, this seems like a waste of time: just like the last one.

From this introduction, the teacher candidate goes on to cite journal articles we read, stories from her peers, and experiences in her field placement as she critiques the reductive approach of giving students a single structure for writing. Because these college juniors are still close enough to their high school experience to viscerally remember their feelings of boredom and defiance, they can put that in their writing in powerful ways. Ideally, they will use their experiences to adjust their future teaching rather than assuming imposed boredom is a tradition that must be maintained.

Another teacher candidate began her position paper with a first-person narrative describing how her teacher introduced her freshman class to the five-paragraph essay structure:

A House in a Hurricane: A Parable of the Five-Paragraph Essay

I remember my very first day of English class during my freshman year. It was an honors English course consisting of only twelve girls. We were anxious to excel in one of our first high school classes. My teacher put up a picture of a hurricane. "This is me," he said. "I am hurricane Dan. I will wipe out any paper that doesn't have structure that can stand the storm." We laughed. He put on screen a house that had been severely damaged in a hurricane. "This will be your paper after I grade it." Nervous laughter continued and got quieter.

A few key ideas emerge from these examples. First, students have fun with this assignment. They are given permission to play with their writing, to try out new techniques and new voices in an academic essay. They practice making authorial choices while considering the impact on the audience. Second, the authors lay the groundwork for making a strong argument by engaging their audience. There are key ideas in each narrative introduction that can be examined later in the essay. Third, these essays are a joy to read. The process of assessment and feedback is more effective when the professor can be in conversation with an active voice that comes through in the writing.

When I assess these position papers, I share comments in the margins as the teacher candidates take me on an emotional and logical journey through an unfolding argument. This style allows me to model feedback on student writing that celebrates risk taking, acknowledges literary techniques, and comments on the effectiveness of persuasion—all things I want my teacher candidates to do with their future students.

Besides using narrative to engage the reader at the beginning of the essay, many teacher candidates use anecdotes throughout to argue for or against the use of five-paragraph essays in their future teaching. Teacher candidates draw on experiences from their field placements as evidence of the impact of rigid, structured writing. For example, one teacher candidate described her host teacher's use of the five-paragraph essay with her classroom of juniors. She detailed the way the teacher gave the students a graphic organizer that dictated what each sentence of their essay would be and then helped them fill in the organizer:

> One week later, on the day after the deadline of the essay, my host teacher informed me that she put nearly fifty grades of 0% in the gradebook for plagiarism and missing work. She felt she had designed an engaging assignment, and it turned out to be the opposite for her students.
>
> Demoralized, she complained to me, saying "I can't make this any easier for them."
>
> Maybe, I thought to myself, that was the problem.

Teacher candidates' use of anecdote and narrative within their position papers demonstrated a deep understanding of argumentation and rhetoric. Through this assignment, preservice teachers engage with ways to approach academic writing that differ greatly from their own high school experiences. And they are highly effective.

DEVELOPING METACOGNITION: REFLECTING ON WRITING PROCESSES

After each major assignment in the Methods course, the teacher candidates reflect on the process of completing the assignment. They tie their final product to the readings and theories they have engaged within the class. They discuss the implications for how they will organize teaching and learning in their future classrooms. These reflections comprise a unique genre of writing. I require MLA-style citations to substantiate ideas from course readings and encourage personal voice and a relaxed dialogic style. In their reflections on writing the position papers, the students revealed how their thinking had evolved (figure 4.1).

Reflection Excerpts
1. Okay so... I'm going to be honest and divulge the fact that I was not excited to write this paper. At all. I didn't really know what my opinion was, didn't really know how to process that lack of opinion, didn't really know where to start... BUT, after going through the entire writing process from start to finish, I actually had a lot of fun creating this".
2. I want to keep reading about how to teach students to write creatively, and what the line is between supports and freedom (especially for the baby freshman that I'll probably be teaching)"
3. Writing the personal narrative felt more like writing a creative story. I was trying to draw my audience in through details, setting the scene, adding in dialogue, and other things like that. With an evidence-based argument, though, it was more straightforward, and I had to be more intentional in adding my voice into the text. I would say that both were fun to accomplish, but I think that I had more fun writing this 5PE paper. I'm kind of surprised to say that, but it was overall a really enjoyable experience for me."

Figure 4.1 Student Reflection Excerpts.

Students learn about the writing process as they think metacognitively about their own writing. In the reflection on this essay, one student explained:

This assignment was a journey, that's for sure. My first draft of this paper hit around the eight-page mark, and when I looked back over what I had read, I realized it made no sense at all. More than anything, it was a winding road of ideas leading back to a problematic truth; I was still figuring out my beliefs about the FPE. It wasn't cohesive, it wasn't convincing, and it wouldn't lead anyone to trust that I had an understanding of course concepts. It might even do the opposite. All that said, I don't consider that draft a waste. It helped me to sort out my thoughts. In a roundabout way, it led me to accept that "sometimes," (or "yes, and") was a valid answer to the question of when to use the FPE.

This student describes a vital piece of the writing process that is frequently erased by the five-paragraph essay: the discovery draft. As Elbow (2000) and others argue, freewriting, sacrificial drafts, shitty first drafts (Lamott, 1995), and other labels for getting raw ideas on the page are powerful ways to discover what one thinks about a topic through writing.

The common process for writing the five-paragraph essay involves generating a thesis statement and outline before doing any drafting. This is the opposite of most good writing that uses the process to explore a concept. My students frequently comment on the value of this iterative process of writing and talking before they settle on what they want to say.

Other students described the change in their writing process as a transformational experience that they will pass on to their future students.

- I wouldn't have dreamed of putting a chart in my essay or ending it with a poem, but why not? It is part of what I want to say and how I wanted to say it! It was almost therapeutic: to loosen the chains of structure I have carried for years as I wrote about how I wanted to liberate my students from it in the future.
- I realized how much more effective of a writer I could be when I had different ways of communicating. By starting with a personal story, my readers could see the personal nature of this topic to me, and how I felt as a student. I would never have dared to ask if I could include a personal anecdote like that in a high school paper.

In the epigraph for this chapter, one student summed up her experience of this assignment in a way that gives me hope for the future of writing classrooms. She attends to "the nature of teaching and learning" as described in the *Beliefs Statement* (Gallo et al., 2020) by highlighting the social aspect ("debating writing formats and structures with my peers"), the research aspect ("understanding educator and expert perspectives on writing instruction"), and the engagement aspect ("writing my own piece of argumentative writing on the subject") of this assignment. She has weighed the issue thoroughly and come down with a principled purpose for writing instruction: to help students interact with the world. She is focused on what students want to do with their writing, not simply compliance to a particular convention.

CONCLUSION

A critical inquiry into the use of prescriptive, structured writing (the five-paragraph essay) does important work of disrupting the apprenticeship of observation (Lortie, 2020). Students who have been taught one "correct" way to write may not be able to envision alternative possibilities for how writing instruction might unfold. As one teacher candidate explains in her reflection:

> In all honesty, I always thought that my teachers taught the five-paragraph essay because it was required by the state standards. Therefore, I always thought that I, too, would have to teach my students to write in this way. Even better, I thought that the reason we had to write this way was because that is what the "professional" and "academic" world required. I was surprised to learn that creativity, choice, and variation is often encouraged and celebrated outside of the high school classroom.

This inquiry approach to explore instructional approaches aligns with the *Beliefs Statement's* recommendation to "prepare candidates to become engaged and effective teachers who can plan, implement, assess, and articulate rationales for pedagogical decisions" (Gallo et al., 2020). Through developing a principled stance, teacher candidates learn to critique traditional approaches and to question when efficiency gets in the way of authentic learning. They become reflective, metacognitive, learners as well as teachers with the confidence to ask questions about curriculum as they advocate for authentic student learning.

REFERENCES

Caplan, N. A. and Johns, A. M. (2019). *Changing practices for the L2 writing classroom: Moving beyond the five-paragraph essay*. University of Michigan Press.
Elbow, P. (2000). *Everyone can write: Essays toward a hopeful theory of writing and teaching writing*. Oxford University Press.
Elbow, P. (2012). *Vernacular eloquence: What speech can bring to writing*. Oxford University Press.
Gallo, J., Hallman, H. L., Parsons, C., Pastore-Capuana, K., Pet, S. R., and Searcy, L. (2020). Beliefs about methods courses and field experiences in English education. https://ncte.org/statement/methodsinee/.
Hillocks, G. (2011). *Teaching argument writing, grades 6–12: Supporting claims with relevant evidence and clear reasoning*. Heinemann.
Kittle, P. and Gallagher, K. (2021). *4 essential studies: Beliefs and practices to reclaim student agency*. Heinemann.
Lamott, A. (1995). *Bird by bird: Some Instructions on writing and life*. Knopf Doubleday Publishing Group.
Lane, B. (2015). *After THE END: Teaching and learning creative revision* (2nd ed.). Heinemann.
Lortie, D. C. (2020). *Schoolteacher: A sociological study*. University of Chicago Press.
Newkirk, T. (2014). *Minds made for stories: How we really read and write informational and persuasive texts* (Illustrated ed.). Heinemann.
Seo, B. I. (2007). Defending the five-paragraph essay. *English Journal, 97*(2), 15–16.
Smith, K. (2006). In defense of the five-paragraph essay. *English Journal, 95*(4), 16–17.
Thomas, P. (2016, September 17). How the 5-paragraph essay fails as warranted practice. *Dr. P.L. (Paul) Thomas*. https://radicalscholarship.com/2016/09/17/how-the-5-paragraph-essay-fails-as-warranted-practice/.
Warner, J. (2019). *Why they can't write: Killing the five-paragraph essay and other necessities* (Reprint edition). Johns Hopkins University Press.

Chapter 5

The English Classroom as a Contested Space

Fostering Critical Dialogue and Antiracist English Language Arts Practices

Hilary Lochte and Kristen Pastore-Capuana

"One of the paradoxes of education [is] that at precisely the point where you begin to develop a conscience, you must find yourself at war with your society."

–Baldwin (1963/2008)

THE ENGLISH CLASSROOM AS A CONTESTED SPACE

The English language arts classroom represents a space for telling and writing stories, for sharing lived experiences, for looking through windows of other worlds, and for cultivating empathy. It is also a space where teachers deserve the professional space to make choices and take up methods that are centered on justice, equity, and antiracist teaching practices that counter linguistic oppression, racial violence, and cultural hegemony (Baker-Bell, 2020).

This, however, is no easy task at a time when the pursuit of humanizing, culturally sustaining spaces is often met with politicized views of the educational field that misrepresent teacher preparation and assert that classrooms are too full of "woke ideology" (Contorno, 2022). References to ideology serve as popular dog whistles for those who assert that social issues do not belong in classrooms, but such arguments conveniently ignore the reality that schools are regularly relied upon to help students make sense of the world.

Classrooms continue to be positioned as battlegrounds, or contested spaces, within the context of rising culture wars and face increased scrutiny over curriculum, certification, and oversight while simultaneously being called upon to meet the holistic needs of students, created by real-world demands.

Ayers et al. (2008) state that "Education exists as a space of competing interests..." (p. 308). Curricular interference by forces outside of education, from parents to politicians to corporate interests result in an "assault on thinking—on being able to look at the world through one's own eyes, to name it, to decide for oneself what is fair and just and true, to question one's circumstances" for teachers and students (Ayers et al., 2008, p. 317). Further, it must be acknowledged, "ELA classrooms are contested spaces that are dominated by white, monolingual, middle-class perspectives that lack criticality and racial consciousness" (Johnson, 2022, p. 3).

When we conceptualize today's English classroom as a "contested space," we acknowledge the ways parents, community members, administrators, and politicians, attempt to shape the English classroom—even when their ideas may counter what educational research and theory recommends or what experienced teachers know their students need and deserve. It is a place of conflict where folks wrestle over who has the right to the space, whose voices are heard in the space, whose stories are told, and who is excluded or policed. English teachers must fight to define how the space presents possibilities to be reimagined and reconstructed.

In this fraught landscape, English language arts teachers must not only be prepared with and supported by tools to advocate for pedagogical autonomy, but they also need professional networks to lean on as they negotiate polarizing stakeholder perspectives in education's diverse landscape and divided social world.

This places more importance on English language arts methods courses to not simply couch themselves in instructional practices but to reconcile the fact that teaching is neither apolitical nor neutral. Teacher candidates need space and opportunities to engage in culturally sustaining and antiracist practices and fieldwork that allows them to bear witness to and participate in the myriad ways teachers design academically rich, justice-centered English language arts spaces.

Tensions within the English Language Arts Methods Course

The tension between externally imposed, traditionalist expectations of ELA classrooms and growing calls within the profession for the adoption of antiracist, culturally sustaining practices was at the heart of reimagining ENG 311: Methods of Teaching Language. ENG 311 presents an opportunity to create space to discuss issues of justice through a focus on linguistic consciousness; moreover, teacher candidates in this course identified issues of language as a specific point of negotiation or tension within the contested space of secondary English language arts. Professors and teacher candidates wrestled with the following core questions:

- How do English teacher educators reconcile connecting the theoretical aspects of English teaching with practical instructional strategies within an English methods course?
- How do English teachers contend with the historical role of cultural transmission that overtly or covertly embraced linguistic supremacy?
- How can English education programs help future teachers navigate the contestation of their English classroom spaces?

The authors acknowledge the ways that the English classroom has been used as a tool to tell an inaccurate tale about language, one couched in notions of neutrality while hiding its connections to power (Andrews, 2015; Johnson, 2022). English classrooms, with all of their expansive creative possibilities, also serve as gatekeepers, protecting standard English from the incursion of lesser linguistic rivals and their speakers.

To decolonize the English classroom, teacher educators have to first face up to the ways it has served as a tool of cultural supremacy. This means doing much more than giving all students a cultural touchpoint, an acknowledgment that each of their cultures matters and has a place in the classroom. Representation is important but it is not everything; at its most superficial, representation is merely lip service or, perhaps, cultural tourism. A core objective in the revised ENG 311 methods course is to interrogate how representation serves students when the remainder of their school year is spent reinforcing existing sociolinguistic power dynamics that undermine their cultures.

In this chapter, the authors explore their experiences wrestling with these questions in the context of a larger English education program revision and the very real challenges facing the community where they teach. The comprehensive overhaul of the English education program will be outlined, but the specific redesign of ENG 311: Methods of Teaching Language, both the course and fieldwork requirements, will be discussed as a model for supporting teacher candidates as they negotiate the tensions of English language arts practices in diverse contexts.

REIMAGINING ENGLISH EDUCATION PROGRAM DESIGN

To confront issues of teacher retention and declining enrollments in teacher education programs along with the sociopolitical and standardized curricular pressures facing local teachers, the Buffalo State English education program was redesigned to be a regional hub under the organizational structure of the Center for English Teaching. The Center for English Teaching encompasses the English education undergraduate and graduate program, the Western New

York Network of English Teachers (WNYNET), the Western New York Writing Project (WNYWP: affiliate of the National Writing Project), and the English Education Alumni Association.

Along with the development of the center, the program redesign was accompanied by a large-scale revision to the BS program. English education coursework is the skeletal structure of the program, but the courses were ill-conceived to reflect the progress in this field and meet the needs of students in local communities.

Previously, fieldwork was conducted only in the first and last classes of the program, which created a problematic gap in the continuity of clinical placements and coursework and the real-life inner workings of an English classroom. The BS program revision restructured fieldwork to be included in courses across the English education pathway.

The final stage of course redesign is focused on centering antiracist and antibias teaching practices at the core of academic and clinical work. Both NCTE's 2021 Standards for the Initial Preparation of Teachers for English Language Arts 7–12 (NCTE 2021) and New York State's 2018 Culturally Responsive-Sustaining Education Framework (CR-S; NYSED 2018) affirm the need to acknowledge and fight racism and bias as they continue to be pervasive in society and affect all students and their education.

Historically, program coursework had superficial and singular opportunities for teacher candidates to consider antiracist/antibias work, but the redesign process identifies opportunities for authentic engagement with this work across multiple courses. Local and national racist events solidified the urgency for centering antiracist/antibias teaching practices across program coursework, underscoring a need to focus on the role of language and rhetoric in an antiracist English classroom.

The Old ENG 311: Methods of Teaching Language

ENG 311: Methods of Teaching Language is the critical course at the center of both the initial and current redesign process. It was clear that ENG 311 needed to change; it touched upon topics like cultural forms of expression and honoring home languages but within a larger framework of traditional English teaching. It was outdated and, in some instances, oppressive. Built upon a prescriptive linguistics foundation, it promoted a hierarchical approach to the English language, one that denigrated nontraditional versions of English. It made English feel like a difficult-to-attain prize, rather than an inalienable right. The course also did not have any fieldwork, so teacher candidates did not have opportunities to work directly with in-service teachers and students on any of the course topics.

The national and local pressures on English teachers that have politicized English language arts teaching have changed the landscape of English teacher preparation; teacher candidates not only deserve space to share fears and concerns over outside pressures on teachers, but they also need specific spaces to explore and design practices that honor students' languages and identities. In the next section, the specific shifts and tensions with ENG 311 are explored in detail as they serve as a microcosm for the challenges facing English teachers and programs today—and perhaps always.

The previous ENG 311 course was designed and approved in 1997, and it focused on "language instruction that secondary education majors should have." The central objectives of the course were written to acknowledge diverse languages, but they failed to, as Baker-Bell (2020) argues, "analyze language through the lens of race and racism, where we ignore how linguistic violence and racial violence go hand in hand" (p. 16). While course objectives can be intentionally vague to carve out room for an instructor's academic freedom, these objectives were painfully broad. They were also fighting each other; for every nod toward culture, such as addressing family literacy, there was an affirmation of linguistic hierarchy.

Particularly problematic, the 1997 course proposal defined understanding the concept of "right to one's own language" through a "discussion of pupil's mastery of 'the dominant code' for public use as advancing pupil participation in society, economically and otherwise, while noting socio-political forces affecting what is 'standard'" (1997 Proposal, p. 2). The 1997 ENG 311 course overview included instructional methods focused on creative ways to teach grammar, but it did not include methods for engaging adolescents in exploring their relationship to language, language development, or cultivation of their own voices.

In addition, the previous iteration of ENG 311 did not include any fieldwork. As noted, the fieldwork design was part of the program changes; teacher candidates went from engaging with fieldwork only in the semester prior to student teaching to participating in fieldwork across a sequence of four English education courses.

Furthermore, the position statement *Beliefs about Methods Courses and Field Experiences in English Education* (Gallo et al., 2020) prompted further rethinking of ENG 311's fieldwork identity. As noted in the belief statement, Pasternak et al.'s (2017) research indicated a need for methods and fieldwork that are focused on preparation for racial, cultural, and linguistic diversity. ENG 311 presented an opportunity to focus on this area in both the teacher education classroom and during fieldwork.

The *Beliefs Statement* posits, "English teacher education programs should structure opportunities for candidates to reflect on, unpack, and learn from their field experiences" (Gallo et al., 2020). Fieldwork is vast and candidates in this program are often focused on strategies for classroom management or lesson plan design. Teacher educators redesigning this course felt that fieldwork for ENG 311 should reflect an explicit focus on the ways real teachers consider their own linguistic, racial, and cultural biases and showcase how English teachers design instructional strategies that center their students.

THE NEW ENG 311: LANGUAGE, LITERACY, AND CULTURE IN TEACHING

The new ENG 311 course revision began with a critical name change, which helped guide the shifts in both course content and pedagogy. Shifting ENG 311: Methods of Teaching Language to ENG 311: Language, Literacy, and Culture in Teaching established a clearer, more contemporary approach to language instruction in secondary schools.

New student learning outcomes focus on exploring the ways we use language and multiliteracies, exploring theories of language use, understanding the history of language instruction in schools, exploring the right to one's own language and other social dimensions of language, and English language arts instruction grounded in social justice. Ultimately, these shifts directly addressed the need to make the social justice focus of the class explicit and address the need that teacher candidates voiced for a place to unpack the tensions resulting from the English class's existence as a contested space.

Students serve as the primary inspiration for the revision of this ENG 311. In teaching an earlier iteration of this course it became clear that candidates were very heavily invested in issues of equity and social justice and wanted to explore ways to incorporate those into their future classrooms, and the course was not affording them the opportunity to explore those issues.

Teacher candidates expressed a desire to learn about the role that these issues could take in classrooms, but they also stated they often felt unsafe engaging in open discussions about race, class, gender, sexuality, ethnicity, and identity. They described feeling judged by peers or professors when they attempted to interrogate these topics; they were afraid to say the wrong thing or to admit to ignorance or confusion about them. It became clear that ENG 311 could become a place where students could explore the issues they valued within a framework they cared deeply about, English education.

In the new ENG 311, the floor has been opened to students so that they can wrestle with the issues that interest and inflame them. They worry about the exclusivity of the English classroom; they worry about dogma. They worry about giving their students a voice and honoring their cultural forms of expression, while also preparing them for jobs. They want to support cultural forms of expression but do not want to set their students up to be judged by the dominant society. They want to create exciting, energizing, and inclusive spaces filled with joy. They want to foster a love of reading and writing just as was once fostered in them. They want to be inspirational teachers.

Through a combination of key readings, student-centered discussions, and revised assignments, ENG 311 gives them an opportunity to explore how the English classroom can be different from the stereotypes we hold of English class. They read about teachers who emphasize voice over mechanics, who foreground expression before rules. They learn about teachers who embrace inquiry to help students understand the cultural rules that underlie prevailing views about "correct" English (Christensen, 2017; Smitherman, 2017).

They explore descriptive linguistics and the origins of our current English classroom doctrines along with teaching language as a set of context-specific registers rather than a zero-sum game of correctness or incorrectness through Andrews's (2015) *Language Exploration and Awareness: A Resource Book for Teachers*. They explore the importance of examining identity to foster confident writers in *Cultivating Genius* (Muhammad, 2020). Boyd's (2017) *Social Justice Literacies in English Classrooms: Teaching Practice in Action* helps students learn about teachers who value social justice and antiracism just as much as they do; moreover, teacher candidates unpack how these justice-centered pedagogical models align with state standards and create academically rich experiences for adolescents.

Centering Student Voice through Inquiry-Based Dialogue

A key element of this course is authorizing student voice, and this is accomplished through class discussion boards and in-class discussions. Rooted in modeling dialogic teaching practices (Freire, 2005), students are encouraged to shape discourse by posting and responding to discussion questions prior to class. Students are divided into two groups, and they alternate as posters and responders to every reading. Posters are expected to pose a question inspired by the next day's reading, with a brief explanation of what inspired their query; responders are charged with choosing one question to address on the board.

In class the students choose which discussion questions they most want to discuss, and an open-ended conversation ensues. This works well, in part, because the discussion boards serve primarily as a springboard for a deeper discussion, but one that has not already unfolded. Students are not required to flesh out their ideas entirely before getting to class, just to express their curiosities. In this way, class discussions remain fresh because they are not a rehashing of a previous discussion.

This exchange between two students in a discussion board illustrates the nature of these conversation starters:

Student 1: These two chapters illustrate invaluable points about viewing the use of language through context and function, rather than as a traditional, corrective study. As future educators, I'm sure we can all agree that we want our students to feel empowered by language, not forced to abandon their authentic selves because of it. . . . My question in response to this reading is, how can we balance teaching our students how to succeed in academic/business settings with allowing them to share their voices? While I understand the need for more formal language usage in certain settings, I would also never want to give my students the impression that their own use of language (whether it be use of AAVE, local vernacular, or words from other languages) is wrong or inferior (Fall 2021).

Student 2: I would be interested in discussing the question that [XXX] has laid out in class today. . . . I think it centers around the disconnect that focusing full bore on prescriptive rules creates between the writer and their words. If we demand that the "rules" be followed, then we risk eliminating their voice and making their writing hollow; technically correct but devoid of their personal voice. If we toss all the rules out the window completely, are we failing to prepare them for settings and people that will be looking for technical perfection? How do we best serve our students? (Fall 2021)

Ultimately, the student-generated discussion questions provide enough focus to keep the in-person conversations productive. Having the discussion started online also lends voice to the students who tend to be quiet during in-class discussions. This assignment provides students with the opportunity to collectively reason through issues in an effort to build understanding, an essential practice for teachers to develop when negotiating through the contested space that English classes have become.

The Language History Project

The Language History Project is an exercise in self-reflection, which asks teacher candidates to situate themselves as cultural beings whose language use has been shaped by their lived social experiences. Self-reflection is an essential aspect of any meaningful cultural work and is especially important for teachers (Hooks, 1994; Gay, 2018).

In the Language History Project, students are asked to reflect on their linguistic identities by identifying and defining at least three different language groups they belong to and examining how they use language differently depending on the group they are with. Students must also explore the ways they learned to use language and how their language use has changed over time. Lastly, they are asked to consider how their relationship to language has influenced their desire to become English teachers. Students pull this together in a multimodal presentation, incorporating audio, video, and images to present their findings.

This project challenges students to frame culture in the broadest of terms—moving them beyond the common demographic categories of race, ethnicity, religion, sexuality, and social class, toward a focus on the other groups that have shaped them and their language use. Perhaps they are gamers, knitters, home brewers, or participants in any other group that manipulates language to fit its needs. Teacher candidates come to see that their linguistic lives have been shaped in a multitude of ways beyond the formal registers they may have been taught in school and that for most, traditional language use is not their linguistic norm.

Students are invited to explore the ways that their language use influences how others view them and how they learned to "code switch" depending on the audience or environment. Encouraging students to examine their own language histories helps them understand that regardless of background, each person has a unique linguistic culture; it also undermines the anthropological tendency to treat other cultures as worthy of study while normalizing one's own.

The Fieldwork Synthesis Paper

Shaping the fieldwork into a meaningful experience has been a key goal of the revisions to ENG 311. The course now requires fifteen hours of fieldwork, which is included in their total of 100 hours of fieldwork prior to student teaching in New York State. The Center for English Teaching has a strong relationship with a K-12 charter school, located less than a mile from the campus. This relationship has been central to strengthening the role of fieldwork in this course; moreover, students in ENG 311 are granted access to the seventh- and eighth-grade ELA classrooms, without restrictions.

Coupled with this in-class experience is the synthesis paper, devised to ground these observation hours within the course readings and discussions. Students are asked to reflect on what they have observed in middle school classrooms, building connections between class readings and their field experiences. For example, students examine the degree to which they see culturally authentic language practices being embraced in classrooms. Are the teachers they observe incorporating student identity into the lessons they teach, and if not, how could they do so?

This assignment helps students make sense of the tensions that always exist between theoretical or practical readings done in class, which can feel idealized when juxtaposed with the realities of daily classroom life. This exercise also provides students with a critical lens while observing; they are asked to think about the type of language pedagogy they are seeing, what role, if any, culture plays in those rooms and the multitude of choices the teachers make within a single ELA class.

The fieldwork and synthesis paper continue to be a work in progress with ENG 311. The course professor is working with the local charter school to cultivate an expanded view of fieldwork that not only provides opportunities for teacher candidates to work with students, but also designates time for teacher candidates to talk directly about the issues, themes, and tensions at the core of ENG 311.

Acknowledging the continued "two-worlds pitfall" between what is taught in teacher preparation programs and what happens in secondary schools (Feiman-Nemser and Buchman, 1985), developing the relationship with one school for course fieldwork is a specific choice to open dialogue about research-based literacy practices and the unique needs of students at a specific school.

The Curriculum Revision Project

The culminating assignment for this course is a Curriculum Revision Project, in which students are asked to take existing curriculum, such as the Engage NY Learning modules[1] and adapt them in ways that make them culturally and historically responsive, antiracist, and socially just (Boyd, 2017; Muhammad, 2020). The inspiration for this assignment is the recurring theme of the "real world" that pops up in class continuously. Students regularly express concern that the readings and discussion from class exist in an idealized bubble; they wonder how any of the issues they feel so passionately about can be brought into classrooms, where they may not have any say in the curricula they teach.

Their concerns are valid, and this assignment pays them due respect. It additionally provides them with the opportunity to become familiar with curricular materials, which they have not worked with in detail yet. Students are tasked with choosing a seventh- or eighth-grade unit from a module, assessing it for ideological and practical goals, and then closely analyzing three lessons from it.

They must assess the goals and objectives, how they relate to the overall unit's goals, to the approach to language and language use, and to the content itself. For example, students are provided with guiding questions such as: If a unit is about racism, how are students asked to think about it? Are students encouraged to critically examine the issue? Are there opportunities to make connections to students' lives? Whose stories are told and whose are not?

After this analysis, students are asked to fill in any existing gaps they find and apply the lessons learned in class, providing critique and supplemental materials. They do so using the following three guiding questions: What opportunities do you see to infuse lessons with culturally and historically responsive pedagogy? What opportunities do you see to connect these lessons with antiracist and social justice pedagogies? What materials, small or large, would you use to supplement these lessons, to better connect them to students' lives?

The opportunity to apply their theoretical readings to real-world curriculum empowers the students while also demystifying the curriculum design process. Students learn that there is room for teacher autonomy, even within a prescribed curriculum, and enjoy applying their criticality and creativity to the modules. This project was created to give teacher candidates experience with not only speaking back to scripted curricular models but also to strategically reenvision them to align with academic and socially just learning goals. Below, a student analyzes a module lesson focused on the Civil Rights Era as part of the Curriculum Revision Project:

> This lesson opens the unit of civil rights, students begin with a gallery walk of texts and photographs that introduce the Civil Rights Era, which is followed by a brief discussion and then wrapped up by reading the first few pages on their main text for the unit. In general, I think this lesson acts as a nice opening to the unit, however I wonder if this lesson asks enough of the students. In eighth grade the idea of Civil Rights and racism is not brand new, I feel that this lesson hits only a surface level discussion of the issues and focuses more on the skills and less on the material. As it is the first lesson in the unit this could be a harsh judgment however this seems to be a common theme throughout the entire unit. Students can think about racism and the class can discuss it, but there doesn't seem to be carved out time dedicated to these conversations. Students are being asked to think about social justice but only as it pertains to perfecting their reading comprehension skills. (Fall 2021)

This student's work reflects the overall critical pedagogical objectives of the Curriculum Revision Assignment and of the course. The goal is to help empower students in the face of external challenges and obstacles, providing them with opportunities to cultivate their skills as culturally responsive educators.

LOOKING FORWARD

In the final weeks of working on this chapter, the authors have heard directly from both experienced English teachers and first-year educators about the challenges they are experiencing in local schools. From parents expressing concern over teachers' asking for preferred names and pronouns to questions over text selections in a classroom, English educators are navigating a landscape increasingly filled with scrutiny, misunderstanding, and questions when implementing antiracist and antibias pedagogy.

Admiration and emotional solidarity are not enough; teachers and teacher candidates deserve support that helps dismantle institutional pressures at schools and speaks back to misinformation about teachers and instructional practices. Redesigning the English education program, with a focus on ENG 311, is one step in advocating for linguistic justice, but the authors acknowledge these issues require larger systems in place to not only discuss the contested spaces of classrooms but to engage in meaningful professional learning at the point of need.

Methods courses and fieldwork are sites of possibility for teacher candidates and in-service teachers alike to engage in critical dialogue about literacy practices and the theory and hierarchies imbued in the practices we engage in every day. From this collective consciousness building, it is the authors' hope that classrooms will become more humanizing places for all, spaces where both teachers and adolescent students feel seen, heard, valued, and free.

NOTE

1. https://nysed.sharepoint.com/sites/P12EngageNY-ELA-EXTA/Shared%20Documents/Forms/AllItems.aspx?id=%2Fsites%2FP12EngageNY%2DELA%2DEXTA%2FShared%20Documents%2FEnglish%20Language%20Arts&p=true&ga=1

REFERENCES

Andrews, L. (2015). *Language exploration and awareness: A resource book for teachers* (3rd ed.). Taylor and Francis.

Ayers, W., Quinn, T., Stovall, D., and Scheiern, L. (2008). Teachers' experience of curriculum, policy, pedagogy, and situation. In F. M. Connelly, M. F. He, and J. Phillion (Eds.), *The SAGE Handbook of Curriculum and Instruction* (pp. 306–26). Sage Publications.

Baker-Bell, A. (2020). *Linguistic justice: Black language, literacy, identity, and pedagogy*. Routledge.

Baldwin, J. (2008). A talk to teachers. In *Handbook of Research on Teacher Education* (pp. 202–7). Routledge.

Boyd, A. S. (2017). *Social justice literacies in the English vlassroom: Teaching practice in action*. Teachers College Press.

Christensen L. (2017). *Reading, writing and rising up: Teaching about social justice and the power of the written word* (2nd ed.). Rethinking Schools.

Contorno, S. (2022, August 13). *Florida students return to schools reshaped by Gov. DeSantis' anti-'woke' education agenda*. CNN. Accessed August 15, 2022. https://

www.cnn.com/2022/08/13/politics/desantis-florida-schools-anti-woke-education-agenda/index.html.

Feiman-Nemser, S. and Buchmann, M. (1985). Pitfalls of experience in teacher preparation. *Teachers College Record, 87*(1), 53–65.

Freire, P. (2005). *Pedagogy of the oppressed* (30th anniversary ed.). Continuum.

Gallo, J., Hallman, H. L., Parsons, C., Pastore-Capuana, K., Pet, S. R., and Searcy, L. (2020). Beliefs about methods courses and field experiences in English education. Accessed January 12, 2022. https://ncte.org/statement/methodsinee/.

Gay, G. (2018). *Culturally responsive teaching: Theory, research, and practice* (3rd ed.). Teachers College Press.

Hooks, Bell. (1994). *Teaching to transgress: Education as the practice of freedom.* Routledge.

Johnson, L. L. (2022). *Critical race English education: New visions, new possibilities.* Routledge.

Muhammad, G. (2020). *Cultivating genius: An equity framework for culturally and historically responsive literacy.* Scholastic.

National Council of Teachers of English. (2021, November 11). *NCTE standards for the initial preparation of teachers of English language arts 7–12.* Accessed May 12, 2021. https://ncte.org/wp-content/uploads/2021/11/2021_NCTE_Standards.pdf.

New York State Education Department. (2018). *Culturally responsive-sustaining education framework.* Accessed January 21, 2019. http://www.nysed.gov/common/nysed/files/programs/crs/culturally-responsive-sustaining-education-framework.pdf.

Pasternak, D. L., Caughlan, S., Hallman, H. L., Renzi, L., and Rush, L. S. (2017). *Secondary English teacher education in the United States.* Bloomsbury.

Smitherman, G. (2017). Raciolinguistics, "mis-education," and language arts teaching in the 21st century. *Language Arts Journal of Michigan, 32*(2), 1–10.

Chapter 6

Planning Units to Work Within and Subvert the System by Critically Viewing Canonical Texts through Literature Circles

Julie Bell

Instructors of methods courses have a responsibility to prepare teacher candidates (TCs) for the realities of full-time classroom teaching by approximating common aspects of the job, including unit planning (Grossman et al., 2009). Unit plans can be cumbersome for TCs to create and instructors to assess. Coplanning and collaboration are integral to teaching; consequently, TCs may be better served by developing unit plans in pairs or small groups.

Smagorinsky (2019) suggested teachers should begin with a unifying concept for English Language Arts (ELA) unit design. However, the reality is many teachers are handed curriculum guides and expected to build units around mandated texts instead of concepts. To simulate this typical scenario, TCs might practice collaborative unit planning by developing a unit with colleagues around a literature circle text.

Given the area schools' expectation that secondary students will read canonical texts, ELA TCs participate in literature circles in their methods class to examine one way they could maintain dialogic instruction and honor students' voices with classic texts. As Garcia and O'Donnell-Allen (2015) acknowledged, "It's possible to work within the system and simultaneously maintain your commitment to a given pose [teaching stance]" (p. 11). Thus, TCs begin by trying traditional literature circle roles (Daniels, 1994; Ragland and Palace, 2017) to work within the system and transition to more critical viewing through updated roles (Thein et al., 2011; Chisolm and Cook, 2021) to subvert the system.

Through group unit development around canonical texts they discuss in literature circles, TCs have an opportunity to explore more diverse texts by developing text sets that take students' cultural backgrounds into account (Smagorinsky, 2019; Gallo et al., 2020). This chapter will address the rationale, implementation, successes, and challenges of unit planning around literature circle texts in an ELA methods course.

BACKGROUND AND CONTEXT

The ELA methods course described in this chapter is offered through the Teacher Education Department at a mid-size university in the Midwestern United States. The university is a member of the Coalition of Urban and Metropolitan Universities; thus, TCs are placed mostly in a large urban district and surrounding suburban districts. Prior to methods, TCs take three semesters of introductory coursework in Teacher Education, including beginning, intermediate, and advanced practicum teaching placements. Final practicum is associated with methods, and then TCs complete a semester of student teaching, known as clinical practice.

In Fall 2021, there were twenty-four TCs enrolled in the ELA methods course. Their demographics mostly matched the current teaching force and that of their professor (e.g., white, cisgender women) (Milner, 2020). Most of them were traditional college students, pursuing a bachelor's degree and initial teacher certification immediately after high school, though six of them already held bachelor's degrees and were pursuing initial teacher certification with coursework that could lead to a master's degree.

Prior to being released from class for five weeks for practicum teaching, TCs read and responded to a variety of texts. Their main course text was *Adventurous Thinking: Fostering Students' Rights to Read and Write in Secondary ELA Classrooms* (Blackburn, 2019). Major assignments before practicum included writing an initial teaching philosophy, participating in a literature circle, and working with a small group of colleagues to write a unit plan.

For practicum, the TCs were placed across six districts in seven high schools and six middle schools. The largest district serves over 50,000 students, while the smallest district serves around 3,000 students. During practicum, TCs submitted three videos of themselves teaching and completed a student work analysis to focus on assessment. When they returned to class, TCs presented to their colleagues about an instructional strategy they implemented during practicum.

RATIONALE FOR UNIT PLANNING AND LITERATURE CIRCLES

The instructors of the various content area methods courses (i.e., business, ELA, mathematics, science, social studies, and world languages) collectively determined that unit planning should be required in all methods courses. However, each instructor has the freedom to decide the logistics of the unit plan. Due to both the number of candidates and the typical nature of unit planning, ELA TCs work in small groups of three, four, or five to create their plans. Working with colleagues this way helps to simulate planning and curriculum discussions teachers frequently hold in schools.

As outlined in the NCTE Beliefs about *Methods Courses and Field Experiences in English Education* position statement, "Methods coursework should prepare candidates to become engaged and effective teachers who can plan, implement, assess, and articulate rationales for pedagogical choices" (Gallo et al., 2020). TCs must include a rationale and unit assessment as part of their unit plan. Their rationale is aimed at convincing parents/guardians and administrators that this is a worthy unit of study, and their assessment must be something other than a test. These elements are described in more detail in the next section.

Another recommendation in the NCTE position statement that is relevant to unit planning and literature circles is the following: "Methods coursework should emphasize the diversity of literacies, texts, and learners that constitute our field and our work as English language arts teachers" (Gallo et al., 2020). While TCs read classic, canonical texts in their literature circles, they design a text set with a variety of accessible texts (Tovani, 2004) to take their students into account. This element is also described in the next section.

IMPLEMENTATION OF LITERATURE CIRCLES AND UNIT PLANNING

Over time, the instructor of the ELA methods course has gathered curriculum guides and text lists aligned with grade levels from area practicum teachers. This information is used to build a questionnaire for TCs to select their top three choices from twelve options (two texts per grade level, grades 7–12). TCs are instructed not to select any texts they have read since graduating high school, and they must briefly explain why they made each selection. The instructor then places TCs into literature circle groups, aiming to assign their top choice text.

In Fall 2021, twenty-four TCs were evenly divided into groups of four to read, discuss, and unit plan around six different texts. One group planned for seventh grade by reading *A Wrinkle in Time* by Madeleine L'Engle. Their self-selected unifying concepts included the theme of nonconformity and individualism along with the archetype of the child hero. The other group that planned for seventh grade read *The Outsiders* by S.E. Hinton with a focus on a coming-of-age theme. The one group that planned for eighth grade read *The Giver* by Lois Lowry and also focused on the theme of coming of age.

For high school, one group read *To Kill a Mockingbird* and planned for tenth grade around the theme of the moral nature of human beings. Another group read *The Crucible* by Arthur Miller and planned for eleventh grade around a variety of archetypes. The final high school group focused on twelfth grade, read *Hamlet* by William Shakespeare, and selected the unifying concept of theme—seeking justice through revenge.

During the literature circle's inaugural meeting, TCs discuss their familiarity with the text using the following questions as a guide:

1. Have you previously read this text?
2. If the answer to #1 is yes, when was the last time you read it?
3. What stereotypes do you think exist about this text and author?
4. Why do you think this text is [still] taught in schools?
5. What do you want students to get out of reading this text?

One (or more) group member(s) acts as a recorder during the discussion so that the instructor may learn more about their background knowledge. During this meeting, the group also sets their reading schedule, divided across four weeks.

To prepare for their first text-based discussion, TCs read an article by Ragland and Palace (2017) in which the authors reported the results of an action research study implemented in a remedial ELA classroom. TCs' focus while reading is to make note of the results: How did the literature circles go? What is the evidence? The authors found that twenty-nine out of thirty-five students had increased comprehension scores on the Degrees of Reading Power test after participating in literature circles using traditional roles (Ragland and Palace, 2017).

Concurrently with reading the article, TCs complete a traditional literature circle role (Daniels, 1994) for one to two chapters or one act of their text. Each group is required to have a discussion director who facilitates the day's conversation. See figure 6.1 for a list and short description of each possible role.

During the second week of reading their text, TCs shift to unit planning. While the grade level is assigned with the text they selected, each group chooses an area school to serve as the context in which they could potentially teach their unit. They begin by looking at the demographics of the school and grade level (i.e., number of students, race, gender, percentage of students classified as English language learners, percentage of students receiving free/reduced lunch). They also explore the website to determine what the school values in terms of teaching and learning based on the school's mission statement and what is featured.

Planning Units to Work 79

Table 6.1 Traditional and Revised Literature Circle Roles

Traditional Literature Circle Roles	Revised Literature Circle Roles
Discussion Director: Your job is to develop a list of questions that your group can discuss about this part of the book.	*Problem Poser:* Your job is to locate and pose five key problems or dilemmas for which there are no easy answers in the text. You may want to pose these problems as questions.
Literary Luminary/Passage Master: Your job is to locate a few special sections of the text. The idea is to point out a part of the book that is *interesting, powerful, funny, puzzling, well written, thought-provoking, confusing, or an important section* of the text.	*Perspective Taker:* Your job is to try on and represent the perspective of a character or characters whose actions are problematic or confusing.
Word Wizard: Your job is to select four to seven new words in this section. These could be words you've never seen before, words that you don't understand in this context, or words you think are especially important to understanding today's passage.	*Difference Locator:* Your job is to point out the differences between how groups of people are represented in the text. Notice how these different groups of people are constructed and maintained.
Summarizer/Summary Supervisor: Your job is to write a paragraph summary of the main idea of this section. Do give us the main idea, but do not explain details.	*Stereotype Tracker:* Your job is to locate and "talk back" to dominant discourses or stereotypes the author evokes intentionally or unintentionally in the language and structure of the text.
Illustrator/Art Director: Your job is to make a *visual representation* of one section of the text. The idea is to show your group a little of the movie that is playing in your head.	*Critical Lens Wearer:* Your job is to consider the assigned reading through the lens of a relevant critical literary theory. *You must choose ONE of the following:* feminism, Marxism/social class privilege, historicism, new historicism, postcolonialism, or formalism. This person may consult Appleman (2015) for an explanation of the lenses.

Based on the demographic information and their knowledge of the text, TCs then identify a unifying concept. Smagorinsky (2019) suggested eight options: theme, archetype, works by a single author, literary time period, movement, region, reading strategy, or genre. They create a Google doc following a provided template for easy collaboration and to share with the instructor.

In week three with their text, TCs return to literature circle roles. This time, they read an article by Thein and colleagues (2011) in which the authors question the ability of traditional roles to push students beyond surface-level discussions and reifying stereotypes. TCs are asked to consider the authors' criticisms of traditional roles along with their recommended changes. They are also tasked with looking for elements of an empirical research article for an assignment they complete later in the semester. Revised roles were previously described in textbox 1.

During the final week of reading their text, TCs go back to unit planning, this time concentrating on composing a rationale to defend or justify their unit (Gallo et al., 2020). At this point, they complete a graphic organizer. They submit a thorough-composed rationale, organized like an argumentative essay, with the final draft of their unit plan. They include one or more types of justification (Smagorinsky, 2019) with a claim, evidence, and warrant to accompany each. They also acknowledge counterarguments and provide rebuttals.

When the TCs finish reading their text, they concentrate their time completely on unit planning. They select standards and write unit goals. They create a text set (Tovani, 2004) that must include examples of the following types of texts: fictional short story, nonfiction article/essay/book chapter, poem or song lyrics, two photos or pieces of art, one video clip that is not just a movie version of the text, and one additional text of their choice. TCs are encouraged to keep in mind principles of culturally relevant teaching and to select texts that coincide with whom they understand their learners to be as people (Gallo et al., 2020).

They develop a final summative assessment that cannot be a test, accompanied by a rubric or other tool with which to evaluate students. The group is also required to create at least one example response to this assessment. TCs include a weekly calendar with the following elements listed for each day: objective(s), standard(s), text(s), main activities, and assessment(s). Typically, each person in the group is responsible for creating the calendar for one week. Finally, each individual in the group must submit one lesson plan for a particular point in the unit (beginning, middle, or end).

The following is a list of the unit plan components:

1. Cover page: names of TCs, title of the novel, demographics of the selected school and grade level, summary of the school's values related to teaching and learning
2. Unifying concept or topic
3. Rationale justifying unifying concept and main text
4. Unit standards and goals
5. Text set
6. Summative assessment with rubric or other evaluation tool and example response
7. Weekly calendar including objective(s), standard(s), text(s), main activities, and assessment(s) for each day
8. Individual lesson plan from each group member

OUTCOMES OF LITERATURE CIRCLES AND UNIT PLANNING

Following the recommendation in NCTE's *Beliefs about Methods Courses* that TCs should be reflective (Gallo et al., 2020), TCs respond to a series of reflection questions each time they complete a literature circle role. They post their responses to a class discussion board, so all their colleagues see them. The questions are as follows:

- What did you learn about your novel by completing your literature circle role?
- What did you learn about your novel by participating in your literature circle discussion?
- Provide one comment OR question about applying literature circles in your own teaching. REMEMBER: Everyone would probably want more time, and in your own classroom, you would be able to plan for more time. Think about some other aspect of literature circles for reflection.

For the first reflection about the traditional roles (Daniels, 1994; Ragland and Palace, 2017), the instructor read and categorized their responses to the final prompt as questions, positive, logistics, or other. Many of the TCs (46 percent) had questions about how to best implement literature circles. For example, Maddie[1] asked, "How can we ensure that all students have equitable time to share their thoughts?" The instructor compiled all the questions and gave each literature circle one or more questions to discuss and share with the class.

The next most frequently occurring type of response was positive (25 percent). Responses categorized as positive were those in which the TC commented in a positive way about participating in or implementing literature circles. One example came from Erika: "I think literature circles would be a fun way to get everyone involved in discussion and build community within the classroom." Overall, TCs viewed this strategy as one that would get students talking in a productive, less intimidating way about text.

Some TCs made comments about the logistics of literature circles (17 percent). For example, Courtney wrote, "I think with literature circles it would also be cool to see the students maybe sharing to the class or other groups reading the same book what they got out of it and discussed compared to other groups/class." TCs commenting on logistics tended to think about ways they could slightly alter the format they experienced in class to better fit their own classroom vision.

A few TCs had responses categorized as other (12 percent). These were responses that did not fit within the questions, positive, or logistics categories.

Avery stated, "I love the idea of having students reading a book they chose because it should motivate them more to get the reading done, and they should be excited to discuss it with their peers."

When they responded to the prompts about the revised roles (Thein et al., 2011; Chisolm and Cook, 2021), most TCs continued to ask questions (39 percent). One question Ben asked about the revised roles was the following: "How do you get beyond surface-level interpretations of the text? For college students it's one thing to have a more nuanced reading, but how do we as secondary teachers push students past their own understanding of the world into new frames of thinking?" Due to time constraints following their reflection on the revised roles, the TCs did not have an opportunity to discuss their responses in small groups. Instead, the instructor briefly responded to the questions, periodically inviting input from the TCs.

Like 15 percent of respondents, Charles made a critical statement: "I think some of these more complicated roles would not work well for certain classes or novels. Some of the roles seemed forced because characters or groups of people in [our text] do not fit well into the critical roles." While Ben asked a question and Charles made a statement, the instructor responded similarly to both, reminding the TCs of the importance of modeling and scaffolding. All students, regardless of grade or perceived ability level, are capable of having rich discussions. The roles themselves are not enough to achieve high-level discussions, though. This question and statement also suggested that the instructor may need to engage in more modeling of the revised roles for TCs.

In addition to questions and critical statements, several TCs commented again about logistics (31 percent). Mary's statement about logistics mirrored the instructor's response to Ben and Charles. She wrote, "I definitely would give examples and model what type of answers I am looking for with each role to my students, because while I think they can do it, for roles like Critical Lens Wearer or Problem Poser, they need guidance in the beginning." While TCs were encouraged to read Appleman's (2015) definitions and examples of critical lenses, they may have benefitted from viewing a completed example of the Critical Lens Wearer role based on a text TCs were not reading.

A few TCs did make positive comments about the revised literature circle roles (15 percent). For example, Breyah noted, "I really like the new literature circle roles. It is honestly fun to complete your role individually and then have the opportunity to speak with others about their thoughts as opposed to, or in conjunction to, your own. It also makes reading the novel (play, in our case) more enjoyable too."

TCs also complete a self-reflection on their unit plans, which is modeled after a tool provided by Carnegie Mellon University (2022). They answer a series of Likert scale questions with an explanation for each response. Most TCs (nearly 70 percent) said they did about the same amount of work on their unit plans as the colleagues in their groups. All TCs said they always or almost always completed assigned tasks on time.

In response to the prompt "I displayed or tried to develop a wide range of skills in service of the project; I readily accepted changed approaches or constructive criticism," one TC said they sometimes did, while the rest responded they almost always or always did. They returned similar responses (i.e., one sometimes, the rest almost always or always) for the communication skills prompt that they were "effective in discussions, a good listener, and proficient at documenting work." The self-reflection closed with two open-ended prompts giving the TCs an opportunity to share additional information about their group members' participation or their own participation.

SUCCESSES AND CHALLENGES OF LITERATURE CIRCLES AND UNIT PLANNING

Based on candidates' feedback and the instructor's evaluation of their unit plans, group unit planning around literature circle texts has been successful overall. TCs work collaboratively in a way that mirrors the planning process for most secondary teachers. They develop a collection of unit and lesson plans that they may use in their practicum (preservice) field placements and beyond.

Some TCs have never experienced literature circles before as a student or teacher. Thus, they have an opportunity to participate like a student while simultaneously reflecting on how they might incorporate them as teachers. They get the experience they crave (Whitney et al. 2013) supported by reading research about the instructional strategy (Thein et al., 2011; Ragland and Palace, 2017).

There are some challenges with this approach to unit planning. As with any collaborative endeavor, TCs sometimes have interpersonal conflicts. The instructor encourages them to resolve the conflicts quickly and respectfully, reminding the TCs that they will likely work through challenges with colleagues in the future. Additionally, the unit planning assignment is not completely authentic for a few reasons, particularly that TCs start with a text instead of a unifying concept (Smagorinsky, 2019).

Even though the instructor consistently reminded TCs that well-scaffolded literature circles are a solid instructional strategy for ALL students, regardless of grade level or perceived academic ability, some TCs continued to think only high school or "advanced" students would be able to participate in literature circles. This was especially true for the updated literature circle roles outlined by Thein and colleagues (2011), which require more critical thinking.

FUTURE DIRECTIONS FOR UNIT PLANNING AND LITERATURE CIRCLES

Even though TCs may have to work within the system by teaching classic, canonical texts, they may subvert the system by designing engaging units around those texts that invite students to think critically. Just as teacher educators ask candidates to reflect, instructors also benefit from reflecting on their practice. Based on reflections of the TCs described in this chapter about literature circles, the instructor likely needs to model the Critical Lens Wearer role from the revised roles (Thein et al., 2011) to better help TCs understand the expectations and think more deeply about their texts.

Implications for other teacher educators who want to incorporate unit planning around literature circles in their own methods classes include the following:

1. Connect with teachers at area schools to incorporate texts and instructional strategies from their curriculum.
2. Contact former TCs to find out if they have used traditional or revised literature circle roles with their students with any degree of success.
3. Determine if TCs will focus on the original roles, revised roles, or some combination.
4. Consider how much class time to offer TCs for discussing the text in a literature circle versus how much class time to offer for planning their collective unit.
5. Decide how much feedback to give TCs on draft portions of their unit plans.

When thoughtfully scaffolded, literature circles are a helpful strategy for secondary students and TCs alike to engage in authentic discussions about texts and unit plan in a unique way.

NOTE

1. TCs gave permission to use their first names or selected their own pseudonyms.

REFERENCES

Appleman, D. (2015). Classroom activities. *Critical encounters in secondary English: Teaching literary theory to adolescents* (3rd ed.). Teachers College Press.

Blackburn, M.V. (Ed.). (2019). *Adventurous thinking: Fostering students' rights to read and write in secondary ELA classrooms.* National Council of Teachers of English (NCTE).

Carnegie Mellon University. (2022). *Assessing group work.* Accessed February 3, 2023. https://www.cmu.edu/teaching/assessment/assesslearning/groupWork.html.

Chisholm, J. S and Cook, M. P. (2021). Examining readers' critical literature circle discussions of Looking for Alaska. *Journal of Adolescent and Adult Literacy, 65*(2), 119–28.

Daniels, H. (1994). *Literature circles: Voice and choice in the student-centered classroom.* Stenhouse Publishers.

Gallo, J., Hallman, H. L., Parsons, C., Pastore-Capuana, K., Ringler Pet, S., and Searcy, L. (2020). *Beliefs about methods courses and field experiences in English education.* https://ncte.org/statement/methodsinee/.

Garcia, A. and O'Donnell-Allen, C. (2015). *Pose, wobble, flow: A culturally proactive approach to literacy instruction.* Teachers College Press.

Grossman, P., Compton, C., Igra, D., Ronfeldt, M., Shahan, E., and Williamson, P. W. (2009). Teaching practice: A cross-professional perspective. *Teachers College Record, 111*(9), 2055–100.

Milner, IV, H. R. (2020). Disrupting racism and whiteness in researching a science of reading. *Reading Research Quarterly, 55*(S1), 249–53.

Ragland, J. and Palace, C. (2017). Literature circles for adolescent developmental readers. *English Journal, 116*(6), 35–40.

Smagorinsky, P. (2019). *Quick reference guide: Unit design in the ELA classroom.* National Council of Teachers of English (NCTE).

Thein, A. H., Guise, M., and Long Sloan, D. (2011). Problematizing literature circles as forums for discussion of multicultural and political texts. *Journal of Adolescent and Adult Literacy, 55*(1), 15–24.

Tovani, C. (2004). *Do I really have to teach reading?: Content comprehension, grades 6–12.* Stenhouse Publishers.

Whitney, A. E., Olan, E. L., and Fredricksen, J. E. (2013). Experience over all: Preservice teachers and the prizing of the "practical." *English Education, 45*(2), 184–200.

Chapter 7

Using Text Sets and Mini-Lessons to Develop Sense of Authority as Teachers of Reading

Allison Wynhoff Olsen and William J. Fassbender

When preparing preservice teachers (PSTs) to become English teachers, programs consider how and when to promote a shift in positioning from student to teacher. Methods coursework aims to "empower" PSTs and teach them how to "articulate rationales for pedagogical choices" (Gallo et al., 2020). Located in the American Mountain West, this educational program attempts to honor the varied backgrounds of students and prepare them to teach in sub/urban areas as well as extremely rural spaces.

The focal preparation program in this chapter dedicates six courses to English education, one of which is *Teaching Reading and Literature.* This course is aimed at supporting PSTs in planning varied learning opportunities for readers and giving support to building and sustaining readers. The course emphasizes how to approach and entangle literature into students' lives rather than just using literature as a prop to help achieve a skill. Through the course, PSTs are expected to make textual choices (Gallo et al., 2020) while considering their future students' backgrounds, cultures, and places.

Figure 7.1 provides the course signature assignment in which PSTs create a text set using Lupo et al.'s (2017) quad text framework pursuant to a theme of their choice. The framework consists of a target text and then surrounding texts to surround, enhance, and bolster the reading and comprehension of ideas; the surrounding texts are categorized as visual, informational, and accessible. The framework encourages a pluralistic approach to meaning-making with texts and does deliberate work to enhance and support PSTs' emerging sense of authority as teachers of reading and literature.

Within the full assignment, PSTs layer in critical lenses (Appleman, 2015) to help articulate their textual choices and rationale. They also script three mini-lessons (Roberts, 2018), aligned with the standards, and create two sequencing

TEXT SETS

Objective: Building text sets helps teachers foreground intertextuality and offers students multiple avenues into a topic. Given connections we naturally make as we read, this assignment offers opportunity to build a text set on a theme of interest. Teaching with text sets also promotes intertextuality and dialogue across perspectives.

Foundation: We will use the Lupo, Strong, Lewise, Walpole, & McKenna (2017) article as a touchstone for this work. I recommend reading this piece in full, as well as referencing it during text set work this month. The article is in D2L under "Resources" tab.

Components
All underlined components are required by the draft deadline.
All components must be in place by the final deadline.

- <u>A named theme & rationale for the full text set</u>
- <u>Indication of the grade level(s) to whom you imagine teaching this set</u>
- 2-4 focal Common Core State Standards [this element is NOT on the sample text set]
- <u>Mini-Lessons</u>
    o Write 3 mini-lessons to use within this text set. When these are delivered is noted in the sequencing options.
    o [Base formatting on Roberts, pp. 71-77; this text selection is found on D2L under the "Resources" tab]
- <u>Two sequencing options for navigating the texts:</u> be sure to also note where mini lessons occur.
- 2 critical lenses:
    o Provide a rationale for EACH lens selected.
    o Also, write a paragraph that explains how the two intersect toward this text set.
- <u>Works Cited or References list</u>
    o <u>This list includes all texts from the text set as well as any additional found within the mini-lessons</u>

QUAD TEXTS: Review Lupo et al. for the quad-text framework. I have written some options under each text type but those are not extensive; you likely have your own ideas, here.

- <u>Target text (a novel that you deem literature)</u>
    o <u>Novel indicates that this target text is one of substantial length</u>
- <u>Visual texts (2-3)</u>
    o Art
    o Picture books
    o Videos
- <u>Informational texts (1-2)</u>
    o <u>These are often nonfiction: nonfiction books, articles or essays, for example</u>
- Accessible text (3-4 total texts; select from the genres below)
    o poems
    o music (both the song + the lyrics, if there are lyrics)
    o memes
    o <u>Ted talks</u>
    o Blogs/Vlogs
    o Videos

Figure 7.1 Text Set Assignment Sheet.

plans on how to experience the texts and topics. To clarify, the required scripts do not promote a scripted curriculum; rather, the planning and script writing provide time for PSTs to focus on their teacher talk so they can practice how to explain and articulate their ideas, receive feedback from peers and their professor, and (hopefully) gain more confidence in their lesson planning abilities.

Additionally, the scripts afford PSTs opportunity to display their knowledge and skills they have cultivated as English majors. Across the signature assignment, professors lean into the beliefs for English methods courses (Gallo et al., 2020).

Prior to offering this signature assignment in the undergraduate course, professors noticed that PSTs were struggling to position themselves as teachers, a struggle made evident in conversation and lesson plans. PSTs were solid at building lessons that moved students across participant structures (e.g., small group examinations, whole-group discussions, independent work time), yet were uncomfortable asserting themselves as teachers who had specific knowledge to share.

Given that the overall teacher prep program is built on student-centered classrooms that believe in cultivating genius (Muhammad, 2020) and leaning into complexities and wobble (Fecho, 2011), it made sense that students emphasized social constructions of learning; yet, the resulting byproduct meant that PSTs shied away from any sort of direct teaching and primarily planned small group work, learning stations, independent reading time, Socratic seminars, and Harkness discussions. The missing piece was a teacher authority who had knowledge to share and opportunities to directly teach students what they needed. PSTs also shied away from writing lessons on canonical literature because they were concerned with how to make it engaging.

Through this signature assignment, professors were able to have more practical conversations about how to move across texts and how to put texts in dialogue with one another. The creation of interrelated text sets offers more relevance because the full text set connects the literature to social contexts and text types across genre, modes, and difficulty; text sets also increase the volume of works being read on the focal topic.

The signature assignment is built on core foundations in the field and articulating teacher moves in curriculum planning—moves that are often invisible because they occur in preparations for teaching rather than PSTs classroom observations. Such moves are grounded in theory and tied to research. This signature assignment, then, allows professors to invite PSTs to "approach our work as English language arts teachers in our classrooms and as part of an engaged professional community" (Gallo et al., 2020).

ASSIGNMENT FOUNDATIONS

To build knowledge before planning, PSTs read the Lupo et al. (2017) article and the class discussed the benefits and challenges of teaching across texts, rather than engaging in a mono-study of text (an approach most of them experienced in high school). Lupo et al. mostly promote quad text sets as a model for in-service teachers; however, introducing this model to PSTs is important for several reasons.

First, professors recognized that, in spite of the reading/writing workshop approach promoted across the English education course offerings, many

PSTs enter less progressive classroom settings. This limits the likelihood that they will work with mentors who will be implementing the workshop model. Text sets, thus, serve as a reasonable compromise and provide a curricular heuristic: a way to think about programming various texts and text modalities for a robust dialogic opportunity (VanDerHeide et al., 2023) and a way to amplify the study of whole class novels in a way that augments students' meaning-making.

Additionally, professors found that examining Lupo et al.'s (2017) article and creating text sets responded directly to theory/practice concerns and invited undergraduate students to engage with research in a generative way. Rather than just read about a pedagogical idea as PSTs, the English teaching program uses research as a foundation for lesson planning and as a way to shift positioning from teacher to student in a continual, reciprocal manner.

Professors also used Robert's (2018) textbook, *A Novel Approach*, and emphasized the four-part framework for "adequate" mini-lessons as a lesson planning model. Similar to the use of Lupo et al. (2017) work, PSTs read Roberts to learn the lesson's four components—connection, teaching, active involvement, and link. PSTs also viewed and debriefed a handful of Roberts' teaching videos, specifically listening to Roberts's language and pacing.

Professors helped PSTs understand how teachers can scaffold information for students and directly offer busts of information that are needed (a need established from kid-watching and formative assessments done in workshop classrooms). In the assignment, PSTs wrote three mini-lessons' scripts to show their understanding of how they (1) connect to previous concepts/skills, (2) teach new concepts/skills, (3) elicit active involvement to practice new skills individually or in small groups, and (4) link new learning to future reading. Via mini-lessons, PSTs practiced teaching with emphasis on synthesizing ideas and articulating their teacher talk; they also gained practice in lesson pacing.

Lesson planning (e.g., mini-lessons) within the signature assignment also facilitated valuable "approximations of practice" (Grossman et al. 2009) for our PSTs. According to Grossman et al. (2009), "Approximations of practice refer to opportunities for novices to engage in practices that are more or less proximal to the practices of a profession" (p. 2058). Such opportunities provide authentic opportunities to "approximate," or get as close to the real experience of teaching, while still providing scaffolding.

Authenticity with these proximate experiences matters in establishing activities that will guide PSTs toward teaching practices they may choose to adopt when they have a classroom of their own. For example, a PST may lead a brief five-minute discussion during a practicum course to get a feel for whole class teacher–student interactions. Experiences like these help students to practice skills while allowing for potential failure in lower stakes settings so that they can make improvements for future iterations when they assume a role as a more permanent fixture during future student teaching experiences.

Whereas it is more typical for approximations of practice to occur through embodied practice of teaching, either through early interactions with students in K-12 settings or in role-play in college classrooms, writing lessons is a critical element of teaching which requires opportunities for "trying on" parts of the teaching profession (Schutz, Grossman, and Shaughnessy, 2018, p. 62) as well. As such, the signature assignment allowed professors to adopt a broader conception of approximations of practice that recognized planning as a process that benefits from rehearsal in the same ways that low-stakes teaching demonstrations provide scaffolding and feedback to PSTs before they assume their own classrooms.

Approximations of practice also attempted to elucidate the text selection process that teachers must consider, not only when choosing a whole class novel, but in looking for moments to interrupt that target text with supporting texts that can bring that novel to life and be in dialogue with other texts and students. As PSTs build their quad text sets for the assignment, most do not push back on putting texts into conversation with one another; however, they lack student experiences reading multiple texts simultaneously and need careful guidance on how to put their texts together meaningfully—an example of how a pedagogical recommendation entices PSTs in theory but asks them to figure out how to use researcher's ideas in their planning/teaching.

The sequence of texts asks PSTs to be thoughtful in their ability to not only choose supporting texts but consider the temporal rationale for how to use them with students. In these considerations, professors attend to a core recommendation from the Methods Commission, "to support teacher candidates in becoming critical, agentic, active, ethical, reflective, and socially just educators." When curating a text set, the *when* and *why* are equally important as the *what*.

ASSIGNMENT DETAILS, ILLUSTRATED

This section provides more detail and illustrates the signature assignment (see figure 7.1) using excerpts from PSTs work. Early in their text set building, PSTs chose a theme and wrote a rationale. Next, they imagined the target grade level, ranging from grades 5 to 12 because while some text sets may be compelling to a wide range of youth, professors expected PSTs to write a rationale that revealed how they understood the texts in dialogue with one another for a particular student population in a particular community.

Unstated in the assignment sheet, the rationale was also a place for PSTs to articulate their understandings of place as well as the sociopolitical moment.

PSTs also selected two-four state standards to emphasize across the text set. PST Harper's[1] rationale illustrates this:

This text set is designed to meet common core standards and engage students through the use of related, multimodal texts (Lupo et al., 2017). I imagine teaching this set to eleventh and twelfth graders. The target text is *There There* by Tommy Orange, a "multigenerational story about violence and recovery, memory and identity, and beauty and despair woven into the history of a nation and its people" (Orange, 2018). This text follows twelve characters, urban Native Americans, and their connection to the Big Oakland Powwow. In order to scaffold deeper, more nuanced understandings of this complex text, I picked supporting texts that give background knowledge on the periods of federal policy toward Native Americans and that dissect stereotyped essentializing portrayals of Native Americans.

Harper's rationale focused on Native American experiences and federal policy with the goal of supporting students in considering how policy impacts people's lives and opportunities. She took a few courses in Native American Studies and made deliberate moves in her planning to incorporate Native authors, build connections to the land, and question Eurocentric ideologies.

PST Sam's rationale shows a different take on the assignment. Given his location in the mountain west, Sam's project theme of survival seemed unremarkable at first given that students are often drawn to the university based on its proximity to national parks and many spend their leisure time in nature, priding themselves on self-sufficiency as it relates to hiking, camping, and fishing. In line with that concept of survivalism, it would have made sense for Sam to build his project around a target text like Gary Paulsen's *Hatchet* or Jon Krakauer's *Into Thin Air*. Instead, Sam offered a more socially aware topic of survival, choosing stories of survival that came from the perspective of people with disabilities—a pedagogical decision made by an athletic, able-bodied, male.

> Survival can seem as a simple and outdated construct with the world we live in today. First-world countries, along with the technology that is available for higher, middle, and lower middle class individuals in these countries, may make it appear as though many individuals do not have to focus on survival to thrive anymore. However, surviving in the world today can have many diverse challenges that can introduce students to perspectives they have not been exposed to before due to their background. A person with a disability has a different method of surviving in the world than an impoverished individual, a minority in a predominantly white country survives with different tactics than a woman living in a male-centered patriarchy. This unit will introduce how human survival and success is greatly influenced by our inequalities.

To note, Sam's awareness of his own privilege as well as the experiences of others was typical for him, yet is not always an articulated move professors see in PST or early-career teachers.

Authors also note that Sam was a double major in English education and economics; his interdisciplinary focus enriched the connections across texts and was a visible thread in his mini-lessons. Sam's work took a deep dive across human and economic issues, using his visual, informational, and accessible texts to build knowledge and think across disciplines.

Sam continued his rationale for each textual choice, again making his interdisciplinary approach visible as he asked students to consider regions of the world due to (dis)abilities and socioeconomics, while acknowledging that one's race also intersects with one's survival—a concept he nuanced and complexified throughout his work. Furthermore, he defended his choice of texts by exploring a pluralistic notion of legacies of oppression that have forced different marginalized groups historically into a mode of survival.

Colson Whitehead's *The Underground Railroad* is a fictional piece that illustrates some of the horrific actions and acts of survival that slaves commonly had to preserve through to survive in an oppressive nation. It is the target text for this text set because it lays the groundwork for how the American ideology forces different modes of survival for different individuals with diverse backgrounds.

American Progress is a painting by John Gast that exemplifies the manifest destiny and our predominantly white culture's rationale for our future and further mistreatment of Native Americans and nature. It is included to demonstrate the troublesome actions that the United States thought was needed to survive and how the manifest destiny led to many different acts of survival for Native Americans.

"How the U.S. stole thousands of Native American Children" is a documentary video by Vox that provides insight on the negative impacts that Indian boarding schools had a lasting impact on Native Americans. They were essentially forced to assimilate to survive in their own country and land.

Surviving in a world with a disability is an aspect of life that most people in the world are unaware of. Judith Heuman's Ted Talk will serve as the talking point of a perspective of how some people still need additional help to survive in the world.

"Anywhere but Here" by Johnathan Newton is a recent article depicting the dreams of Montana basketball player Mya Fourstar and her desire to get off the reservation to play college basketball. For her basketball is her mode of survival.

"Life of Privilege Explained in a $100 Race" is an incredibly insightful and applicable YouTube video for this unit. It intertwines both critical race theory and social class theory to produce a visual exemplifying how privilege impacts who wins the game of life.

Sam's focal text was *The Underground Railroad* by Colson Whitehead, yet he wrote in his final draft that this text "can be substituted with other texts like Reyna Grande's memoir *The Distance Between Us*." In this remark, Sam indicated his understanding that in order for readers to sustain attention on the focal text, it needs to be carefully selected for them.

Providing opportunities for Sam to explicate various options organized toward different pedagogical aims demonstrated his ability to honor "[attend] to the cultural backgrounds of students and choosing texts and learning opportunities that nurture students' unique literacies" (Gallo et al., 2020).

Once PSTs set their rationale, target grade level, and standards, they built three mini-lessons. As they wrote their mini-scripts according to Roberts' four components (connection, direct teaching, active involvement, and link), professors reminded them that connection and link are critical in lesson planning of any length. While a lesson may be brilliant, its use for students is lessened if connections and transfers are not made. Harper's connection illustrates how she reminded students what they had done and how they would add a step in order to do a deeper analysis of the same poem.

> We just read "Living History" by Kimberly Blaeser and had a great discussion about the poem. Now we're going to take our analysis a step further by applying a new thinking framework to the poem. *[Pull up the Pyramid of Violence]*. This is a thinking framework sort of like the Systemic Awareness chart. If you remember from yesterday, the Systemic Awareness chart looks at how individual experiences and oppressions are influenced by trends at different systemic levels. The Pyramid of Violence is a thinking tool designed to help us dig into individual experiences and understand how acts of violence build upon one another. Using this chart, we can also see possible ways to prevent violence and oppression (If you eliminate the base support of the pyramid—language—all the other violences have nothing to stand on). It's the responsibility of readers to use thinking frameworks like these charts to critically analyze what power dynamics are functioning in a text to create violences. None of us, including authors and characters, exist in a vacuum where we don't feel the impacts of power structures, reinforce power structures, or fight against power structures.

Teacher talk (noted by the mini-lesson script) was the most difficult for PSTs to compose in the teaching and active involvement components. Thereby, professors offered their own mini-lessons on these two elements, modeling for PSTs how to language a focused concept and how to offer a

gradual release of responsibility: I do, we do, you do. Harper's sample illustrates how she wrote the teaching section of the mini-lesson.
Let's take a deeper look at the Pyramid of Violence. *[Explain how the different levels are put in this order for a reason—they build on each other. As you quickly go through the pyramid, ask students questions like, "how do you see language and jokes creating rigid stereotypical roles?" And, "What is your understanding of objectification? Dehumanization? How do rigid stereotypical roles create objectification and dehumanization?"]* Ok, now let's apply this to the poem we just read.

So first I ask myself "where do I see tension in this poem?" Follow your gut here. I start to feel the tension in these lines, "Pinches my arm, but I guess it's yours/he touches./Hell, wasn't even looking at me./Wonder if I'm what they call living history?" I get the feeling that some sort of violence is happening here. The speaker is touched without her consent and feels like she wasn't even seen. So now, I need to try and narrow in on what's causing that tension and I can do this by using the Pyramid of Violence.

I can look for keywords or themes that could clue me in to what's happening in this scene. I get the keywords and themes from the Pyramid of Violence. So I see how the language and actions are dehumanizing the speaker to the point where she doesn't feel like she's seen or her own person. With this, I now get a deeper view into tensions and power dynamics within the poem. What do you think this means?

Harper's teaching ended with a direct question to students and served as a bridge into the active involvement component of her mini-lesson. Notice that while her teaching section was not lengthy, it was direct and used a pyramid document to which all students would have access to examine with her (an important scaffold). Harper's invitation for students to engage also came quickly after she told students her own steps as a reader—making herself vulnerable and using her processes as a model.

Writing mini-lesson scripts allowed PSTs to focus on their teacher talk, especially their ways of explaining concepts to others—an important component of identity work that supports PSTs "in becoming critical, agentic, active, ethical, reflective, and socially just educators" (Gallo et al. 2020).

Taking these mini-lessons and determining when to offer them in the textual study matters as well, which is why PSTs were required to create two sequencing options. To build these sequences, PSTs reviewed their text selections and articulated rationale; they then determined how to order texts (e.g., when to interrupt the reading of one for the study of another), and how to use their mini-lessons to develop their students' skills and go deeper with their themes. Pacing was highlighted.

Harper's sequencing notes provide a glimpse into how PSTs considered these arrangements.

Option 1
This sequencing track foregrounds applying thinking frameworks and circular lessons.

This sequencing options begins with "A History of Federal Indian Policy" by Pevar and the mini-lessons *Thinking Frameworks: Pyramid of Violence and the Systemic Awareness Chart*. Starting with Pevar's piece gives students the necessary background to contextualize the various historical time periods present throughout *There There*, the target text. This will allow students to make sense of temporal shifts within the target text and will provide students with a nuanced view of shifting federal policies toward Native Americans. The thinking frameworks mini-lessons will help students recognize and challenge various biases and stereotypes through understanding how violence is created and how systemic structures impact lived experiences. The rest of the sequencing interweaves support texts with the target text. The support texts are placed alongside specific points in *There There* to deepen students' understanding of the themes, characters, and tensions present at that textual moment in *There There*.

Option 2
This sequencing is front-loaded with various support texts which allow students to expand and nuance their definitions of "Native American." By beginning with modern Indigenous projects, this sequencing quickly combats ideas of Native Americans as trapped in the past through showcasing the agency and work of contemporary Native Americans from many different tribes. The pacing of this sequencing is slower with a lighter homework load. This sequencing allows for more sustained immersement (sic) in a single text for longer periods of time.

Harper's explanation for different sequences for her text set illustrated why order matters. Introducing a particular topic through a supporting text early in the text set foregrounded certain knowledge toward a specific pedagogical purpose. Option 1 privileged the need for students to have a strong grasp on the history of violence against Native Americans before reading the target text, whereas Option 2 contextualized the reading of *There There* by defining what is meant by *Native American* and discussing how the naming of tribal communities is an act of colonization.

While Option 1 focused on the wrongs of the past, Option 2 offered students a more speculative and progressive lens for discussing modern tribal communities depicted in *There There*. In addition to the curricular considerations, Harper mentioned how deploying different texts at certain points through a unit might impact the pacing of reading—an important consideration when considering how to support varied young adult readers.

Finally, PSTs had to select two critical lenses to help examine their texts and meet their goals. As English teaching majors, they took a literary criticism course. They also read Appleman's (2015) *Critical Encounters in Secondary English* in this course. The lens work in the signature assignment provided opportunity for extended practice on applying critical lenses and how to function with them as they intersect. Harper selected New Historicism and gender, explaining that "The combined Gender and New Historicism lenses will help my students untangle these power dynamics because New Historicism will help us see how the socially constructed category of gender actives various notes of power in society."

DISCUSSION

The signature text set assignment helped PSTs foreground intertextuality and apply practical strategies that good readers use when engaging with text. This assignment offers the opportunity to build a text set on a theme of interest, while promoting intertextuality, multimodality, and dialogue across genres and perspectives (VanDerHeide et al., 2023). Importantly, it also provides a step beyond the "mono-text study" by asking PSTs to make connections across and then communicate the pedagogical moves they are making to help students make similar connections.

Although professors did not ask PSTs to role-play or teach any of their mini-lessons, the teacher script allowed teachers to write, revise, and receive feedback on their teacher talk. Over the course of the English education program, there are minor, yet significant, shifts in PSTs' efficacy, which led to an increase in their sense of authority as readers and writers. The teacher talk in mini-lesson scripts offered powerful insight into the role reversal that often accompanied their newfound sense of authority, as PSTs shifted from thinking like a student to thinking like a teacher. Lesson planning is just one of the approximations of practice (Grossman et al., 2009) implemented in order to ease PSTs into the teaching profession.

Professors noticed that PSTs who struggled with the signature assignment were unsure how to articulate reading practices. In the undergraduate course, professors worked to slow readers down, asking them to pause and notice questions they ask, rereading they do, and the connections they are making. In class discussions, PSTs helped one another name these moves and often, a range of readers emerged, with some asking questions as to how (questions that well benefit the articulations professors are aiming for) and others encouraging their peers for creative and insightful ideas they themselves hadn't experienced.

Other times, PSTs worried about reading levels and how *to know* or imagine what their students may be capable of doing with their selected texts.

This, again, was fodder for class conversation on reading habits, how to use standards as guides, and how to build and sustain readers over time. In such discussions, professors encouraged PSTs to avoid a deficit model toward youth readers and reminded them that much of what stresses them out in the university classroom is due to the theoretical nature of preparing for *class*—a falsified, theoretical version of the actual people they may someday teach.

Because the Teaching Reading and Literature course is one of the final classes before student teaching experiences, professors often see students naturally take up themes around social justice and place-based pedagogies—two core principles addressed early in the program and in line with English Methods Beliefs Statement (Gallo et al., 2020). Through the signature assignment, PSTs were asked not only to consider how young people read and analyze challenging texts, but to build curricula that fit with the teacher they want to be in the place they hope to be as a teacher.

The signature assignment brought to bear the types of questions that are important to developing the dispositions and philosophies PSTs hope to one day inhabit in their future classrooms. Asking PSTs how they feel as future English teachers is one way to begin speaking about one's sense of belonging (Wynhoff Olsen et al., 2022): both in the field and in place. Asking them to articulate their teaching, defend their decisions, and reflect on ways to make reading meaningful provides an opportunity to "try on" (Schutz et al., 2018) reading pedagogies in low-stakes classroom settings in order to help PSTs begin to build a teaching repertoire that they can carry into their first years into the classroom.

NOTE

1. All names are pseudonyms.

REFERENCES

Appleman, D. (2015). *Critical encounters in secondary English: Teaching literary theory to adolescents* (3rd ed.). Teachers College Press.

Fecho, B. (2011). *Teaching for the students: Habits of heart, mind, and practice in the engaged classroom.* Teachers College Press.

Gallo, J., Hallman, H. L., Parsons, C., Pastore-Capuana, K., Ringler Pet, S., and Searcy, L. (2020). *Beliefs about methods courses and field experiences in English education.* Accessed February 7, 2023. https://ncte.org/statement/methodsinee/.

Grossman, P. L., Compton, C., Igra, D., Ronfeldt, M., Shahan, E., and Williamson, P. W. (2009). Teaching practice: A cross-professional perspective. *Teachers College Record, 111*(9), 2055–100.

Lupo, S. M., Strong, J. Z., Lewis, W., Walpole, S., and McKenna, M. C. (2017). Building background knowledge through reading: Rethinking text sets. *Journal of Adolescent and Adult Literacy, 61*(4), 433–44. https://doi.org/10.1002/jaal.701.

Muhammad, G. (2020). *Cultivating genius: An equity framework for culturally and historically responsive teaching.* Scholastic.

Orange, T. (2018). There there: A novel. Knopf.

Roberts, K. (2018). *A novel approach: Whole-class novels, student-centered teaching, and choice.* Heinemann.

Schutz, K. M., Grossman, P. L., & Shaughnessy, M. M. (2018). Approximations of practice in teacher education. In P. Grossman (Ed.), *Teaching core practices in teacher education* (pp. 57–83). Harvard Education Press.

VanDerHeide, J., Newell, G., and Wynhoff Olsen, A. (2023). Conceptualizing dialogic literary argumentation: Inviting students to take a turn in important conversations. *Written Communication.* https://doi.org/10.1177/07410883221148680.

Wynhoff Olsen, A., Long, D., Olsen, K., and Fassbender, W. (2022). Rurally motivated? How English teachers negotiate rural sense of belonging. *English Education, 54*(3), 196–218.

Chapter 8

English Pedagogy through Critical Lenses

Empowering English Teachers as Agents of Change

Katharine Covino

Those who educate and mentor the next generation of English teachers stand charged "to support teacher candidates in becoming critical, agentic, active, ethical, reflective, and socially just educators" (Gallo et al., 2020). This directive has become even more important in the current social, cultural, and political moment. Classrooms are more diverse than ever before. Differences of perspective and experience, which exist both within English classrooms and without, reflect and reinforce larger, overarching trends of bias and inequity that exist in American society.

Preservice teachers arrive at their first positions amid a minefield of "racial injustice, failed insurrections, detention centers, unemployment caused by the pandemic, and disproportionate COVID-19 rates among Indigenous, Black, Brown, and Latinx people" (Nyachae, 2021, p. 38). These struggles are not new, but rather they are "deeply embedded in the social, economic, and educational fabric of our nation's history" (Ebarvia, 2021, p. 581).

Frustratingly, the tumult of the times has led to a backlash in the ways society views teachers. Legislators, rather than teachers or librarians, have claimed an active and all-to-often decisive role in determining what books are appropriate for students to read in schools. Under the guise of protecting innocence, book banning is serving instead to silence and marginalize students, teachers, and, in point of fact, entire underrepresented and often vulnerable communities (Burke and Greenfield, 2016). Decisions about the texts, stories, and voices students encounter in school shine a light on those who inhabit realms of power in society and those who do not. As books are forcibly removed from classrooms and libraries, teachers' professionalism and autonomy continue to erode.

And yet, even as teachers face unrelenting headwinds regarding their professional abilities and encounter day-to-day challenges that emerge from the complex social, cultural, and political contexts in which they serve, their larger mission remains the same. English teachers must care for, support, and appropriately challenge the students who sit in front of them each day. English classrooms have long offered students safe spaces to have tough discussions about difficult topics—including identity, belonging, and power.

It is through such charged conversations that students can begin the lifelong process of learning to recognize, respect, and internalize divergent points of view. With that goal in mind, English teachers must find ways to infuse the curriculum with diverse authors, voices, and perspectives. Through this daunting but vital work, teachers can play a role in disrupting trends that would silence and disenfranchise them, their students, and the communities they serve.

TAKING A CRITICAL APPROACH: RECONCEIVING TEACHER IDENTITY THROUGH METHODS COURSEWORK

With so much asked of classroom teachers today, it is imperative that teacher preparation programs offer thoughtful, rigorous, and progressive curriculum and instruction that intentionally entwines coursework and field experiences. Such plans of study must be bolstered and enhanced by diverse mentoring relationships and authentic opportunities for reflection. Methods courses and accompanying field placements often serve as the cornerstone of such programs.

Through Methods coursework and time spent in the field, preservice teachers learn to consider and apply different skills and strategies that help them understand, integrate, and critique the intersections of literature, pedagogy, and sociocultural issues. In many teacher training institutions, methods courses are frequently designed to reflect and embody lofty programmatic goals, such as the desire to embrace inclusivity and teach through a lens of restorative justice (Ebarvia et al., 2020). Shipp (2017) agrees, contending that methods courses should be designed to support budding English teachers as far more than servants of standardized tests, but rather as purveyors of "justice, hope, and consciousness" (p. 40).

Morrell (2005) goes further. He rightly argues that English teachers at all levels should be reimagined as explicitly political agents, activists, and intellectuals committed to the struggle for social justice (p. 319). Methods classes created in this framework can empower young teachers as agents of change. Bolstered by such training, program graduates will move into classrooms of their own, emboldened by their academic and professional experiences.

Such teachers will be able to embrace the identity of a critical pedagogue—galvanized to challenge and disrupt the status quo. Morrell explains:

> Those who believe in a critical English education see language and literacy learning as political acts, realize literacy as tied to power relations in society, and recognize literacy educators as political agents capable of developing skills which enable academic transformation and social change. (p. 313)

Never has there been more impetus for teacher educators to devote time and attention to redesigning English Methods courses that consistently innovate and productively disrupt norms and conventions. Drawing on literature from the field as well as recently collected qualitative data, this chapter will outline three areas of focus useful to those interested in applying the tenets of critical pedagogy to teacher education.

Specifically, the chapter will explore (1) critical awareness of self, (2) critical engagement with texts and discourse, and (3) critical dialogue. Each area offers those who train teachers research-informed methods and strategies to consider for inclusion in English methods courses. Theory, practice, and on-the-ground experience and expertise offer guidance for teacher educators as they help their students develop "deep understandings about not only *what* to teach in English language arts curricula, but also *how* to approach our work as English language arts teachers in our classrooms and as part of an engaged professional community" (Gallo et al., 2020).

CRITICAL AWARENESS OF SELF

As part of its *Beliefs about Methods Courses and Field Experiences in English Education*, the following stance is shared: "Methods coursework should foster candidates' professional identity development. Coursework should be designed to support teacher candidates in becoming critical, agentic, active, ethical, reflective, and socially just educators" (Gallo et al., 2020). This statement is part aspiration and part common sense. It is impossible to turn a critical eye on school texts, discourses, and practices without first gaining a close and critical awareness of one's self.

Ebarvia's (2021) recent work explores this issue deeply. She claims that preservice teachers must understand themselves before they can begin to understand those around them. Identity, particularly teacher identity, is multifaceted and dynamic. There are many ways to probe and explore such issues in English Methods courses. A unit focused on diversity and multicultural education, for example, may spend time engaging with readings which ask teacher candidates questions regarding their impressions about who belongs in school. Burke and Greenfield (2016) use this approach to question the status quo by exploring how and why some groups' experiences in schools are accepted as normal while other groups' experiences in schools are othered. Such discussions, penetrating and probing issues of power and privilege, can do much to support teacher candidates in thoughtfully questioning their own expectations and assumptions.

There are, of course, other approaches English Methods instructors can use to help their preservice teachers turn an inward reflective eye on themselves. Young adult literature, for example, stands as a well-chosen tool for helping young teachers begin to explore the links that exist between literature, identity, and power. A piece that serves this purpose particularly well is *The Absolutely True Diary of a Part-Time Indian* (Alexie, 2009). This unique and emotive coming-of-age story not only allows university instructors and their students access to a novel frequently taught in high schools but also provides a powerful springboard for identity work.

Professors can ask students to explore the facets of themselves, just as Junior, the protagonist, does in the story (see Figure 8.1). Exploring and reflecting on the various components of their identity, students will gain insight into themselves—their values, expectations, and ideals. Through the act of sharing their reflections with others, they will directly encounter and grapple with Ebarvia's (2021) contention that identity depends not "only on how we see ourselves but also on how the critical awareness of self—identity work—intersects with teaching in real and important ways."

Understanding themselves, their identities, their experiences, and their innate biases can help young teachers anticipate ways their identity may

Figure 8.1 Student-created "Who Are You, Really?" project based upon an illustration in The Absolutely True Diary of a Part-Time Indian (Alexie, 2009) exploring all aspects of the protagonist's character.

affect their engagement with texts, issues, experiences, and students. Again, Ebarvia's (2021) writing about disrupting texts supports this position: "It's critical that teachers do this intensive identity work on themselves."

"As teachers, we must persistently ask ourselves how our own racialized, gendered, and other socialized identities affect how we choose texts, deliver instruction, and most importantly, engage with students" (p. 584). Her work provides some grounding questions that teacher educators can use and adapt to help their students consider how their own identities may be self-limiting. Examples of such questions are paraphrased here: (1) How might my identity limit my ability to understand this issue? (2) How might my identity inform my response when I encounter experiences that are different from mine? (3) How might my feelings of resistance or defensiveness be rooted in my identity? (pp. 583–4).

Moving this lens outward, English Methods instructors can help their preservice teachers begin to apply what they have learned about the importance of identity in consideration of the identities of their future students. Specifically, Methods instructors can support their teacher candidates in thinking about the ways in which their future students' home lives, cultures, and communities intersect with their learning expectations and classroom experiences (Ervin, 2021).

Assessments in Methods classes that ask preservice teachers to consider contextual factors of a specific middle or secondary classroom, school, and community can be enormously enriching. Such assignments first prompt the young teacher to investigate the classroom setting in which they are completing their field experience. As the candidates gain more insights into the identity of their students, their families, and the larger community, they can begin to reflect on how this knowledge can improve their instruction and assessment.

BOX 8.1. EXCERPT FROM STUDENT-WRITTEN CONTEXTUAL FACTORS ASSESSMENT.

The second factor I am considering when creating classroom norms is the importance of having a safe and positive environment for all of my students. With classroom sizes that average 14 students, [Smithville] is a tight-knit community that I want to make sure is safe for all students.

There are students that identify as non-binary, and my classroom norms will include respecting all students and peers' various sexualities and genders. I will establish this by including inclusive instruction. I will include readings by authors who identify as non-binary and introduce literary work by a variety of authors with diverse backgrounds and various sexualities to make sure that all students see themselves in their work and feel included in the classroom environment. I will also make sure to include literary works that feature diverse characters and cultural backgrounds that identify with the students in my classroom. It is important for students to see themselves represented in what they are learning about.

The student-crafted example (see figure 8.2), written by a senior in Special Methods in Teaching English II, reveals the power of identity work when it shifts from an internal to external focus. Of course, it must be said that the point of focusing on identity in English Methods coursework and field experiences is not to promote one particular identity practice, but instead to help young teachers realize that there are many ways to be in the world. A dynamic and inclusive understanding of identity can help preservice teachers create classrooms where students are free to embrace all facets of themselves, while at the same time learn to value the different identities and experiences of those around them.

When teachers and students feel free to offer and inhabit themselves wholly and authentically, when they learn to appreciate both similarities and differences in others, they become more open-minded and more empathetic. They will, as Ervin (2021) suggests, be open to learning and embracing new points of view. Identity work in Methods classes, not only embraces an important and powerful stance of critical pedagogy, it also empowers both students and teachers to reshape their thinking as they encounter and embrace new understandings and ideas (p. 325).

CRITICAL ENGAGEMENT WITH TEXTS

In addition to analytical identity work, Special Methods courses can prepare future English teachers to foster deep, evaluative thinking by emphasizing critical engagement with texts. This goal echoes and reinforces language from NCTE's (2020) *Beliefs about Methods Courses and Field Experiences in English Education.*

> Methods coursework should emphasize the diversity of literacies, texts, and learners that constitute our field and our work as English language arts teachers. To do this, coursework must support teacher candidates in attending to the cultural backgrounds of students and choosing texts and learning opportunities that nurture students' unique literacies. (Gallo et al., 2020)

Special Methods instructors can guide novice teachers in the practice of selecting materials for the classroom by creating assessments that ask teacher candidates to consider and include voices and stories that reflect the "racial, linguistic, and cultural backgrounds" (Nyachae, 2021, p. 37) of their students. Asking candidates to create a text set, for example, around an essential question, can pose an essential learning opportunity for young teachers.

Figure 8.3, from a Special Methods of Teaching English I course, provides an example of such an assessment. The Puerto Rican American undergraduate student who designed this text set started with a central question—"What Does it Mean to Belong to a Community?" The first text she selected, *How The Garcia Girls Lost Their Accent* (Alvarez, 2010), looks closely at the struggle of the Garcia sisters to inhabit two worlds. Supplemental readings, including *Ordinary Girls* (Díaz, 2019) and the free verse poetry of Mexican American author—Pat Mora, all shed light on the themes of belonging and struggle that exist for those who bridge two cultures.

Designing units that showcase "a variety of experiences, realities, histories, knowledges, and contexts" (Nyachae, 2021, p. 38) can empower young educators by offering them low-stakes opportunities to select instructional materials and design units of study that may differ from or even directly challenge those they encountered as high school students themselves.

BOX 8.2 EXCERPT FROM CLASS-WRITTEN RATIONALE FOR *DRAMA*.

This book is likely to be challenged because administrators may not being comfortable with their students reading a book that has leading gay characters. In addition to this, the characters are exploring their sexualities at a young age. While some parents or administrators may not be comfortable with this, this is the reality of what adolescents are experiencing. Some parents may be scared that reading this book will influence their child to be gay. However, adding a book with gay characters to the curriculum is important, so that students can see themselves portrayed in the content that they are learning about. If students are reading books that they cannot connect with, a meaningful learning transaction will not be made and opportunities to connect the text with students' life experiences will not be possible. For this reason, it is important to include academic content that features real life experiences and issues that middle school age students can relate to. More likely than not, teachers will have students in their classrooms that already identify with the LGBTQ+ community or exploring their sexualities, and need to see a physical example of it being safe to come out and how welcoming their friends and family will be. It is important that these students experiencing these challenges feel safe and comfortable in their classroom and respected by both their teachers and

> their peers. It is important for parents or those in opposition to note that just because teachers are including books with a wider variety of characters, teachers will still be teaching all the frameworks and standards, just in a more inclusive and relatable format to their students.
>
> Source: Telgemeier, 2012.

Qualitative data from a recent study of teacher candidates reveal that some students in today's English Methods classes are decidedly ahead of the curve when it comes to their ability to engage critically with texts. The study, an intervention designed to support teaching candidates in their ability to select and use inclusive literature, had three open-ended questions. The researcher delivered the set of identical questions twice; once before a unit focused on LGBTQ+, history, issues, and texts, and then again at the end of the unit.

The questions are as follows:

(1) As a future teacher, I believe it is appropriate/inappropriate to include texts that depict diverse gender and sexual identities in secondary school classrooms.
(2) As a future teacher, I believe it is necessary/unnecessary to include texts that depict diverse gender and sexual identities in secondary school classrooms.
(3) As a future teacher, I feel comfortable/uncomfortable bringing texts that depict diverse gender and sexual identities into secondary school classrooms.

While the researcher hypothesized that post-data would differ markedly from pre-data, ultimately, that did not prove to be the case. For many participants, the second round of open-ended responses only further cemented their previously held views. In her post responses, Sally[1] stated, "I am further convinced now after studying the history of LGBTQ+ books that it is very necessary to teach them. Many old books portray [queerness] as something to be ashamed of, which indicates that it is something we *need* to incorporate in schools."

Ryan had the same idea: "Before I believed it was necessary to include texts with diverse gender and sexual identities, and I have been furthered reinforced on this idea." Most students seemed to agree regarding the importance of including such texts. When it came to their comfort level, however, some students seemed more diffident. Morgan highlighted these complex views in her response to the third prompt: "I still feel somewhat comfortable teaching these types of books. I just don't have all the answers." Those who teach Special Methods courses can draw upon students' interest in using diverse texts, and, through guided practice in the form of course assessments and field experiences, help them gain confidence as empowered decision-makers interested in choosing texts that reflect the diversity of their students.

And yet, just as teacher educators want to inspire their preservice candidates, they must also recognize that as these young teachers graduate and come to serve in their first classrooms, their inclinations toward selecting diverse, inclusive texts may face resistance in the form of institutional expectations and practices. Anticipating this possible eventuality, instructors can take steps in Methods classes to ensure that "the work of examining biases, deconstructing, and reconstructing the canon" (Ebarvia et al., 2020, p. 100) does not falter at the first hurdle.

One way teacher educators can help support their candidates' critical engagement with texts, while at the same time connecting them to a vast network of supportive allies in the field, is by mentoring them through the process of writing rationales for NCTE. While NCTE has long offered its database of rationales for all members to use, the recent assault on English teachers' professionalism has prompted a resurgence of interest in the national project. Methods instructors can explain the importance of rationales, and then explore the process of writing them. Detailed information about the process, exemplars, instructions, and the full database is included within the *This Story Matters* website.

The portion of the rationale included below, written collaboratively by members of Special Methods in Teaching English II, highlights the importance of presenting preservice teacher with opportunities to use their knowledge, skills, and professional expertise regarding inclusive literature in the service of colleagues across the country.

Though censorship and book banning are real issues facing today's classroom teachers, university instructors can support and prepare their candidates by offering different avenues designed to critically engage with texts in Methods classes. As young teachers gain confidence in selecting, integrating, and defending diverse and inclusive materials, they not only enrich themselves and their practice, but they buttress themselves against the coming headwinds. While there are likely many university instructors who feel more comfortable teaching and sharing classics, it is important that teachers at all levels feel at least some impetus to embrace a broader spectrum of voices and experiences.

Such work ensures that all students see themselves and their struggles reflected in the curriculum (Burke and Greenfield, 2016). Critical engagement with texts is challenging. There is no doubt about it. But, even small victories are worthy of celebration. Any steps Special Methods instructors can take to support the next generation of teachers in gaining experience and master bridging the gap between their students' lives, experiences, and interests and the school curriculum will pay dividends in terms of the secondary students' academic outcomes (Shipp, 2017).

CRITICAL DIALOGUE

Selecting, integrating, and defending diverse and inclusive texts and curricular materials is important work that should be built-in to contemporary English Methods courses and field experiences. Just as vital to meet NCTE's (2020) *Beliefs about Methods Courses and Field Experiences in English Education* statement, however, are programmatic experiences in the classroom and the field that give preservice candidates experience engaging in critical literacy practices; specifically, those that forefront critical dialogue with authors, texts, peers, instructors, and society at large. But what is meant by critical literacy? The following excerpt offers one conceptual definition.

> Critical literacy, which may be viewed as a subset or outgrowth of critical pedagogy, provides a way for literacy educators to develop a critical practice of literacy instruction. Grounded in practices that disrupt common assumptions, interrogate multiple perspectives, foster critical conversations, problematize issues of inequity and injustice, and lead to transformative action, critical literacy works toward developing compassion and critical awareness. (Covino and Malcahy, 2020, pp. 7–8)

One place to begin such critical dialogue in English Methods classes is through conversations, activities, and assignments that pose thoughtful, probing, and evaluative questions of authors preservice teachers encountered during their own time in middle and secondary school. Revisiting culturally accepted writers, often taught more from habit and convenience than choice, gives young teachers practice applying "their knowledge and experiences to question the position of the author and how that position impacts the narrative and read to connect understandings of power, equity, oppression, and social positioning" (Ervin, 2021, p. 322). Instructors can also explicitly develop and assign assessments that ask English Methods students to pair traditional texts with more progressive selections. Or, if teacher candidates are placed in prepracticum placements where the curriculum is settled, then university professors can support them in applying new ways of reading and interpreting conventional texts.

Reading *Lord of Flies* (Golding, 1954) through the lens of toxic masculinity, for example, provides new insight into almost every element of the story (Consalvo et al., 2021). Learning to experiment with the process of challenging accepted authors in the safety of a Methods classroom is an important way university faculty can support preservice teachers' abilities to engage in critical dialogue with texts.

Building on their work interrogating canonical authors, English Methods instructors can provide candidates explicit practice in asking critical questions. Such dialogue, designed to investigate issues of "stereotypical and damage-centered representations of diverse groups, dominant narratives, missing voices, and societal implications" (Nyachae, 2021, p. 38) alerts young teachers to issues of power, privilege, and marginalization.

Ebarvia and her colleagues (2020) offer some questions that can be used when engaged in critical dialogue with texts: "Who is centered? Who is marginalized? Who is missing? And what does this mean and why does it matter?" (p. 101). In a recent Methods of Teaching English I course, a Latinx student, looking at the texts she had been given by her field placement mentor, designed her own set of critical questions focused on norming and othering. She asked, "Whose history is this book reporting? Whose point of view is centered? Whose culture holds power? Whose language tells the story?" Practicing and applying strategies to read texts deeply and evaluatively can help Methods students gain practice and confidence engaging in critical dialogue with the curricular materials.

Preservice teachers also need explicit guidance and practice engaging in dynamic class conversations wherein instructors decenter their own voices and views, and privilege instead of the voices and perceptions of students. While there are many ways this approach can be included within English methods coursework, Socratic seminars offers an accessible means of practicing critical dialogue. Socratic seminars enable students to take an active role in negotiating and co-constructing meaning (Barker et al., 2017). Such seminars require clear, shared expectations for preparation, implementation, and success.

Methods teachers can collaboratively shape these with their university students. Common requirements include active reading and annotation prior to the discussion, coupled with the creation of "thought-provoking questions, revelations, or predictions" (p. 93) to spur the conversation forward. Recently, preservice teachers led a Socratic seminar exploring the issues facing migrant families and children while reading *The Circuit* (Jimenez, 1997). They came to class with annotations, questions, and links and stories connecting the text to the struggle of today's migrant workers. Throughout the course of their discussion, the university professor remained completely silent; modeling the practice of decentering in favor of the voices, ideas, and perspectives of her students.

Another method for facilitating and modeling critical dialogue is dialogic teaching. Employing this approach, teachers demonstrate yet another means of stepping to the side and ceding power and expertise to their students. Nyachae

(2021) elaborates: "Dialogic teaching asks teachers to listen to all students, welcome diverse perspectives, prompt students for more talk, and scaffold learning while disrupting traditional teacher-students hierarchies" (p. 38).

These critical literacy practices answer and address two underlying goals. First, young teachers gain exposure by listening to and considering the views of others. Second, engaging in this work in the university classroom provides a model that candidates can take with them into the field. Learning to facilitate critical dialogue that "transforms, disrupts, and dismantles oppressive ideologies and structures" (Nyachae, 2021, p. 38) lays the groundwork for future conversations in their own classrooms.

Of course, it must be said that the purpose of critical dialogue is never to promote or espouse any one worldview but rather to help teaching candidates learn to feel more comfortable inhabiting spaces where both agreement and disagreement occur. To that end, English Methods classrooms should be spaces that promote freedom of expression. Ervin (2021) explains: "The class dynamic should be one that values new perspectives, where students feel safe challenging authority as it is presented within the text or by the teacher, and comfortable pushing back on their peers if necessary" (p. 325).

Empowered by this type of training and support, young teachers will feel ready to incorporate critical dialogue into their classrooms creating a sophisticated and engaging learning environment where their middle and high school students feel safe asking critical questions of authors, texts, and peers (Barker et al., 2017). In turn, their students will gain independence. They will develop confidence in their ability to think critically. To quote Morrell (2005), they will no longer

> need a teacher to make sense of the text for them and let them know how close to the 'truth' of the text they had gotten; instead, they [will] became empowered within their own interpretations and learn that any text can be read multiple ways. (p. 318)

EMPOWERING ENGLISH TEACHERS AS AGENTS OF CHANGE

Teachers today face tests and trials from within the school building and without. To equip young teachers to face these challenges, teacher educators must prepare them to serve and to lead as agents of change (Morrell, 2005). With this powerful goal in mind, university instructors in teacher preparation programs can reexamine their English methods courses and field experiences to ensure that these arenas are enabling teaching candidates to gain practice consistently innovating and productively disrupting norms. In the name of creating a new generation of teachers who exhibit empathy and compassion, those who train teachers must embrace rigorous instruction, explicit modeling, and well-paced scaffolding (Burke and Greenfield, 2016).

With a full commitment to embracing various aspects of critical pedagogy; university professors can guide their students in the processes of (1) critical awareness of self, (2) critical engagement with texts and discourse, and (3) critical dialogue. Deep, demanding encounters with critical pedagogy will embolden young teachers to stand against those who seek to sideline them, their students, and the communities they serve. There are resounding and powerful results of such course redesign. Preservice teachers will enter the profession better prepared to empower students to become engaged members of society, driven in equal measure by critical minds and empathetic hearts. In their work supporting their students and the communities they serve, young teachers will embrace a liberatory consciousness and reclaim their professional status.

NOTE

1. All names used are aliases.

REFERENCES

Alvarez, J. (2010). *How the García girls lost their accents.* Plume.

Barker, L. M., Tensen, T., and Shea, B. (2017). Under discussion: Teaching speaking and listening: Socratic seminars: Risk, revision, and magic. *English Journal, 107*(1), 92–95.

Burke, B. R. and Greenfield, K. (2016). Challenging heteronormativity: Raising LGBTQ awareness in a high school English language arts classroom. *English Journal, 105*(6), 46–51.

Consalvo, A., Covino, K., and Chase, N. (2021). Decentering the book(room) and (re)centering students' interest contemporary issues: Theories, questions, and relevance. *Teaching/Writing: The Journal of Writing Teacher Education, 10*(1), 1–9.

Covino, K. and Mulcahy, C. (2020). Social justice in the classroom: How critical literacy can help teachers and students move toward empowerment, equity, and transformative change. *The Leaflet, 117*(1), 7–19.

Diaz, J. (2019). *Ordinary girls: A memoir.* Algonquin Books.

Ebarvia, T., Germán, L., Parker, K. N., and Torres, J. (2020). #DISRUPTTEXTS. *English Journal, 110*(1), 100–2.

Ebarvia, T. and Parker, K. N. (2021). Starting with self: Identity work and anti-racist literacy practices. *Journal of Adolescent & Adult Literacy* 64 (5), 581–84. https://doi.org/10.1002/jaal.1140.

Ervin, J. (2022). Critically reading the canon: Culturally sustaining approaches to a prescribed literature curriculum. *Journal of Adolescent & Adult Literacy, 65*(4), 321–29.

Gallo, J., Hallman, H. L., Parsons, C., Pastore-Capuana, K., Ringler Pet, S., and Searcy, L. (2020). *Beliefs about methods courses and field experiences in English education.* https://ncte.org/statement/methodsinee/.

Golding, W. (1954). *Lord of the flies: A novel.* Perigee.

Jimenez, F. (1997). *The circuit.* Albuquerque: University of New Mexico Press.

Morrell, E. (2005). Critical English education. *English Education, 37*(4), 312–21.

Nyachae, T. M. (2021). Got diverse texts? Now what? *Literacy Today, 38*(6), 36–39.

Shipp, L. (2017). Revolutionizing the English classroom through consciousness, justice, and self-awareness. *English Journal, 106*(4), 35–40.

This Story Matters. NCTE. (2022, July 6). Accessed July 22, 2022 from https://ncte.org/book-rationales/this-story-matters/.

Telgemeier, R. (2012). *Drama.* Graphix.

Chapter 9

Figuring Out the Path Forward Together

The Power of Collaborative Reflection and Problem-Posing in Field-Based English Language Arts Teacher Education

Michelle Fowler-Amato

In a recent special issue that invited teacher education scholars to consider the theories that support us in understanding the intricacy of teacher learning, Strom and Viesca (2021) argue, "Teaching is not something the teacher does as an isolated actor, but rather is jointly produced by the collective. Therefore, teaching activity, as well as teacher learning, has to be considered as heavily mediated, multiply produced co-constructed phenomena" (p. 218). This understanding reinforces the importance of inviting preservice teachers (PTs) to participate in field-based teaching and learning, across coursework, not just in classes with an associated practicum.

This invitation to "learn in practice" (Hallman, 2012) allows preservice and early-career teachers to link the theory and research introduced in methods courses to real-world teacher and student interactions, negotiating moments of success and struggle with the support of a methods instructor, a cooperating teacher, and a community of educators who are participating in a shared journey of becoming (Strom and Viesca, 2021).

In the NCTE position statement, "Beliefs About Methods and Field Experiences in English Education," Gallo et al. (2020) encourage ELA teacher educators to innovate, considering new opportunities for field-based teaching and learning that allow preservice and early-career teachers to "reflect on, unpack, and learn" as they negotiate problems of practice. Through these invitations for collaborative reflection and revision, we can simultaneously demonstrate that ELA teachers learn with and from each other, highlighting the importance of building a network of mentors and colleagues who challenge one's thinking and support their professional growth across their career.

In their study of secondary ELA teacher education in the United States, Pasternak et al. (2018) define field experience as an encounter taking place "outside of the university classroom in which candidates observe, teach, and/or engage with students with university or K-12 supervision" (p. 34). They note that field experiences have varied widely in ELA education and have involved "applying English content," "learning the social context of schools," "connecting theory to practice," and "reflection" (Pasternak et al., 2018, p. 52).

This chapter discusses an invitation for preservice and early-career teachers to participate in field-based teaching and learning in my first-year composition (FYC) class. In doing so, the design of the field experience is highlighted as well as the stories that describe preservice and early-career teachers' participation. Next, the impact of this field experience is discussed as it pertained to me, the methods instructor, and cooperating teacher, as well as the impact it had on students in both courses. The chapter concludes with a discussion of the importance of providing new opportunities to move from "awareness" to "application" (Pasternak et al., 2018, p. 45) with guidance and support, throughout ELA teacher education programs.

A TEMPORARY SOLUTION WITH FUTURE POTENTIAL

Despite my commitment to incorporate field experiences across my ELA methods courses, it was unknown what this might look like during the 2020–2021 academic year. The labor that cooperating teachers take on when participating in these partnerships is often tremendous, and while these efforts are worth the time commitment because of the ways these partnerships support all participants in their professional growth, asking K-12 teachers to take on more work during the COVID-19 pandemic did not seem right.

While working on my syllabus for my FYC course, I had an "Ah-ha" moment. What if I took on the role of "cooperating teacher" this semester, inviting my teaching composition students to learn in practice in my FYC course? How might this partnership serve not only preservice and early-career teachers' growth as writing teachers, but also my FYC students' growth as writers? What might be lost, and what might be gained in serving as both the methods instructor and cooperating teacher across this field experience? How might I address the limitations of this model of field-based teaching and learning, so students grow as writers and as teachers of writers?

A PARTNERSHIP BETWEEN THE FIRST-YEAR COMPOSITION AND TEACHING COMPOSITION COURSES

To support my FYC students' development as writers and my teaching composition students' growth as teachers, a partnership across both courses in the spring of 2021 was planned. In addition to conferring with the instructor while working on multiple pieces of writing, students in the FYC course were invited to participate in digital conferences with one to two preservice or early-career teachers enrolled in the composition course. Preservice and early-career teachers also had an opportunity to review and respond to student writing, developing understandings of the potential impact of the conferences they facilitated. When responding to student writing, the participating teachers were invited to name strengths and offer a strategy to support student writers in their growth.

FACILITATING CONFERENCES

Prior to conferring with student writers, participating teachers in the teaching composition course were introduced to Ray and Laminack's (2001) process for conferring. Across these conferences, they were encouraged to *research*, posing questions to writers to better understand what they hoped to accomplish through their writing and learn what support might benefit them. Next, they would *decide*, determining whether to respond to the writer's request or offer an alternative strategy. They would then *teach* through modeling, sharing a strategy, recommending a resource, and so on. Finally, they would *record* what they learned about the student, note how their instruction grew out of this learning, and think toward future conferences.

RESPONDING TO STUDENT WRITING

Drawing on Bomer's (2010) framework for response and assessment, the participating teachers were invited to read each piece of student writing once, expecting that meaning existed. They then returned to student drafts, responding first as a reader, and then naming what was working in the student's writing. Moving beyond the framework to continue practicing what they learned through conferring, the participating teachers were encouraged to share one strategy that built on what they saw the writer doing in the draft. The strategy they chose could support the writer in revising the piece and/or trying something new when negotiating future writing projects.

Professional Learning through Teacher-to-Teacher Conversation

Though I served in the dual role of methods instructor and cooperating teacher during this field experience, I remained committed to expanding my preservice and early-career teachers' network of mentors and colleagues who could support their growth and development. The university writing center tutors who had taken on this role during previous field-based teaching and learning experiences in my teaching composition course became part of the course as well (Fowler-Amato, 2020). These writing center tutors, with expertise in individualizing instruction, drew on research and theory as well as their own experiences working in the university writing center (and in the FYC course) to ensure that preservice and early-career teachers were prepared to engage in writer-to-writer conversations with FYC students. They also visited with the participating teachers after the teachers conferred and responded to student writing, offering support in thinking through their experiences.

In addition to reading research and theory about the teaching of writers across the course, participating teachers were invited to explore blog posts featured on the *Teachers, Profs, Parents, Writers Who Care* blog, as well. The writers of these blog posts became additional writing teachers in our classroom, communicating the importance of taking on a listening stance (David and Consalvo, 2018), building on writers' agendas (Taylor, 2019), avoiding "criticism overload" and committing to naming strength (Dunn, 2016).

Because teachers who participate in the teaching composition course take this class at different points in their teaching journeys, their confidence varied. As a result, they were given the option of independently conferring or conferring in pairs. It was my hope that all of these invitations served as reminders that teachers learn in practice with and from writers *and* other teachers of writers.

THINKING TOWARD CONFERENCES

Before conferring with and responding to writers, the participating teachers met with the writing center tutors to prepare for the experience of offering individualized support to students in the FYC class. During this meeting, the writing center tutors each shared a lesson learned in practice with the preservice and early-career teachers to support them in interacting with student writers. The participating teachers then had opportunities to pose questions to the writing center tutors and to the methods instructor. One PT asked how to go about sustaining a balance of teacher and student talk throughout a conference. A first-year teacher working toward licensure wondered how teachers knew if they were leading student writers in the right direction.

Though the writing center tutors and I shared experiences and strategies in response to questions the preservice and early-career teachers posed, we understood that these questions often did not have simple answers. The opportunity to learn in practice, with the support of other writing teachers, would allow many of the preservice and early-career teachers to come to this understanding, too. In addition, engaging in writer-to-writer conversations would lead to new questions, worthy of collaborative exploration.

LEARNING IN PRACTICE

While each of the teachers who participated in this experience has a story worthy of revisiting, two vignettes highlighting the potential of expanding opportunities for field-based teaching and learning across ELA teacher education programs will be shared. These vignettes ensure that preservice and early-career ELA teachers receive "emotional and instructional support" (Zeichner and Conklin, 2008, p. 275) as they strengthen their content and pedagogical knowledge through the collaborative negotiation of problems of practice.

Vignette #1: "Writing Has a Complex Relationship to Talk" (NCTE, 2016). New to taking on the identity of a teacher of writers, Anna (all participants' names are pseudonyms) was concerned she would not have anything to offer the student whom she would support. To prepare, Anna reviewed the assignment description for the personal essay that her student, Kayla, would be negotiating. In addition, she read through multiple mentor texts Kayla was introduced to in the FYC course to consider the possibilities of composing in this genre.

Upon meeting Kayla, Anna engaged in research, asking the writer to share how things were going as she drafted. Though Kayla had started this process, she was unsure how to continue. Anna invited Kayla to read her draft. Anna's initial noticing, highlighted in her conference notes, was that Kayla's writing seemed "more academic" and "less personal" than the mentor texts Kayla's class had explored when inquiring into the genre. In an effort to help Kayla find her own voice and journey through her own thoughts (Bomer, 2016), Anna asked Kayla questions in response to her personal essay, inviting Kayla to consider what she wanted to make sense of through the writing of this piece. As the two engaged in this writer-to-writer conversation, Kayla began to see a new path forward.

Upon reviewing Kayla's final draft, Anna recognized Kayla's efforts to make sense of her thinking and noted Kayla's developing "comfort with the writing style" in her conference notes. Anna highlighted moments in which Kayla might have considered adding additional "anecdotes" and "personal definitions/explanations," as a means of further developing her thinking in this genre. Anna concluded her notes pointing out that this might be something to discuss during future conferences, if it served Kayla at that time.

Anna had the opportunity to confer with Kayla again later in the semester. Kayla arrived at this conference with an understanding of the argument she planned to make in her opinion piece. However, upon recognizing that Kayla had not been drafted, Anna found herself concerned, once again, about what support to provide. Anna decided to meet Kayla where she was that day. Thinking back on her prior experience conferring with Kayla, Anna had come to see, firsthand, that talk could support a writer in building one's thinking as well as in imagining a piece of writing (NCTE, 2016).

Drawing on these understandings, Anna posed questions that invited Kayla to clarify her argument, reflect on the research she had done, and think about the next steps. In addition, Anna invited Kayla to consider how this argument might be structured in an effort to accomplish her intended purpose.

In her conference notes, Anna wrote, "This wasn't much of a writing conference . . . It was a brainstorming/brain-picking conference." Though Anna anticipated offering support in response to a piece of writing, she recognized that the conversation she had with Kayla before Kayla drafted had value, too. Reflecting on the conference, Anna wrote, "Talking to a student about a topic or just their knowledge is not necessarily a waste." I affirmed Anna's thinking through my commentary on her conference notes and shared that writing teachers confer across a writing process. This might even include a conversation before putting words on a page.

Vignette #2: "Assessment of Writing Involves Complex, Informed Human Judgment" (NCTE, 2016). After introducing herself to the writer she would support, Jasmine, like Anna, began her conference by engaging in research, reviewing Josh's essay. Upon doing so, *she* felt stuck. Josh had found a topic that he was passionate about. Throughout his personal essay, he confidently explored the life lessons that surfing taught him, highlighting the importance of finding a hobby/interest that served as an outlet, an opportunity to connect with others, a teacher, and so on. Jasmine was unsure what she could offer this writer to support him in strengthening the piece, so she suggested that Josh "read the writing out loud, making sure his sentences sound good outside his own headspace" and then concluded the conference.

After this interaction, Jasmine shared that she felt as if she had failed this writer. Feeling pressure to offer the "perfect" strategy led Jasmine to panic. In doing so, she did not take the time to learn about Josh's experience drafting or to ask about the support Josh thought he needed to create the piece he envisioned. The pressure to respond the "right" way led Jasmine to overlook the different kinds of assistance she might have provided.

As we thought together about this problem of practice, I shared that writers often benefit from thinking with a reader about their work. Even coming to understand a reader's experience negotiating a text can support a writer in revisiting a draft. I explained that a teacher can certainly support a writer through teaching editing strategies, as well. But before choosing any strategy, it is important to consider what might benefit the writer at that particular moment in time. At the conclusion of our conversation, Jasmine recognized this would be harder to determine if the conversation was limited.

Though Jasmine did not have another opportunity to confer with Josh, she did have the chance to respond to Josh's opinion piece that he wrote later in the semester. This time, Jasmine shared her takeaways, as a reader. In doing so, she pointed out what she found interesting in his draft and made connections with the writer's way of seeing the world. In addition, she offered feedback on Josh's organization of the piece.

Though she effectively communicated her experience negotiating Josh's opinion piece, Jasmine reflected that she would have preferred the opportunity to confer with Josh when he was actively working on this piece, acknowledging the value of thinking with a writer about possibilities for organization, rather than just providing direction through written commentary at the end of the process. In addition to recognizing the importance of understanding the writer's intentions, Jasmine worried that her commentary might come across as "critical" rather than supportive, as the conversation between the two was, once again, limited.

In class, we had previously discussed that different kinds of feedback might better serve writers earlier or later in their writing processes. In addition, we had called attention to the fact that a teacher's words have the potential to help and to hurt a writer. Jasmine did not seem to internalize these lessons until *she* was invited to gather information about a writer in order to make decisions about how best to support him.

EXPLORING PROBLEMS OF PRACTICE

Though seemingly hesitant to pose questions during the first meeting with university writing tutors, participating preservice and early-career teachers shared thoughtful wonderings during the debriefing sessions that took place after conferring. They asked whether it was possible to ask too many questions when thinking with a writer about their work. They questioned how best to negotiate awkward silences that might exist within a conference and gave thought to when these silences might, in fact, be productive. They deliberated over when it might be useful to offer direction and when it might be necessary to position the writer as the sole decision-maker. In response to these questions, this teacher community reflected on our own experiences as writers and teachers of writers, sharing strategies and insight that would later live on in other teachers' practices.

THE METHODS INSTRUCTOR AS A COOPERATING TEACHER

Because I aim to teach writing in ways that I prepare preservice and practicing teachers to, recognizing differences in context, of course, the students in my FYC course and my teaching composition course came into this experience having used a writer's notebook to pay attention to their thinking and to think toward pieces designed for audiences (Bomer and Fowler-Amato, 2014). After reading Dirk's (2010) "Navigating Genres" to grow understandings of what a genre is and how genres function, students in both courses were invited to participate in inquiry-based genre study. They later had opportunities to practice composing in the genres they explored with the support of in-class mini-lessons, peer-writing groups, and opportunities to confer. Preservice and early-career teachers built on these shared experiences to support student writers during their conferences.

In addition to participating in the debriefing experiences, I thought with participating teachers about their experiences by posing questions and providing commentary on their conference notes and written reflections. To do so, I made use of the comment feature on Google docs, inviting teachers to engage in dialogue. While these conversations varied, we often discussed how to build confidence through conferring. We gave thought to the support a writing teacher might provide across a writing process. In addition, we often engaged in conversation about how teachers might encourage students to take ownership of their writing after years of positioning their teachers as their primary audiences.

As seen in Jasmine's vignette, it was not uncommon for the preservice and early-career teachers to think with me over email about their experiences, as well. Often, they wanted reassurance that the choices they made in their conferences were productive. However, there were also circumstances in which they offered insight into writers' developing understandings and decision-making that led me to reflect on my own teaching practices, giving thought to what *I* could do differently to better support individual writers in my FYC course. Just like the preservice and early-career teachers benefited from teacher-to-teacher conversation in response to the conferring they were doing, I grew because of the discussions we had about our shared students' growth as writers.

One advantage of taking on the role of methods instructor and cooperating teacher was that I was able to share my decision-making when preservice and early-career teachers questioned the experiences that my FYC students had or made suggestions about the kinds of support different students needed. I believe this transparency led the preservice and early-career teachers to better understand the thinking behind a teacher's decision-making. I hope that my willingness to listen, learn, and adjust was impactful, as well, communicating that teachers are always becoming (Strom and Viesca, 2021).

STUDENT PARTICIPATION IN FIELD-BASED TEACHING AND LEARNING

Having reviewed conference notes, responses to student writing and written reflections, the invitation to confer and reflect with other teachers of writers across the process led the preservice and early-career teachers to recognize the importance of establishing trust and building relationships with writers. In addition, they developed understandings of the necessity to ask questions and gather information before deciding what or how to teach. Many saw, firsthand, that naming and building on strength often increased comfort, confidence, and encouraged student agency. This said, the participating teachers continued to negotiate how to support writers while encouraging them to take ownership of their writing.

In written reflections and conversations in class, FYC students voiced recognition that talking about their writing during conferences gave them new ideas for how to approach their essays and opinion pieces. In addition, they shared that the conversations they had with the preservice and early-career teachers increased their confidence and allowed them to see strengths and areas for improvement that they had not previously recognized. Students also noted that they learned new writing strategies and came to new understandings about negotiating the genres they were exploring through this collaboration.

INNOVATING TO SUPPORT THE TRANSITION FROM AWARENESS TO APPLICATION

In the NCTE position statement *Beliefs about Methods Courses and Field Experiences in English Education*, Gallo et al. (2020) argue,

> Field experiences must prepare English teacher candidates for many and diverse contexts and with awareness of the richness and variety of the profession as a whole; therefore, field experiences should connect candidates to the widest available variety of students, teachers, schools, and communities.

While field experiences have varied across institutions and programs, they have often invited PTs to learn in practice in K-12 schools, working closely with K-12 teachers. The methods instructors' participation in these field experiences and the opportunity for PTs to apply what they have learned in their methods courses has sometimes been limited (Pasternak et al., 2014, 2018).

Although meaningful partnerships with secondary teachers and schools when implementing field-based teaching and learning in my methods courses had been done for many years, my desire to ask less of practicing K-12 teachers during a time in which so much was expected of them led me to recast the role of "cooperating teacher" and locate a new context in which participating preservice and early-career teachers could begin to transition from awareness to application, with the support of other teachers of writing.

This opportunity likely strengthened the participants' disciplinary and pedagogical knowledge, further preparing them for the work they would later do with writers in other contexts. While the context in which they were invited to learn in practice was different than the one in which most of the participating PTs would go on to teach, we attempted to address this by continually thinking together about these differences. In addition, they regularly reflected on how the larger lessons they were learning about the teaching of writers impacted their beliefs and the choices they would go on to make in our own classrooms.

Though it is certainly important that PTs have opportunities to practice what they are learning in secondary schools, as well, ELA teacher educators who participated in Pasternak et al.'s (2018) study voiced concern about the "two-worlds pitfall" (Feiman-Nemser and Buchmann, 1985) noting that without adequate scaffolding and support, preservice ELA teachers often struggled to link theory and research explored in the ELA methods class to practice in this new context.

Is it possible that opportunities to move from awareness to application, explicitly linking pedagogical and disciplinary-specific theory to practice in new spaces, with the support of a methods instructor, might better prepare PTs to negotiate this pitfall upon beginning their work in schools? If so, what new kinds of field experiences might we design *and actively participate in*, keeping this goal in mind? Who might we invite to join us as "cooperating teachers," supporting our efforts to expand opportunities for our preservice and early-career teachers to learn in practice, throughout their ELA teacher education programs? What efforts might we need to engage in to ensure transfer?

Pasternak et al. (2014, 2018) remind us how limited the research is on clinical experiences within ELA education. While 73 percent of the ELA teacher education programs participating in Pasternak et al.'s (2018) study claimed that their program included connected field experiences as part of their ELA methods courses, 40 percent of the syllabi submitted did not provide details about this experience. In addition to innovating in an effort to better support teachers as they transition from universities to secondary classrooms, it is necessary to clarify what, in fact, we already do and to engage in research to better understand what works and what might be reenvisioned to ensure that PTs have the disciplinary and pedagogical knowledge to not only negotiate new contexts but also to disrupt practices and approaches that continue to limit equity, access, and justice.

REFERENCES

Bomer, K. (2010). *Hidden gems: Naming and teaching from the brilliance in every student's writing*. Heinemann.
Bomer, K. (2016). *The journey is everything: Teaching essays that students want to write for people who want to read them*. Heinemann.
Bomer, R. and Fowler-Amato, M. (2014). Expanding adolescent writing: Building upon youths' practices, purposes, relationships and thoughtfulness. In K. A. Hinchman and H. D. Sheridan-Thomas (Eds.), *Best practices in adolescent literacy instruction* (2nd ed.) Guilford Press.
David, A. D. and Consalvo, A. (2018, November 26). Advice to teachers: What do young people have to say about writing? *Teachers, Profs, Parents: Writers Who Care*. Accessed March 1, 2023. https://writerswhocare.wordpress.com/2018/11/26/advice-to-teachers-what-do-young-people-have-to-say-about-writing/.
Dirk, K. (2010). Navigating genres. *Writing Spaces: Readings on Writing*, *1*, 249–62.
Dunn, P. (2016, July 18). What teaching driver's education taught me about giving writers feedback. *Teachers, Profs, Parents: Writers Who Care*. Accessed January 27, 2023. https://writerswhocare.wordpress.com/2016/07/18/what-teaching-drivers-education-taught-me-about-giving-writers-feedback/.
Feiman-Nemser, S. and Buchmann, M. (1985). Pitfalls of experience in teacher preparation. *Teachers College Record*, *87*(1), 53–65.
Fowler-Amato, M. (2020). New possibilities for field experiences: Learning in practice in a university writing center. *Teaching/Writing: The Journal of Writing Teacher Education*, *9*(1), Article 22.
Gallo, J., Hallman, H. L., Parsons, C., Pastore-Capuana, K., Pet, S. R., and Searcy, L. (2020). Beliefs about methods courses and field experiences in English education. Accessed February 10, 2023. https://ncte.org/statement/methodsinee/.
Hallman, H. L. (2012). Community-based field experiences in teacher education: Possibilities for a pedagogical third space. *Teaching Education*, *23*(3), 241–63.
National Council of Teachers of English. (2016). Professional knowledge for the teaching of writing. Accessed March 1, 2023. https://ncte.org/statement/teaching-writing/.
Pasternak, D. L., Caughlin, S., Hallman, H. L., Renzi, L., and Rush, L. S. (2014). Teaching English language arts methods in the United States: A review of the research. *Review of Education*, *2*(2), 146–85.

Pasternak, D. L., Caughlin, S., Hallman, H. L., Renzi, L., and Rush, L. S. (2018). *Secondary English teacher education in the United States*. Bloomsbury Academic.

Ray, K., with Laminack, L. (2001). *The writer's workshop: Working through the hard parts (and they're all hard parts)*. NCTE.

Strom, K. J. and Viesca, K. M. (2021). Towards a complex framework of teacher learning-practice. *Professional Development in Education*, *47*(2–3), 209–24. https://doi.org/10.1080/19415257.2020.1827449.

Taylor, L. A. (2019, July 29). The radical possibilities of "What are you working on?": Student-driven learning in writing conferences. *Teachers, Profs, Parents: Writers Who Care*. Accessed February 15, 2023. https://writerswhocare.wordpress.com/2019/07/29/the-radical-possibilities-of-what-are-you-working-on-student-driven-learning-in-writing-conferences/.

Zeichner, K. and Conklin, H. (2008). Teacher education programs as sites for teacher preparation. In M. Cochran-Smith, S. Feiman-Nesmer, D. J. McIntyre, and K. E. Demers (Eds.), *Handbook of research on teacher education* (3rd ed., pp. 269–89). Routledge.

Chapter 10

Using the NCTE SPA Program Review as a Catalyst for Change

Moving Beyond the Methods Course

Lara Searcy

For many English Language Arts Teacher Educators (ELATE) who have completed the Specialized Professional Association (SPA) program assessment process for accreditation, "SPA" is not the right acronym—there is no relaxation with program review. It is a tedious and cumbersome process with lengthy template reports that include narrative alignments to data findings and assessment analysis with tools, scoring guides, and data charts. The use of data charts alone can bring about a statistical dread for many English Language Arts (ELA) teachers.

Yet, SPA program review does provide an opportunity for rejuvenation—especially with the adoption of the new *2021 National Council of Teachers of English (NCTE) Standards for the Initial Preparation of Teachers of Secondary English Language Arts Grades 7–12* standards. Programs can use this adoption time as a catalyst for personal, professional, and programmatic growth through the redevelopment of content pedagogical knowledge, program outcomes, coursework, and assessments.

In general, standards guide the development of curriculum and instruction to ensure that it is appropriately engaging, challenging, and sequenced (OAS-ELA, 2021). Standards simply indicate what should be taught, not how content should be taught. As Gallagher (2015) notes, standards are helpful, and a necessary starting point for building curriculum. Since standards establish expectations about what students should know and be able to do, they should provide opportunities for meaningful changes (Goering, 2021), such as during program review. The NCTE serves as an SPA for ELA teacher preparation programs, and because of that, NCTE defines the content area standards for programs to become nationally recognized as part of the accreditation process (CAEP, 2022). By using the new *2021 NCTE Standards* as "a necessary starting point," programs can apply and demonstrate knowledge of how to plan and assess instruction in English language arts—which are requirements of teacher candidates:

- Standard 1: Candidates apply and demonstrate knowledge of learners and learning to foster inclusive learning environments that support coherent, relevant, *standards-aligned,* differentiated, and antiracist/antibias instruction to engage grade 7–12 learners in ELA.
- Standard 3: Candidates apply and demonstrate knowledge of theories, research, and ELA to plan coherent, relevant, *standards-aligned,* differentiated, antiracist/antibias instruction and assessment.
- Standard 4: Candidates implement planned coherent, relevant, *standards-aligned,* differentiated, and antiracist/antibias ELA instruction and assessment to motivate and engage all learners. (*2021 NCTE Standards*)

From 2019 to 2021, a Steering Committee leadership team of NCTE members from the ELATE group worked to revise, create, gather feedback, and reach consensus on these new *2021 NCTE Standards* used for SPA review (George et al., 2021). Because of their work, the newly revised *2021 NCTE Standards* are NCTE's work created by NCTE members—and they "have the ability to challenge and change what it means to teach ELA" (Goering, 2021, p. 65). The *2021 NCTE Standards* revision work includes four areas of advancement:

1) acknowledging adolescence/ts as a complex and often problematic social construct; using languaging;
2) creating an integration of antiracism throughout all standards and assessments;
3) moving forward the important role critical media literacy must play in the preparation of teachers; and
4) acknowledging that candidates must understand the concept of antiracism/antibias and build knowledge and skill toward this ever-evolving goal. (George et al., 2021, p. 66)

Some may argue that standards "limit certain aspects of the English curriculum or restrict teacher autonomy and agency" (Endacott and Goering, 2014). Goering, one of the ELATE members on the Steering Committee leadership team, challenged educators back in 2014 to consider the "big business values" that have been infiltrated into curriculum with standards-based reforms, such as with the adoption of the Common Core State Standards. Instead of being complicit, as he asks in the article, *Reclaiming the Conversation,* we should be the ones indeed "reclaiming the conversations" about what we can control in our classrooms, such as the creation of standards that accurately reflect the professional knowledge and responsibility of ELA teachers (Endacott and Goering, 2014).

Due to NCTE's role in program review and their collaboration with the Council for the Accreditation of Educator Preparation (CAEP), educators did have a seat at the table to inform practice and be bearers of ethical practice and standards for the profession (CAEP, 2022). Therefore, we should view the new *2021 NCTE Standards* as an asset that holds us accountable for new content and pedagogical knowledge in our field—especially during SPA program review cycles.

With the adoption of these *2021 NCTE Standards*, many programs will need to undergo the process of SPA rejuvenation—reenvisioning their program, curriculum, and assessments to better "apply and demonstrate knowledge and theoretical perspectives, including antiracist/antibias ELA, pertaining to texts, composition, language, and languaging" (NCTE 2021, Standard 2).

In order to practice what programs teach, program reviewers can use the *Beliefs about Methods Courses and Field Experiences in English Education (2020)* position statement and other NCTE resources to think creatively about how to use national accreditation standards and program review as a catalyst for change—programmatically, professionally, and personally.

The *Beliefs about Methods (2020)* position statement (Gallo et al., 2020) can guide reviewers to examine (1) how coursework is integral to the professional lives of prospective English teachers, (2) how to develop deep understandings about what we teach and how we teach, and (3) how to empower candidates for social transformation. It also discusses how research in the field is expanding and provides guidance on how to program coursework—specifically in the Methods course (Alsup et al., 2006, p. 285). This happens through

1) the examination of historical, social, political, global, and economic influences;
2) the exploration of teaching and learning—understanding that teaching and learning are:
    i. social practices;
    ii. the emphasizing of the diversity of literacies, texts, and learners;
    iii. the planning, implementing, assessing, and articulating rationales for pedagogical choices; and
    iv. the fostering of professional identity development. (NCTE, 2020)

The *Beliefs about Methods (2020)* position statement can also push reviewers to expand their thinking about how programs can react to a dynamic English teacher education ecosystem with influences from without (e.g., changing national and state accreditation standards) and within (e.g., candidates' other courses in a specific teacher education program). Programs must help candidates make explicit connections between courses in English Methods, English content area, and the education major, as well as develop concepts of teaching and learning, content knowledge, content pedagogy, knowledge about learners and learning, and professional knowledge and skills (NCTE 2020).

In addition, what is advantageous with the *2021 NCTE Standards*—specifically, the ELA Content Knowledge in Standard 2—is their direct alignment to *Policy Brief* resources provided by the NCTE James R. Squire Office of Policy Research in ELA, in three specific areas: (1) Critical Media Literacy and Popular Culture in ELA Classrooms (Lyiscott et al., 2021); (2) Racial Literacy (Sealey-Ruiz, 2021); (3) Understanding Translanguaging in the US Literacy Classrooms (Seltzer and de los Rios, 2021). These Policy Briefs model how to "use knowledge and theoretical perspectives [. . .] to demonstrate professional learning, and advocacy" (NCTE, 2021, Standard 5).

A PERSONAL AND PROFESSIONAL NARRATIVE ABOUT USING SPA PROGRAM REVIEW AS A CATALYST FOR CHANGE

The Standards Steering Committee Co-Chairs share that numerous colleagues used the "then-new 2012 standards to make fairly significant modifications to both program coursework and assessments used to determine teacher candidates' readiness" (George et al., 2021, p. 56). With the adoption of the new *2021 NCTE Standards*, many ELATE are due once again for a "SPA" experience—full of rejuvenation that is hopefully transformative personally, professionally, and programmatically. This at least was my experience during my first SPA review in 2016 and again in 2022 as I just completed my last review using the *2012 NCTE Standards*. With the adoption of the *2021 NCTE Standards,* I am beginning the process (again) of redesigning courses and assessments to align with the new standards. This process has indeed allowed me to reflect personally in order to grow professionally in order to create the catalytic changes needed in my program.

Almost a decade ago, as a new English Education Specialist for our B.A.Ed. English Education, I did not feel mastery of the standards. For example, when considering NCTE Standard VI (2012): "Candidates demonstrate knowledge of how theories and research about social justice, diversity, equity, student identities, and schools as institutions can enhance students' opportunities to learn in English Language Arts," I asked how I could create, assign, and assess the professional knowledge and skills that I did not have.

To better establish my content pedagogical knowledge, the NCTE position statement, *Beliefs about Social Justice in English Education*, became a text I consulted. This position statement outlines seven beliefs about social justice in schools, detailed assignments, an appendix with teacher educator activities and assignments, considerations for research, and classroom resources. This starting point helped me understand that social justice "is a grounded theory, a stance/position, a pedagogy, a process, a framework for research, and a promise" (NCTE, 2009). In addition, to further my understanding of antiracist instruction, as stated in the new *2021 NCTE Standards*, I read. A lot. Because as Falter, Alston, and Lee address in their article, *Becoming Anti-Racist English Teachers: Ways to Actively Move Forward (2020)*, the "teaching for an antiracist future starts with educators"—in which they offer five steps for actively moving forward toward antiracist ELA teaching: (1) Listen and Reflect, (2) Read, (3) Interrogate, (4) Act, and (5) Repeat.

English Education's *Intentional Praxis in English Education (January 2021)* provided multiple pedagogical articulations of how to develop as equity-minded educators who embody critical thinking, individual agency, ethical awareness, reflective reasoning, and social responsibility through connections with the development of critical, agentic, active, ethical, reflective, and socially just ELA teachers (Shoffner). Yet, in order to enact these tenets myself—both personally and professionally—I had to answer the assumption Goering makes in *Setting the Standard in Antiracist/Antibias Instruction* (2021), that "faculty leading programs will make progress on their own content knowledge when it comes to antiracist instruction" (p. 69). That is why we must

> examine every move [we] make, from the sources [we] use in classes to the ways we spend time, from the conversations we have to the conversations we don't. There is only one way forward for my students and me, and that's toward an antiracist/antibias English language arts. (p. 68)

Ultimately, this starts with my acknowledgment that as a white, female educator, I represent 74 percent and 72 percent, respectively, of the teaching profession. Therefore, to grow in my own work of being antiracist, I choose to actively move forward by being persistent in my self-awareness, constant in my self-criticism, and regular in my self-examination of how the intersections of my identity influence my programmatic and instructional decisions (Kendi, 2019, p. 23). As a result, many of the changes my program has undergone is often a direct result of my own learning.

What social justice looks like in my program is a reflection of my own development of growth. The preliminary actions for adding "social justice" to my course were as limited as my own knowledge. Initially, to meet NCTE Standard VI (2012): "Candidates demonstrate knowledge of how theories and research about social justice, diversity, equity, student identities, and schools as institutions can enhance students' opportunities to learn in English Language Arts," I devoted one class session to discussion with a written reflection for the SPA Assessment:

> Read *Supporting Linguistically and Culturally Diverse Learners in English Education* (2005) and write a reflective summary of each of the Eight Beliefs. Select one activity from *Beliefs about Social Justice in English Education Appendix: Teacher Education Activities/Assignments* to implement in your future classroom.

This reflection, ultimately, was as limited as my own knowledge at the time. As Goering (2021) shares—social justice work, much aligned to antiracist/antibias work—"is a process, a lifelong commitment, a belief system about how to interact with and engage the world. There's (ironically) no standard to check off or meet" (p. 68). What I was haphazardly trying to create—a checked-off assessment requirement for the SPA report—needed instead to be a philosophical change of thinking in how I approached and demonstrated principles of difference and power (NCTE, 2021). This is when I realized that the work of social justice needed more depth and time embedded into my program rather than one class session in my Methods course.

As with the dilemma explored in this book, "the Methods course cannot (and should not) do it all" (NCTE, 2020). At the beginning of my career, my Methods course was the only course situated for content pedagogical knowledge for our English teacher candidates. That meant it housed four of the six required NCTE SPA Assessments: (1) candidates took their state licensure test that semester, so we used Methods to prepare; (2) candidates were in the last semester of their coursework before their final internship, so we used Methods to demonstrate their content knowledge; (3) candidates created content unit plans to demonstrate content pedagogy, so we planned, assessed, and implemented those in the Methods course; (4) candidates were in their second internship, so we practiced professional knowledge and skills in Methods. Needless to say, teacher candidates in the class (and myself) were already overloaded because I was forcing Methods "to do it all." Therefore, adding "plan and implement social justice into their knowledge of students and instructional planning" to my already overloaded Methods course felt confining to a concept that was so broad.

Due to this, I used my upcoming SPA program review deadline to make necessary program modifications—not only because of "influences from without" such as standards and accreditation but also by rethinking how I could use "influences from within" to create more space. As my own learning and understanding of social justice expanded, so did the space for it in my program.

This rethinking, as prompted by my SPA program review, allowed for the creation of two new courses. In Fall 2018, I proposed reassigning a one-hour elective to create a new one-hour required course specific for English Education majors: Critical Issues in English Education. The rationale for this course was to provide more class time to explore "theories and research about social justice, diversity, equity, student identities" (NCTE Standard VI, 2012). Based on positive student feedback and involvement in this one-hour seminar class, another new course was proposed, Social Justice Literacies, as a three-hour "English Studies" elective. Again, with positive student feedback and continuous enrollment, I was able to provide a rationale for the elective course to become a required course for B.A. English Education teacher candidates.

The new course aligns with a more meaningful SPA assessment about "social justice" and "antiracist/antibias instruction." Instead of a one-page reflection assignment within the Methods course, the Assessment for Standard VI (NCTE, 2012) and Standard 1 (NCTE, 2021) now occurs in its own created course as well as more authentic integration across multiple courses. Now the program embeds the "knowledge of learners and learning to foster inclusive learning environments that support [. . .] antiracist/antibias teaching" using multiple avenues, such as by reading NCTE position statements, such as *Educators' Right and Responsibilities to Engage in Antiracist Teaching (2022)* and participating in Anti-Racist Professional Development Book Clubs.

The course also asks students to create Text Rationales to interrogate how to "plan, implement, and assess [. . .] antiracist/antibias instruction" through the creation of content unit plans that are focused on diverse text selection that relate to the diversity of the students in their field experience setting. Finally, we create action plans in our classrooms or community to move from thought to action (NCTE, 2021).

What began with my first SPA review cycle in 2016 continues today with the new *2021 NCTE Standards*. Through my own personal, professional, and programmatic rejuvenation, it is my intention to model for my teacher candidates how to start with self-reflection and use one's personal history as a necessary beginning for antiracist/antibias work because we know how "our own identities and experiences frame our practices and impact our teaching of ELA" (NCTE, 2021, Standard 5).

It is my resolve to (1) support efforts by educators to teach about social injustice and discrimination; (2) acknowledge my role in teacher education to prepare teachers to enact and value a socially just pedagogy; (3) advocate for equity, student dignity, and success; and (4) oppose policies that reinforce inequitable learning opportunities or outcomes for students (NCTE 2010). I continue this work because of the asset and accountability that comes with Standards. "Are these perfect standards? Of course not. Are there flaws and omissions? Naturally. But they are our standards" (Goering, 2021, p. 70). And for that, I am grateful for the guidance they have provided in my eight years as an ELA teacher educator and as an NCTE SPA program writer and reviewer. May you find the same rejuvenation during the program review process to consider how to create catalysts for change—personally, professionally, and programmatically.

REFERENCES

Alsup, J., Emig, J., Pradl, G., Tremmel, R., and Yagelski, R. (2006). The state of English education and a vision for its future: A call to arms. *English Education*, *38*(4), 278–94.

Council for the Accreditation of Educator Preparation. (2022) *Standard 1: Content and pedagogical knowledge*. CAEP. Retrieved August 21, 2022 from https://caepnet.org/standards/2022-itp/standard-1.

Council for the Accreditation of Educator Preparation. (2022). *Navigation*. CAEP. Retrieved August 21, 2022 from https://caepnet.org/accreditation/caep-accreditation/spa-program-review-process.

Endacott, J. and Goering, C. Z. (2014). Speaking truth to power: Reclaiming the conversation on education. *English Journal*, *103*(5), 89–92.

Falter, M. M., Alston, C. L., and Lee, C. C. (2020). *Becoming anti-racist English teachers: Ways to actively move forward* [White paper]. North Carolina State University. Accessed March 2, 2023. https://go.ncsu.edu/antiracist-ela.

Gallagher, K. (2015). *In the best interest of students: Staying true to what works in the ELA classroom*. Portland, ME: Stenhouse.

Gallo, J., Hallman, H. L., Parsons, C., Pastore-Capuana, K., Pet, S. R., and Searcy, L. (2020). Beliefs about methods courses and field experiences in English education. Accessed February 15, 2023. https://ncte.org/statement/methodsinee/.

George, M. A., Pasternak, D. L., Goering, C. Z. (2022). A years' long journey into the 2021 English language arts teacher preparation. *English Education*, *54*(1), 54–64. Accessed March 1, 2023. https://library.ncte.org/journals/EE/issues/v54-1/31632.

Goering, C. Z. (2021). Setting the standard in antiracist/antibias instruction in English language arts and teacher education. *English Education*, *54*(1), 65–71. https://library.ncte.org/journals/ee/issues/v54-1/31633.

Kendi, I. X. (2019). *How to be an antiracist.* Random House Publishing Group.
Lyiscott, J., Mirra, N., and Garcia, A. (2020, November 30). *Critical media literacy and popular culture in ELA classrooms. A policy research brief.* National Council of Teachers of English. Retrieved September 6, 2022 from https://eric.ed.gov/?id=ED612183.
National Council of Teachers of English (NCTE) (2022). Membership. Retrieved August 21, 2022 from https://ncte.org/membership/.
National Council of Teachers of English (NCTE) (2022). Policy Briefs. Accessed September 6, 2022. https://ncte.org/resources/policy-briefs/.
National Council of Teachers of English (NCTE). (2010 November 20). *Resolution on social justice in literacy education.* Accessed September 6, 2022. https://ncte.org/statement/socialjustice/.
National Council of Teachers of English (NCTE). (2012). *NCTE/NCATE Standards for initial preparation of teachers of secondary English language arts, grades 7–12 approved October 2012.* Accessed September 6, 2022. http://www.ncte.org/library/NCTEFiles/Groups/CEE/NCATE/ApprovedStandards_111212.pdf.
National Council of Teachers of English (NCTE). (2018 November 14). *Expanding opportunities: Academic success for culturally and linguistically diverse students.* Accessed September 6, 2022. https://ncte.org/statement/expandingopportun.
National Council of Teachers of English (NCTE). (2020 May 22). *Beliefs about methods courses and field experiences in English education.* Accessed September 6, 2022. https://ncte.org/statement/methodsinee/.
National Council of Teachers of English (NCTE). (2021). *NCTE/NCATE standards for initial preparation of teachers of secondary English language arts, grades 7–12 approved October 2021.* Accessed September 6, 2022. https://ncte.org/wp-content/uploads/2021/11/2021_NCTE_Standards.pdf.
National Council of Teachers of English (NCTE). (2022 March 7). *Educators' right and responsibilities to engage in antiracist teaching.* Accessed September 6, 2022. https://ncte.org/statement/antiracist-teaching/
Oklahoma Department of Education (OSDE 2021). Oklahoma Academic Standards for English Language Arts (OAS-ELA). Accessed September 6, 2022. https://sde.ok.gov/sites/default/files/documents/files/2021%20Oklahoma%20Academic%20Standards%20for%20English%20Language%20Arts.pdf.
Pasternak, D. L., Caughlan, S., Hallman, H. L., Renzi, L., and Rush, L. S. (2014). Teaching English language arts methods in the United States: A review of the research. *Review of Education, 2*(2), 146–85. https://doi.org/10.1002/rev3.3031.
Pasternak, D. L., Caughlan, S., Hallman, H. L., Renzi, L., and Rush, L. S. (2018). *Secondary English teacher education in the United States.* London: Bloomsbury Academic, an imprint of Bloomsbury Publishing Plc.
Sealey-Ruiz, Y. (2020, November 30). *Racial literacy: A policy research brief.* National Council of Teachers of English. Accessed September 6, 2022 from https://eric.ed.gov/?id=ED612185.
Seltzer, K. and de los Ríos, C. V. (2020, November 30). Understanding translanguaging in US literacy classrooms: Reframing bi-/multilingualism as the norm. A policy

research brief. National Council of Teachers of English. Accessed September 6, 2022, from https://eric.ed.gov/?id=ED612186.

Shoffner, M. and Searcy, L. (2021). Intentional Praxis. *English Education*, *53*(2), 158–70. https://library.ncte.org/journals/ee/issues/v53-2/31090.

U.S. Department of Education, National Center for Education Statistics, National Teacher and Principal Survey (NTPS), "Public School Teacher Data File," 2017–18. Accessed September 6, 2022. https://nces.ed.gov/surveys/ntps/tables/ntps1718_fltable01_t1s.asp.

Chapter 11

The Impact of Policies that Promote the Science of Reading on English Teacher Preparation

William Kerns

This chapter addresses the challenge of responding to policy pressures in support of the science of reading within a middle and secondary English teacher education program. The goal of the chapter is to shed light on ways of meeting foundational literacy needs while drawing upon the social turn in literacy and the language arts. The approach to English teacher education that is envisioned contrasts with discourse that is too easily dominated by such divides as nature v. nature (Yaden et al., 2021) or structured literacy vs. whole language.

A statement from The National Council of Teachers of English's position statement, *Beliefs about Methods Courses and Field Experiences in English Education*, grounds this chapter: "Methods coursework should prepare candidates to become engaged and effective teachers who can plan, implement, assess, and articulate rationales for pedagogical choices" (Gallo et al., 2020). The chapter explores implications from policies related to the science of reading for the preparation of middle and secondary English teachers, and strategies that can potentially guide programs in responding to state policies.

DEBATES OVER THE SCIENCE OF READING

The International Literacy Association (n.d.) defined the science of reading as "a corpus of objective investigation and accumulation of reliable evidence about how humans learn to read and how reading should be taught." This definition points to a multidisciplinary outlook. As Afflerbach (2022) suggested, the diverse range of research points to discourse on sciences in reading rather than a single science of reading.

In 2013, Mississippi legislation addressed the science of reading and set the tone for subsequent laws that most states passed (Schwartz, 2022). The approach to the science of reading embraced by reformers in most states since 2013 promotes explicit and systematic instruction of basic reading and writing skills, with an emphasis on Scarborough's Reading Rope (2001), the Simple View of Reading (SVR) (Gough and Tunmer, 1986), and structured literacy (Spear-Swerling, 2022).

Mississippi's Department of Education (n.d.) defines the science of reading as "the research that reading experts, especially cognitive and linguistic scientists, have conducted on how we learn to read. This body of knowledge reveals what happens in the brain during reading and what needs to take place instructionally to enable skillful reading." Importantly, this definition privileges implications from cognitive science and neuroscience, language structure, and the way language is used to make meaning.

DIFFERING MODELS OF READING AND READING INSTRUCTION

Competing understandings of the reading process result in divergent approaches to instruction. Additionally, competing approaches to the type of research which produces valued insights leads to researchers and practitioners who find themselves in competing camps (Stanovich, 2000).

The first battle within the reading wars highlights disagreements over models of reading and the implications of these models for reading instruction. A divide exists between those who favor bottom-up models of reading comprehension and those who favor top-down models. Bottom-up models emphasize learning to read words from part to whole, while top-down models prioritize learning to read from whole to part (Whitehurst and Lonigan, 1998; Stanovich, 2000).

The Bottom-Up Model

The bottom-up model of reading comprehension (Gough, 1972; Laberge and Samuels, 1974) emphasizes building from foundational aspects of language structure, such as sound parts and word parts, then building in a serial process. Those favoring bottom-up models see literacy development as progressing through stages. Chall's stages of reading development stressed the importance of early phonics as children progress toward exploration of diverse literary texts (Semingson and Kerns, 2021).

The SVR (Gough and Tunmer, 1986) highlights the role of decoding and linguistic comprehension in reading comprehension. Hoover and Tunmer

(2020) provide an in-depth elaboration of SVR. Scarborough's Reading Rope (2001) is a framework for understanding the interlinking roles of word recognition and language comprehension in the reading process.

Structured literacy is an umbrella term for instructional approaches that focus on explicit and systematic instruction of foundational areas of reading and writing (Spear-Swerling, 2022). In alignment with bottom-up models, structured literacy involves a scope and sequence of instruction which moves in a serial process from phonemic awareness and phonics toward more complex aspects of learning vocabulary and comprehending texts. Struggling adolescent readers can receive instruction using a structured literacy-based approach that involves explicit instruction in the use of prefixes, roots, and suffixes (Fallon and Katz, 2020).

The Top-Down Model

The top-down approach emphasizes understanding and enjoying texts, gaining meaning and a sense of the big picture by, for example, drawing on background knowledge and making personal connections (Smith, 2011). The whole language movement (Goodman, 2014) contributed to the popularity of literary response and reading workshops. English teachers who are influenced by the whole language movement will often draw upon reader response theory (Rosenblatt, 1978), with the meaning of a text interpreted based on the reader's personal reactions to the text as opposed to the reader seeking an objective standard meaning to the text.

Reading as an Interactive Process

Interactive models of reading (Rumelhart, 2013) stress the importance of adolescents gaining purposefulness in what they read, setting goals, and drawing on background and subject matter knowledge. Subsequent models build on the interactive approach, examining both bottom-up and top-down processes of reading and the contexts, goals, and outcomes of reading. The active view of the reading model (Duke and Cartwright, 2021) builds on the SVR and Scarborough's Reading Rope, while pointing to the importance of background knowledge, self-regulation, context, the use of strategies, and self-efficacy.

The Social Turn

The social turn implies that reading instruction should be informed by the cultural, historical, and political context of students' lived experiences (Lankshear and Knobe,l 2006). Among the concepts to emerge through the social turn include situated cognition (Brown et al., 1989), shedding light on the contextual nature of learning, and a new understanding of the way that learning is shaped by participation in communities of practice (Lave and Wenger, 1991) that have commonly agreed upon goals and rules.

Debates Over Research Methods

Competition over what type of research provides valued evidence represents another front within the reading wars. Positivist-oriented scholars prioritize randomized experimental design and quantitative research such as large-scale statistical analysis (Crotty, 1998). Interpretivist scholars argue that tacit positivist frameworks (Howe, 2009) serve to silence the voices of those who would call for attention to the social aspect of learning and how to teach (Kincheloe and Tobin, 2009).

Positivist Methods

The positivist approach within educational research inherits a claim within the paradigm of logical positivism (Hempel, 1969) that methods of the natural sciences are necessary to systematically classify knowledge within the social sciences. In the reading field, this translates into an emphasis on cognitive, biological, and neurological aspects.

Approaches to understanding the science of reading that have been influential in state legislation since 2013 strongly lean on positivist, privileging cognitive models of reading, implications from biological sciences (e.g., eye movement studies), and implications drawn from neuroscience (e.g., brain imaging and studies of the functioning of parts of the brain).

The understanding of *scientifically based research* embedded within many state laws is the same as that of the National Reading Panel (NICHD, 2000). Two overarching tasks drove the work of the panel: (1) determine relationships between components of instruction and literacy gains and (2) provide a basis for educators to make well-informed instructional decisions. Given the tasks charged to the panel, the panel prioritized experimental and quasi-experimental design studies since these shed light on causal relationships.

A key suggestion from the panel's findings that can inform middle and secondary ELA instruction is the use of a variety of comprehension strategies as appropriate for different modes of texts and genres. Additional recommendations include explicit and systematic instruction of vocabulary words as well as guidance in the use of morphemes (prefixes, roots, suffixes) to make sense of difficult words in context of reading challenging texts. Finally, the panel recommended the explicit modeling of strategies for summarizing texts and reading aloud to model skilled use of comprehension strategies.

Interpretivist Methods

Interpretivists use qualitative research methods to shed light on social and cultural aspects. For example, ethnographic research by Brice Heath (1983) showing a mismatch between language use within communities and the way it is used in school settings provided a touchstone for the social turn.

Beach and O'Brien (2018) conducted a review of research related to methods of instructing students to read that have influenced English Language Arts since the 1920s. Although researchers in the English Education field use experimental design studies as well as both quantitative and qualitative methods, in general since the 1970s and 1980s, the interpretivist approach has been deeply influential in middle and secondary English.

IMPLICATIONS FOR MIDDLE AND SECONDARY ENGLISH EDUCATION

This chapter advocates for the integration of reading instruction into focal areas of an English methods course (Pasternak et al., 2018; Gallo et al., 2020). Methods of teaching reading can be tied into the teaching of writing, assessment methods, alignment of standards with instruction, and the use of technological tools. Additionally, methods courses can address how to plan and implement reading instruction for culturally and linguistically diverse students.

Many teacher education programs require a field experience concurrently with the English methods course (Gallo et al., 2020). Preservice teachers have the opportunity to apply techniques for teaching reading in the middle school or high school setting. Field experiences provide opportunities for preservice teachers to reflect on practice and to engage in research.

Content Area Literacy

Preservice teachers benefit from training in the delivery of explicit and systematic instruction which includes a deep study of implications from Scarborough's Reading Rope (2001). A broad view of literacy leads a program to also provide training related to addressing social and cultural practices, context, and multiple modes of meaning-making, such as digital compared with print texts. Other factors include engagement, purposefulness, and motivation (Frankel et al., 2016).

Field Experiences

Preservice teachers who take field experiences in conjunction with methods courses can apply instructional strategies in a classroom setting. Drawing on both pedagogical content knowledge (PCK) (Shulman, 1987) and technological pedagogical content knowledge (Koehler et al., 2013), there should be a strong connection between a methods course and field experiences. Knowledge and skills of the preservice teacher are shaped by teaching during field experience and then reflecting (Gess-Newsome, 2015).

Methods course instructors should work with the cooperating teacher and university supervisor to help preservice teachers make collective, personal, and enacted connections with literacy instruction (Carlson and Daehler, 2019). Collective PCK about practices of literacy instruction, such as how to ensure that students use different strategies appropriate for understanding fiction compared with nonfiction texts, would be knowledge that is shared among the community of literacy scholars.

Instructional implications from Scarborough's Reading Rope (2001) are gained through individual experience, becoming personal PCK. Concepts related to how middle grade and high school students develop vocabulary knowledge are likewise personalized through field experiences. Preservice teachers build their enacted PCK through opportunities to teach in a classroom setting during field experiences.

Preparation for Racial, Cultural, and Linguistic Diversity

This chapter's recommendations are intended to promote praxis (Freire 1972), with both teacher educators and preservice teachers continuously examining theory, practice, and social contexts (Sailors, 2019). Critical literacies (Luke, 2012) resist forms of oppression including systemic racism (Johnson, 2021) and the privileging of language use within classrooms which is based on deficit models (Baker-Bell, 2020).

Instruction in Linguistically Diverse English Classrooms

Instructional strategies associated with structured literacy can benefit linguistically diverse students, and so can draw on social and cultural background. Preservice teachers should have opportunities to apply effective methods of teaching word parts, vocabulary, and the comprehension of diverse texts (August and Shanahan, 2008). This includes using explicit instruction as typically described within a structured literacy-based framework (Cárdenas-Hagan, 2020).

There is concern about whether discourse on the science of reading adequately takes into account the cultural and linguistic assets of bilingual and emergent bilingual students (Noguerón-Liu, 2020). Preservice teachers would benefit from training on methods that differentiate between the instructional needs of second language learners and students whose only language is English (Goldenberg, 2020).

Translanguaging is both an approach to reading in which two or more languages are in use simultaneously, and it is also an instructional approach that values the simultaneous use of two or more languages as an asset within the curriculum (Garcia and Leiva, 2014). Training in methods of instruction associated with translanguaging would allow students to tap into their primary language as a strength, while also highlighting for preservice teachers the importance of asset-based instruction.

A Social Justice Focus

Morrell's (2015) touchstone 2014 NCTE Presidential Address called for English Education to be "a multilingual, multiliterate discipline focused on social justice" (p. 310). The focus that Morrell proposed in the Presidential Address involves being part of a social justice movement, focused on *critical hope* and *critical love*. Three focal questions would drive the movement forward according to Morrell: how to excite students about learning, how to develop the literate identities of students, and how to make reading instruction relevant for students.

Reading instruction becomes increasingly relevant for students when the teacher values partnerships with communities as sources of strength to inform the curriculum (Kinloch et al., 2021). Curriculum design in English Education that is influenced by critical literacies (Morrell and Scherff, 2015; Compton-Lilly et al., 2022) is empowering to students who are members of traditionally disempowered groups through, for example, affording the opportunity to explore young adult literature in ways that are personally and culturally meaningful (Ginsberg, 2022).

Technology

Methods courses should prioritize the knowledge and skills needed to integrate technology with the planning and implementation of instruction (Schmidt and Kruger-Ross, 2022). Digital texts contain features such as hyperlinks and videos that may help or hinder a student in comprehension of a text (Leu et al., 2015). Preservice English teachers need both training and experience in the use of technological tools that help adolescents to understand texts (Alexander, 2020).

Assessment

Assessment literacy (Popham, 2011) is a key aspect of English teacher education. Ideally, preservice teachers would enter the methods course already possessing awareness and experience with varied types of assessments (e.g., formative, summative, diagnostic, standardized, norm-referenced, criterion-referenced, benchmark, screening, progress monitoring) as applied within literacy and the language arts. This allows preservice teachers to analyze the results of assessments for the purpose of providing feedback that informs the planning of literacy instruction (Black and William, 2010).

Preparation for Conducting Research

Differences between positivist and interpretivist paradigms in research inform debates over the science of reading. The study of research methods enhances the ability of preservice teachers to make informed judgments related to claims that stem from these paradigms, while increasing concept knowledge and pedagogical skill (Kuh, 2008). Involvement in research helps preservice teachers become increasingly skilled in literacy instruction while gaining a more nuanced understanding of relevant content and pedagogical knowledge (Frager, 2010).

The Boyer Commission Report (1998) proposed reforming undergraduate education around a set of student rights. The report is worth revisiting in the context of meeting pressures raised by the science of reading policies. The rights claimed by the commission, when rephrased through the lens of secondary English teacher education, include the right of preservice teachers to opportunities for inquiry and the right to preparation for the challenges involved in becoming English teachers. The commission viewed it as crucial to provide training in the conduct of research.

Case studies can be conducted to better understand aspects of instruction that help or hinder the development of literacy skills in the English classroom (McCann et al., 2021). Clinical and field experiences tied to coursework represent opportunities for preservice teachers to be mentored by professors into the type of critical action research urged by Morrell (2015).

Exploration of progress in literacy can be collaborative among teacher educators, preservice teachers, and classroom teachers (Fine and Torre, 2021). The Boyer Commission's vision for training in research methods included the conduct of inquiry projects during the freshman year, the conduct of research during clinical and field experiences, and the completion of a culminating research project.

CONCLUSIONS

Foundational literacy skills need to be developed. But in doing so, English teacher education programs should ensure that a strong emphasis is placed on attending to the cultural backgrounds of students and on social justice. Teamwork within a program can be enhanced through multidisciplinary collaboration along the focal areas (Gallo et al., 2020) of field experiences, racial, cultural, and linguistic diversity, new technologies, content area literacy, and content standards and assessments. This chapter envisions a program that fosters a deep study of theory and research, classroom practice, and social context along each of these focal areas.

REFERENCES

Afflerbach, P. (2022). *Teaching readers (not reading): Moving beyond skills and strategies to reader focused instruction.* The Guilford Press.

Alexander, P. A. (2020). What research has shown about readers' struggles with comprehension in the digital age: Moving beyond the phonics versus whole language debate. *Reading Research Quarterly, 55*(S1), S89–S97. https://doi.org/10.1002/rrq.331.

August, D. and Shanahan, T. (2008). *Developing reading and writing in second language learners.* Routledge.

Baker-Bell, A. (2020). *Linguistic justice: Black language, literacy, identity, and pedagogy.* Routledge.

Beach, R. and O'Brien, D. (2018). Significant literacy research informing English language arts instruction. In D. Lapp and D. Fisher (Eds.), *Handbook of research on teaching the English language arts* (4th ed., pp. 1–29). Routledge.

Black, P. and William, D. (2010). Inside the black box: Raising standards through classroom assessment. *Phi Delta Kappan, 92*(1), 81–90.

Boyer Commission. (1998). *Reinventing undergraduate education: A blueprint for America's research universities.* Carnegie Foundation for the Advancement of Teaching. Accessed September 6, 2022. https://files.eric.ed.gov/fulltext/ED424840.pdf.

Brown, J. S., Collins, A., and Duguid, P. (1989). Situated cognition and the culture of learning. *Educational Researcher, 18*(1), 32–42. http://doi.org/10.3102/0013189X018001032

Cárdenas-Hagan, E. (Ed.) (2020). *Literacy foundations for English learners: A comprehensive guide to evidence-based instruction.* Brookes Publishing.

Carlson, J. and Daehler, K. R. (2019). The refined consensus model of pedagogical content knowledge in science education. In A. Hume, R. Cooper and A. Borowski (Eds.), *Repositioning pedagogical content knowledge in teachers' knowledge for teaching science* (pp. 77–92). Springer.

Compton-Lilly, C., Ellison, T. L., Perry, K. H., and Smagorinsky, P. (2022). *Whitewashed critical perspectives: Restoring the edge to edgy ideas.* Routledge.

Crotty, M. J. (1998). *The foundations of social research: Meaning and perspective in the research process.* Sage.

Duke, N. K. and Cartwright, K. B. (2021). The science of reading progresses: Communicating advances beyond the simple view of reading. *Reading Research Quarterly, 56*(S1), S25–S44. https://doi.org/10.1002/rrq.411.

Fallon, K. A. and Katz, L. A. (2020). Structured literacy intervention for students with dyslexia: Focus on growing morphological skills. *Language, Speech, and*

Hearing Services in Schools, 51(1), 336–44. https://doi.org/10.1044/2019_LSHSS-19-00019.

Fine, M. and Torre, M. E. (2021). *Essentials of critical participatory action research.* American Psychological Association.

Frager, A. N. (2010). Helping preservice reading teachers learn to read and conduct research to inform their instruction. *Journal of Adolescent and Adult Literacy, 10*, 199–208. https://doi.org/10.1598/JAAL.54.3.5.

Frankel, K. K., Becker, B. L. C., Rowe, M. W., and Pearson, P. D. (2016). From "what is reading?" to what is literacy? *Journal of Education, 196*(3), 7–17. https://doi.org/10.1177/0022057416196030.

Freire, P. (1972). *Pedagogy of the oppressed.* Penguin.

Gallo, J., Hallman, H. L., Parsons, C., Pastore-Capuana, K., Ringler Pet, S., and Searcy, L. (2020). *Beliefs about methods courses and field experiences in English education.* Accessed September 6, 2022. https://ncte.org/statement/methodsinee/.

Garcia, A. and O'Donnell-Allen, C. (2015). *Pose, wobble, flow: A culturally proactive approach to literacy instruction.* Teachers College Press.

García, O. and Leiva, C. (2014). Theorizing and enacting translanguaging for social justice. In A. Blackledge and A. Creese (Eds.), *Heteroglossia as practice and pedagogy* (pp. 199–216). Springer. https://doi.org/10.1007/978-94-007-7856-6_11.

Gess-Newsome, J. (2015). A model of teacher professional knowledge and skill including PCK. In A. Berry, P. Friedrichsen, and J. Loughran (Eds.), *Reexamining pedagogical content knowledge in science education* (pp. 28–42). Routledge.

Ginsberg, R. (2022). *Challenging traditional classroom spaces with young adult literature: Students in community as course co-designers.* National Council of Teachers of English (NCTE).

Goldenberg, C. (2020). Reading wars, reading science, and English learners. *Reading Research Quarterly, S55*(S1), S131–S144. https://doi.org/10.1002/rrq.340.

Goodman, K. S. (2014). *What's whole in whole language in the 21st Century?* Garn Press.

Gough, P. B. (1972). One second of reading. In J. Kavanagh and I. Mattingly (Eds.), *Language by eye and ear.* MIT Press.

Gough, P. B., and Tunmer, W. E. (1986). Decoding, reading, and reading disability. *Remedial and Special Education, 7*(1), 6–10. https://doi.org/10.1177/074193258600700104.

Heath, S. B. (1983). *Way with words: Language, life and work in communities and classrooms.* Cambridge University Press.

Hempel, C. G. (1969). Logical positivism and the social sciences. In P. Achinstein and S. Barker (Eds.), *The legacy of logical positivism* (pp. 163–94). Johns Hopkins Press.

Hoover, W. A. and Tunmer, W. E. (2020). *The cognitive foundations of reading and its acquisition.* Springer.

Howe, A. R. (2009). Positivist dogmas, rhetoric, and the education science question. *Educational Researcher, 38*(6), 428–40. https://doi.org/10.3102/0013189X09342003.

International Literacy Association. (2020). Science of reading. In *Literacy glossary*. Accessed September 6, 2022. https://literacyworldwide.org/get-resources/literacy-glossary.
Johnson, L. L. (2021). *Critical race English education: New visions, new possibilities*. Routledge.
Kinloch, V., Nemeth, E. A., Butler, T. T., and Player, G. D. (2021). *Where is the justice? Engaged pedagogies in schools and communities*. Teachers College Press.
Koehler, M. J., Mishra, P., and Cain, W. (2013). What is TPack? *Journal of Education, 193*(3), 13–19. https://doi.org/10.1177/002205741319300303.
Kuh, G. D. (2008). *High-impact educational practices: What they are, who has access to them, and why they matter*. Association of American Colleges and Universities (AAC&U).
Kincheloe, J. L. and Tobin, K. (2009). The much exaggerated death of positivism. *Cultural Studies of Science Education, 4*, 513–28. http://doi.org/10.1007/s11422-009-9178-5.
LaBerge, D. and Samuels, S. J. (1974). Toward a theory of automatic information processing in reading. *Cognitive Psychology, 6*, 293—323. https://doi.org/10.1016/0010-0285(74)90015-2.
Lankshear, C. and Knobel, M. (2006). *New literacies: Everyday practices and classroom learning* (2nd ed.). Open University Press.
Lave, J. and Wenger, E. (1991). *Situated learning: Legitimate peripheral participation*. Cambridge University Press.
Leu, D. J., Forzani, E., Rhoads, C., Maykel, C., Kennedy, C., and Timbrell, N. (2015). The new literacies of online research and comprehension: Rethinking the reading achievement gap. *Reading Research Quarterly, 50*(1), 37–59. https://doi.org/10.1002/rrq.85.
Luke, A. (2012). Critical literacy: Foundational notes. *Theory into Practice, 51*(1), 4–11. https://doi.org/10.1080/00405841.2012.636324.
McCann, T. M., Khan, E. A., Hochstetler, S., and Chambers, D. (2021). *On the case in the English language arts classroom: Situations for the teaching of English*. National Council of Teachers of English (NCTE).
Mississippi Department of Education (n.d.). *Science of reading*. Accessed June 20, 2022. https://www.mdek12.org/OAE/OEER/Science-of-Reading.
Morrell, E. (2015). NCTE yesterday, today and tomorrow: Toward the next movement. *Research in the Teaching of English, 49*(3), 307–27.
Morrell, E. and Scherff, L. (2015). *New directions in teaching English: Reimagining teaching, teacher education, and research*. Rowman & Littlefield.
National Institute of Child Health and Human Development (NICHD). (2000). *Report of the national reading panel. Teaching children to read: An evidence-based assessment of the scientific research literature on reading and its implications for reading instruction: Reports of the subgroups* (NIH Publication No. 00-4754). Washington, DC: U.S. Government Printing Office. Accessed June 20, 2022. http://www.nichd.nih.gov/publications/nrp/report.htm.
Noguerón-Liu, S. (2020). Expanding the knowledge base in literacy instruction and assessment: Biliteracy and translanguaging perspectives from families,

communities and classrooms. *Reading Research Quarterly, 55*(S1), 307–18. https://doi.org/10.1002/rrq.354.

Pasternak, D. L., Caughlan, S., Hallman, H. L., Renzi, L., and Rush, L. S. (2018). *Secondary English teacher education in the United States.* Bloomsbury.

Popham, J. W. (2011). Assessment literacy overlooked: A teacher educator's confession. *The Teacher Educator, 46*, 265–73. https://doi.org/10.1080/08878730.2011.605048.

Rosenblatt, L. (1978). *The reader, the text, the poem: The transactional theory of the literary work.* Southern Illinois University Press.

Rumelhart, D. E. (2013). Toward an interactive model of reading. In D. E. Alvermann, N. J. Unrau, and R. B. Ruddell (Eds.), *Theoretical models and processes of reading* (6th ed., pp. 1149–79). International Reading Association.

Sailors, M. (2019). Re-imagining teacher education. In D. E. Alvermann, N. J. Unrau, M. Sailors, and R. B. Ruddell (Eds.), *Theoretical models and processes of literacy* (7th ed., pp. 430–48). Routledge.

Scarborough, H. S. (2001). Connecting early language and literacy to later reading (dis)abilities: Evidence, theory, and practice. In S. B. Neuman and D. K. Dickinson (Eds.), *Handbook of early literacy research* (Vol. 1, pp. 97–110). Guilford.

Schmidt, P. S. and Kruger-Ross, M. J. (2022). *Reimagining literacies in the digital age: Multimodal strategies to teach with technologies.* National Council of Teachers of English (NCTE). Accessed May 13, 2022. https://publicationsncte.org/content/books/9780814132036

Schwartz, S. (2022, July 20). Which states have passed "science of reading" laws? What's in them? *Education Week.* Retrieved August 3, 2022 from https://www.edweek.org/teaching-learning/which-states-have-passed-science-of-reading-laws-whats-in-them/2022/07.

Semingson, P. and Kerns, W. (2021). Where's the evidence? Looking back to Jeanne Chall and enduring debates about the science of reading. *Reading Research Quarterly, 56*(S1), S157–S169. https://doi.org/10.1002/rrq.405.

Shulman, L. (1987). Knowledge and teaching: Foundations of the new reform. *Harvard Educational Review, 57*(1), 1–23. https://doi.org/10.17763/haer.57.1.j463w79r56455411.

Smith, F. (2011). *Understanding reading: A psycholinguistic analysis of reading and learning to read* (6th ed.). Routledge.

Spear-Swerling, L. (2022). *Structured literacy interventions: Teaching students with reading difficulties, grades K-6.* The Guilford Press.

Stanovich, K. E. (2000). *Progress in understanding reading: Scientific foundations and new frontiers.* The Guildford Press.

Whitehurst, G. J. and Lonigan, C. J. (1998). Child development and emergent literacy. *Child Development, 69*(3), 848–72. https://doi.org/10.1111/j.1467-8624.1998.tb06247.x.

Yaden, D. B., Reinking, D., and Smagorinsky, P. (2021). The trouble with binaries: A perspective on the science of reading. *Reading Research Quarterly, 56*(S1), 119–29. https://doi.org/10.1002/rrq.402.

Chapter 12

NCTE/ELATE Beliefs Meet Economic Realities

The Struggle to Prepare Students Facing Financial Challenges

Jeremy Glazer and Emily Wender

I am not quite finished, and I have been working non-stop because of the holidays. I work at Safeway and when I am not in class or student teaching I work the majority of the time. Today I am working 12:30 pm to 9 pm. I have the sequence [assignment] started but not to where I want it to be . . . I am also going to struggle financially if I don't take next semester off . . . I don't know if I would able to stay afloat otherwise.

—*Email excerpt from a student teacher in the first of two semesters of field experience*[1]

The NCTE/ELATE *Beliefs about Methods Courses and Field Experiences in English Education* articulates a set of "key recommendations that guide the theoretical and practical purposes of Methods courses" (Gallo et al., 2020). This document guides teacher educators who hope to provide high-quality training for future teachers.

In its emphasis on flexibility and specific program needs, the Beliefs Statement also recognizes that there cannot be a one-size-fits-all approach to ELA teacher preparation, naming "the demands of local schools, state requirements, student characteristics, and other factors" as significant contexts. This chapter uncovers another, unnamed aspect of context which presents a fundamental challenge to instantiating the beliefs articulated in the statement: the financial situation of students in teacher education programs.

As teacher educators in four-year public institutions where many teacher candidates work anywhere from ten to forty hours a week, the authors,

Jeremy and Emily, recognize the financial demands their students face. During a conversation about methods courses and challenges in implementing some of the Beliefs Statement, the authors shared their recognition that many of these challenges are a result of the collision course their students are put on by the expectations of educator preparation programs and the economic realities of their lives.

In these contexts, the authors are caught between Scylla and Charybdis, feeling forced to decide between compromising on fundamental principles of the Beliefs Statement or excluding students from a future as ELA teachers. Put another way, two core commitments to justice are in tension: the commitment to ensuring that rigorous methods courses fully prepare teacher candidates for the profession and the commitment to providing equitable access to the profession, particularly to the many first-generation college students in English teacher education programs.

In this chapter, Emily and Jeremy will flesh out this tension, exploring various ways it challenges their students and their work as instructors in methods courses, and they will make recommendations for ways teacher educators can negotiate this tension more transparently, aiming to serve students and the profession.

INSTITUTIONAL CONTEXTS

The authors each train teacher candidates at mid-tier four-year public institutions in the Mid-Atlantic region, the kinds of schools that prepare the bulk of our nation's teaching force. Their universities fit the description of "working-class colleges," which Leonhardt (2017) calls "engines of social mobility" given their impact on students' incomes in adulthood relative to their parents' earnings. Lower-income and middle-class students, if they attend college, are likely to attend institutions like the authors. In fact, "outside of the top income quintile, four-year college students are 3 to 4 times more likely to be attending a public rather than private college" (Reber et al., 2020, para. 4).

With declining state investment in public higher education, however, such students and families have taken on more and more of the financial burden of a college education. For example, where Emily teaches in Pennsylvania, state funding in higher education has decreased substantially and currently is the sixth lowest nationally (NSF, 2022). At Emily's Western Pennsylvania institution, in 2020, 35 percent of students were awarded Pell Grants, which are only awarded to students who demonstrate "exceptional financial need" (US Department of Education, 2022), and 67 percent of undergraduates received federal student loans; similarly, at Jeremy's institution, 32 percent were awarded Pell Grants and 61 percent received federal student loans.

At both the authors' institutions and nationally, intersections between race and class lead to disproportionate financial burdens for students of color. In 2016 "more than 80 percent of Hispanic, black, and Asian students have a gap between their financial need and grants and scholarships, compared with 71 percent for white undergraduate students" (US Department of Education, 2022). At the same time, enrollment of students of color in higher education is particularly important for educator preparation programs in their efforts to diversify a largely white teacher workforce.

It is also important to note that becoming a teacher in any state brings additional costs beyond tuition costs for teacher education program, including testing fees, background clearances, and certification application fees. Such fees are usually not covered in university financial aid packages.

NEEDING TO WORK

Given these economic realities, it is no surprise that many college students are employed, at least part-time. In 2018, 43 percent of students in college worked (NCES, 2022). Around 6 percent of full-time undergraduates were employed less than 10 hours per week, 7 percent were employed for ten to nineteen hours per week, 17 percent were employed for twenty to thirty-four hours per week, and 10 percent were employed for thirty-five hours or more per week.

In Jeremy's and Emily's educator preparation programs, many teacher candidates fit into one of these categories. The authors know that the students' performance and experiences in methods courses, field experiences, and in the program as a whole can vary depending on how much they work. Just like any other resource, time is not distributed evenly.

METHODS COURSES

Goals

The methods courses at Jeremy's and Emily's respective institutions are designed to be capacious and meaningful learning opportunities that engage teacher candidates in multiple experiences of ELA teaching in middle and high schools and reflect, in many ways, the Beliefs Statement. Specifically, these courses lead teacher candidates to "develop deep understandings" in five ways:

(1) the "social" nature of learning, including the broader contexts surrounding the profession;

(2) how and why to create ELA curricula that is relevant to their students' contexts and their "unique literacies";
(3) how and why to enact adaptive instruction and relationship building in the classroom in ways that honor a "diversity of literacies, texts, and learners";
(4) the continual evolution of English Language Arts as a profession; and
(5) the significance of ongoing reflection, lifelong learning, and social justice in becoming an ethical and effective ELA teacher.

In short, the Beliefs Statement reflects our own governing desires as ELA teacher educators.

A crucial component of the Beliefs Statement is the call for concomitant field experiences (Gallo et al., 2020). In addition to the time spent in the field, the Beliefs Statement authors underscore the importance of "opportunities for candidates to reflect on, unpack, and learn from their field experiences," a core element of methods courses. Consistent with the Beliefs Statement, both Emily's and Jeremy's institutions scaffold field experiences, gradually releasing more responsibility to teacher candidates and providing ample time for candidates to observe and participate in a variety of classroom cultures.

Both institutions also use multiple structures for reflecting on field experiences, such as whole class discussions in methods courses; meetings between the university supervisor, teacher candidate, and the cooperating teacher; various types of written reflection; and one-on-one meetings between the teacher candidate and university supervisor. As articulated in the Beliefs Statement, both authors' programs' field experiences are integral to candidates achieving the learning objectives of their methods courses.

Additionally, the Beliefs Statement explains that methods courses "must support teacher candidates in attending to the cultural backgrounds of students and choosing texts and learning opportunities that nurture students' unique literacies" (Gallo et al., 2020). As teacher educators, Emily and Jeremy strive to model the cultural responsiveness described in the Beliefs Statement in their own teaching, while also endeavoring to situate their methods courses within changing educator preparation programs and contexts. In fact, the Beliefs Statement explicitly calls for that situational flexibility, naming that "English Methods courses exist within, and must react to, a dynamic English teacher educator ecosystem" (Gallo et al., 2020).

Methods Courses Demands

There are unstated assumptions behind the structures and principles articulated in the Beliefs Statement, however. While there is the explicit recognition that field experiences will be "necessarily idiosyncratic" and will reflect context, including "local school contexts and placement availability," the Beliefs Statement—and the authors' individual methods courses—make implicit demands on the time and financial well-being of teacher candidates.

One demand is the time expected for out-of-class reading, often fundamental to a methods course. This reading is where students will (or will not, if they don't do the reading) encounter pedagogical research as well as important writing about the practice of teaching. These are the ideas that may frame their teaching throughout their career.

Another demand is the time students will dedicate to their field experience. The cooperating teachers from whom teacher candidates will be taking over are full-time workers. Teaching, of course, is more than a full-time job. Higton et al. (2017), for example, found that teachers worked, on average, a little more than fifty-four hours a week. Of these hours, 23.6 are in classroom and 29.5 are outside of the classroom. It is important to note that more time is spent outside of the classroom, doing the familiar teacher tasks of grading, planning, calling parents, etc. These are the very tasks that take longer for novices to perform, so one can expect the out-of-classroom time to be even higher for teacher candidates.

This means that for teacher candidates to have a valuable, successful field experience, culminating in a full takeover during student teaching, candidates will be dedicating not just the time they are physically in the classroom, but significantly more time outside of the classroom. In both the authors' programs, teacher candidates are in the classroom between twenty-five and forty hours during their final semester. In reality, to successfully complete this requirement, they may well be dedicating fifty to sixty hours a week to their student teaching.

THE TENSION FOR TEACHER CANDIDATES

The authors' students have demonstrated the economic and physical costs of these expectations. Unlike interns in a business environment, teacher candidates are not paid for their work in schools. The time that teacher candidates must devote to class meetings, coursework requirements, and travel to and from field experience sites—a huge challenge for students without access to a car—is time that they cannot be working to earn money.

Many of Emily's and Jeremy's teacher candidates raise this dilemma in moments of crisis, and the authors explore several of the themes that have emerged from these moments below. Each theme is introduced with a representative example of student communication received while Jeremy and Emily were teaching their respective methods courses.

Balancing School and Work Schedules

I forgot that I picked up an extra shift at work today. Do you think we could move our meeting to noon tomorrow? It completely slipped my mind when we spoke on Friday.

One of the most direct ways the authors observe teacher candidates' time constraints is when they have to be at work instead of attending class, meeting with their university supervisor, or showing up to their field experience. Their work schedules are often unpredictable. Some candidates have shared fear of losing their jobs if they cannot cover shifts for coworkers, a problem only exacerbated by the pandemic. Candidates may also need to add any hours that are offered to them or may have jobs where schedules are constantly in flux. Such situations make it difficult for teacher candidates to build a predictable field experience and can get in the way of course attendance and other required meetings to reflect on the field experience.

Having the Time to Do Quality Work

I am sorry I haven't been showing up to class lately and have not been a good student. I am prioritizing my placement, which has meant I am struggling with courses and managing my job. My placement has also been overwhelming. There is a lot going on with my students, and I am not sure what to do. I feel like I'm bound to fail at some of my responsibilities this semester.[2]

Many of the authors' teacher candidates express concerns as they recognize the demand and impact of being and becoming a quality educator. For example, the above candidate realizes that there is much to learn in her field placement. At the same time, she recognizes that she has not been a "good student" and has not been showing up to her methods class.

It could be that the candidate does not see the value of the methods class—how attending class sessions, for example, might help her deal with the fact that "there is a lot going on" with her students. If that is the case, it is likely that she sees the university context of the methods course as less "real" than the context of the field placement, despite the ways in which the methods course would productively enrich her choices in the field.

It is also likely that this candidate simply has too many conflicting demands on her time, which together are not allowing her to engage with the methods course, blunting her learning in the field placement as well. It should be noted that this candidate has begun to develop what Santoro (2017) terms a *craft conscience*, an ethical commitment to practice the craft of teaching well. She realizes that she is not meeting her own expectations in the field, nor those of the methods course, and she is disappointed in her performance because of that.

Setting Priorities

I'm actually having a hard time coming up with a gateway activity [an assignment for the Methods Course]. *I'm actually having a hard time in general between classes, student teaching, and work. I've been working the past couple of days and trying to work on this which is why I haven't sent anything in yet. I'm actually on my way to work now, and I know this probably isn't the best work I can produce, but I don't really know where to start.*

Another recurring theme in the authors' teacher candidates' expressions of their financial challenges in methods course is that, given the lack of time noted above, they struggle to know what to prioritize. Housing, food, and bills are physiological and safety priorities that teacher candidates cannot ignore, and, for many candidates, there is simply no choice to be made. Emily and Jeremy have both had many conversations with teacher candidates about prioritizing, from struggling to determine if they should work less and how they could economically pull that off to deciding which deadlines are most important given their work demands.

It is no surprise that these conversations often occur when candidates start their methods courses and field experiences. As previously stated, it is in methods courses and their concurrent field experiences where teacher candidates often start to realize how much time it will take to become "critical, agentic, active, ethical, reflective, and socially just educators," what each of those adjectives mean, and the complexity of practicing each descriptor as an educator. Again, they are reflecting the development of a craft conscience in that they are recognizing that they are not performing to their best ability, but that recognition in and of itself is not enough to fix the problem.

Leaving the Career before It Begins

After this last semester, I decided to leave the program and pursue an English degree instead. As you know, I was unable to finish my field experience hours due to work and family obligations, and I don't think I'll be able to manage the increased hours next semester.[3]

Any one of the struggles noted above can derail a teacher candidate, leading to withdrawal from an educator preparation program or from college altogether. Every year, the authors' programs lose promising teacher candidates because they cannot financially manage the expectations of methods courses and field experiences while working and maintaining their outside responsibilities, which may include supporting themselves, contributing financially to their families, and/or caring for family members.

THE TENSION FOR TEACHER EDUCATORS

These email fragments are just a fraction of the students the authors are aware of, the ones who approached breaking points during their courses and reached out. Surely, other teacher candidates who are experiencing these tensions did not. Perhaps many of these other teacher candidates stayed below the radar by completing their required assignments and checking the required boxes, but they may have sacrificed quality in their methods and field experience coursework—and thus in their own development as teachers—because of the number of hours they had to work. These candidates may be able to make it through the program, but they will not be achieving what is in the NCTE Beliefs Statement as fully as they could.

Both Emily and Jeremy teach and write about methods courses and because they believe in their importance. As the Beliefs Statement asserts, these courses and the accompanying field experiences help student teachers "develop concepts of teaching and learning, content knowledge, content pedagogy, knowledge about learners and learning, and professional knowledge and skills."

The authors also believe in the rigor and quality of methods courses and clinical experiences—and that maintaining the rigor for all teacher candidates is a justice issue, as these experiences are fundamental to the development of good teachers for public schools. Compromising the quality of teacher training does a disservice to our own students, but just as importantly, it does a disservice to the many children who will be served by the teachers we prepare.

So, what can be done? Any concessions to the reality of the lives of teacher candidates can feel like a compromise in quality. If programs err on the side of opening up, that hurts students downstream. If programs err on the side of rigidity, they continue to do a silent kind of gatekeeping. It is a Solomonic situation, asking for a split of the baby in ways both Jeremy and Emily find unacceptable. What follows are suggestions for how to begin to address these issues.

RECOMMENDATIONS

In the Methods Course

First, methods course instructors need to get to know students, their responsibilities, and their work identities—until instructors have that information, it is hard to move on. Gathering this information can be a key part of the methods course. One way to do this is by adding questions about work to any opening survey. Instructors can ask questions like: *Do you have a job (or two or three)? What is/are your job(s)? So far, how have you tried to balance your job and school? What practices will you use this semester? What challenges do you anticipate with managing your coursework, your job(s), and your field experience?*

Posing these questions early in the methods course accomplishes multiple goals. First, by putting these questions on an opening survey, the teacher educator legitimatizes the tension between academics and financial responsibilities, paving the way for a teacher candidate to come forward before they reach a crisis. Second, for teacher candidates who may not yet anticipate the demands of the methods course and/or understand the demands of teaching, these questions help alert them to raised expectations and provide a moment of reflection on how to meet those new challenges.

Instructors also need to be honest about what the non-negotiables in methods courses are and why these things are non-negotiable. What texts, assignments, and/or experiences cannot be missed? It needs to be recognized that the field experience tends to take priority over methods coursework because of the built-in accountability that comes from being responsible for a classroom full of students.

Importantly, though, instructors must help teacher candidates understand the importance of a methods course not merely for the day-to-day survival of their student teaching, but as a vital part of their future development as a teacher. This means explaining the potential impact of each text, assignment, and activity—and the rationale for including them.

Third, just as methods instructors need to recognize non-negotiables within methods courses, they also need to identify opportunities for flexibility, whether those are structurally built into the course or worked out individually with teacher candidates. Some examples of course-level structural flexibility are having a preset number of late vouchers for assignments, offering virtual options for activities, or designing meaningful ways to make up a class session. Incomplete grades are also one tool that can be used for teacher candidates if they are on track to finish field experience hours and assignments successfully but simply need more time to complete the requirements of the methods course.

Finally, methods courses are an ideal place to highlight how teacher candidates can set priorities. One way to help students prioritize is to have past teacher candidates talk about the choices and structures that helped them— "Here's how I made time for my field experience coursework," "Here's how I cut down on my hours at work," "Here's how I talked to my parents about needing money," or "Here's how I struggled and why I eventually decided to slow down my time to graduate."

Ideally, teacher candidates can begin methods courses by building awareness of the realistic demands of coursework and field experiences, the choices they are making, and the impact those choices will have. This awareness will help them prepare for their not-too-distant futures in which they will be newly certified teachers, managing student debt and a demanding job, and they will have to continue to set priorities with limited time and resources.

Beyond the Methods Course

As the Beliefs Statement recognizes, methods courses happen within a context. Given the current moment in teacher education in the United States, there are a few things that can be done programmatically.

Program advising is critical to maintain quality in the methods courses and field experiences so that teacher candidates can become well-prepared educators. Advising needs to include honest conversations about what course and program requirements entail. Students should have a sense of the whole trajectory of teacher preparation—of the costs that will pop up (like Praxis exams, background checks, and certification fees) and of the periods when it will be most difficult for them to work (e.g., during their full-time student teaching).

Given such warning, students will be better able to plan for these events. Slowing down is something Emily and Jeremy raise as a possibility for the teacher candidates who come to them in crisis about work and school. Emily recently had a teacher candidate who took seven years to graduate: the candidate took a year off to work and save money and then had to retake methods classes she had previously failed. Now she is a practicing reading specialist in an urban setting.

Jeremy also recently had a teacher candidate take a semester off to work in order to pay for her final semester of student teaching. It wasn't until the middle of her student teaching experience that she realized the financial realities of the time commitments required by the program. Advanced warning of this could have helped make this decision less of an emergency.

Advocacy is also crucial, and teacher educators need to include sustainability and affordability part of our Belief Statements going forward. We need to be honest about the time requirements and external, hidden costs of becoming a teacher, and we need to advocate for funding to help students bear these costs and to be willing to radically reimagine curricular structures and field experiences.

As states confront teacher shortages and concerns for teacher quality, there are models of inclusive policies, including the legislation HB22-1220 in Colorado focused on removing barriers to educator preparation. With a growing teacher shortage nationally, some band-aid solutions can be expected (suspending various requirements, lowering eligibility thresholds), but advocacy for long-term solutions that augment accessibility while maintaining rigor is vital for justice.

As a professional organization and as educators, difficult discussions and difficult decisions are essential: what are the non-negotiables with the NCTE/ELATE *Beliefs about Methods Courses and Field Experiences in English Education*? These discussions and decisions must take place with an acknowledgment of the economic implications of these requirements on teacher candidates. The field needs honesty and realism about the best ways to prepare a well-educated, diverse teaching force for the nation's children. Without it, a statement of beliefs will never be translated into reality.

NOTES

1. Quotes have been altered to maintain student anonymity.
2. This email has been altered to be emblematic of several student emails because permission was unable to be obtained from students who left the program.
3. This is a paraphrase of a few separate communications with one student.

REFERENCES

Gallo, J., Hallman, H. Parsons, C., Pastore-Capuana, K., Ringler Pet, S., and Searcy, L. (2020, May 22). *Beliefs about methods courses and field experiences in English education*. National Council of Teachers of English. Accessed January 19, 2023. https://ncte.org/statement/methodsinee/.

Higton, J., Leonardi, S., Choudhoury, A., Richards, N., Owen, D., and Sofroniou, N. (2017). Teacher Workload Survey 2016. London: Department of Education.

Leonhardt, D. (2017, January 18). America's great working-class colleges. *The New York Times*.

National Science Foundation. (2022). *State support for higher education per full-time equivalent student*. ncses.nsf.gov. Accessed January 19, 2023. https://ncses.nsf.gov/indicators/states/indicator/state-support-for-higher-education-per-fte-student.

National Center for Education Statistics. (2022). *Percentage of 16- to 64-year-old undergraduate students who were employed, by attendance status, hours worked per week, and selected characteristics: 2010, 2015, and 2020*. Accessed January 19, 2023. https://nces.ed.gov/programs/digest/d21/tables/dt21_503.40.asp.

Reber, S., Sinclair, C., and Van Drie, H. (2020). *Public colleges are the workhorses of middle-class mobility*. Washington, DC: Brookings Institution Press. Accessed

January 19, 2023. https://www.brookings.edu/blog/up-front/2020/07/22/public-colleges-are-the-workhorses-of-middle-class-mobility/.

Santoro, D. A. (2017). Teachers' expressions of craft conscience: Upholding the integrity of a profession. *Teachers and Teaching*, *23*(6), 750–61.

United States Department of Education. (2022, July 14). *Federal Pell Grants are usually awarded only to undergraduate students*. Accessed September 5, 2022. https://studentaid.gov/understand-aid/types/grants/pell.

Chapter 13

Pre- and Corequisite Content Knowledge and Pedagogy Development

Antiracist Future English Teachers

Christian Z. Goering and Holly Sheppard Riesco

When the authors prepared to become secondary English teachers in the late 1990s and early 2000s, in Kansas and Arkansas, there were clear and consistent expectations in terms of the content required to earn the title of English teacher. Courses in literature primarily created the focus of the English major, and substantial writing assignments adorned nearly all of the mid-terms and ends of the semester. One semester Chris had no fewer than five literature courses *en route* to his official content knowledge: Shakespeare, American Lit 1, Short Story, Brit Lit 1, and Brit Lit 2.

They each took undergraduate or graduate courses dedicated solely to adolescent and young adult literature. The canonical literature of their English degrees was almost entirely written by white people, and their respective first exposures to literature written by BIPOC happened in the young adult literature courses and through their first years of teaching. Titles such as *Roll of Thunder, Hear My Cry*, *Fallen Angels*, and *Bud, Not Buddy* provided compelling perspectives by people who experienced different versions of America.

Chris and Holly met in the fall of 2019 when Holly applied to and was accepted to the Ph.D. program at the University of Arkansas following fifteen years of teaching in different contexts across the state of Arkansas. Chris, following five years of teaching in Kansas, began a career in higher education in 2007 at the University of Arkansas.

They share some similarities and differences. They are white from middle to middle-class (upper) backgrounds. They are parents to two children each. Their teaching covers the past twenty-two years of education with Chris from 2000 to 2005 and Holly from 2005 to 2020. Finally, they both fully invested in developing intercultural practices in future teachers as they ready themselves for a future version of English language arts, one that is multimodal, multilingual, and multicultural.

But their current mission aside, Chris's and Holly's English education did not address how to become an antiracist or, for that matter, even teach about race or difference in the context of teaching English. They each learned this on the job, a fact that—looking back—causes some discomfort. When the concept was popularized through Ibram X. Kendi's best-selling book *How to Be an Antiracist* (2019), both Chris and Holly read the book and saw many implications for teaching and teacher education and determined to make changes in their approaches.

Chris and Holly both took up the critical work in their respective spaces, following the National Council of Teachers of English which had previously proffered a statement on antiracism that was inclusive in nature:

> Racism consists of two principal components: difference and power. It is a mindset that sees a "them" that is different from an "us." Racism in America is the systematic mistreatment and disenfranchisement of people of color who currently and historically possess less power and privilege than white Americans. In modern times, there has arisen a "cultural racism" that allows for ethnic groups that cannot always be distinguished from the majority, in terms of physical features, but are nevertheless subject to the same kinds of biases as those who have been traditionally marked as a different race. (Moore, Manning, and Villanueva, 2018, n.p.)

This differs from a larger body of scholarship about antiracism that defines the concept as solely race-based, reasoning that race deserves the undivided attention and that the other forms of "othering" do as well (Simmons, 1994; Kendi, 2019). The NCTE statement acknowledges that "racism [. . .] [and] other forms of discrimination continue to be a part of American society, continuing to affect all students and their education" (Moore, Manning, and Villanueva, 2018, n.p.). Their statement continues:

> The Committee Against Racism and Bias in the Teaching of English of the National Council of Teachers of English (NCTE) is committed to working toward the eradication of racism, discrimination, and bigotry in the profession, in the preparation of teachers, and in the administrative decisions made in schools, especially in the teaching and learning of English and the language arts at all levels. (Moore, Manning, and Villanueva, 2018, n.p.)

English—as Chris and Holly were prepared to teach it—was inherently white, heteronormative, and monolingual in nature, focused more on establishing a formal standard register than acknowledging the brilliance of different language abilities. So, the evolution of English teachers since the time in which they entered the field was to broaden who and what counted in the curriculum and class.

In a very real sense, they have committed to continuous learning about others and themselves, and this is the goal for all future teachers—not that they know everything they will need to know, but that they are committed to continuing the journey, to evolving, to learning so they can help all of their students develop skills relevant to ELA. Unfortunately, most English teachers and most English teacher educators are still not prepared in antiracist/antibias methods of teaching the discipline. This fact, coupled with the adoption of the new NCTE teacher preparation standards in 2021, provides a significant challenge to the profession, especially in times when even the word antiracist has been declared illegal.

In this chapter, Chris and Holly take up the notion and challenges that antiracism is now part of what the profession must account for in the pre- and corequisite knowledge of English teachers and offer a practical approach to starting those conversations. Specifically, the Antiracism is a Verb project (ARVP) (Goering, 2021) tied into and built from a blog post published by NCTE, "Being an Antiracist Educator is a Verb," in which Rembert, Harris, and Hamilton (2019) argue, "Teaching is not apolitical. Antiracist educators must make discussions of racism and bias an everyday practice" (n.p.).

The ARVP also addresses the 2021 NCTE Standards for Initial Preparation of English Language Arts Teachers, Grades 7–12. These issues are examined across two cohorts of secondary English language arts teaching methods courses followed by recommendations for practice and potential research.

BACKGROUND

As mentioned, Chris and Holly worked together at the University of Arkansas (UA) at the time of writing this chapter. UA is a primarily white institution. Initiating conversations about antiracism and supporting mostly white preservice teachers (PSTs) toward those goals is essential to their professional development and their future in the field of education. Since Chris was a co-chair (with Donna Pasternak and Marshall George) of the national committee that created the new standards that put this language into English teacher preparation standards, this perspective and implementation of the ARVP over two years is unique. A process that spanned multiple years, the new standards were released in July 2021 and were born illegal.

Anti-"CRT" laws have swept across the nation since September 2020, when the notion that anything that made white people uncomfortable—often including real American history or books—should fall under a category deemed "Critical Race Theory." Disturbingly, the actual, previously defined term Critical Race Theory could have predicted this kind of move being employed by white supremacists to protect white supremacy in America.

The standards were in full form and being prepared for submission to the accrediting body in May 2020 when George Floyd was murdered, and Floyd's death and the countless murders of non-white people in America in recent years led the group of scholars gathered to revise the standards to use the term antiracism. While these teacher education standards were vetted and further revised, the concept of antiracism literally became a crime in several states, lumped together with anti-"CRT" legislation and faux outcry.

What is not uncertain is the fact that these laws are impacting the new standards and will continue to do so. In Wyoming, for example, an English educator attempted to share the new standards on a public college and university's website, a request that was denied by the webmaster due to the term "antiracism." Even in states that have not enacted specific laws about this yet, like Arkansas, Attorney General Leslie Rutledge wrote a legal opinion on the matter, stating that, "With certain qualifications set forth below, instituting practices based on critical race theory, professed 'antiracism,' or associated ideas can violate Title VI, the Equal Protection Clause, and Article II of the Arkansas Constitution" (Rutledge, 2021, n.p.).

THE STANDARDS THEMSELVES

Every eight to 10 years the profession is implored to update the standards for teacher preparation. Most recently, NCTE adopted in 2012 a set of standards for teacher preparation that, for the first time, called for social justice as part of what English teachers had to know and teach to enter the field.

Standard Six, or *The Social Justice Standard*, as it is known, reads, "[c]andidates demonstrate knowledge of how theories and research about social justice, diversity, equity, student identities, and schools as institutions can enhance students' opportunities to learn in English Language Arts" (NCTE/NCATE Standards for Initial Preparation of Teachers of Secondary English Language Arts, Grades 7–12 2012). The 2021 standards shifted from *The Social Justice Standard* to the *Social Justice Standards*, featuring the language of antiracism/antibias in four of five core standards.

Upon their release, then NCTE President Alfredo Lujan, commented,

> Our field deals directly with the human condition through shaping the literate lives of our learners and is uniquely positioned to act on the complexities we collectively face [. . .] Bigotry, discrimination, oppression, divisiveness, and racism are part of the world in which future teachers of English are working.

These new standards seek to support educators as they prepare to go into the classroom. (Lujan cited in Finkel, n.p., 2021)

- Standard 1: Candidates apply and demonstrate knowledge of learners and learning to foster inclusive learning environments that support coherent, relevant, differentiated, and antiracist/antibias instruction to engage grade 7–12 learners in ELA.
- Standard 2: Candidates apply and demonstrate knowledge and theoretical perspectives, including those that critically address antiracist/antibias ELA, pertaining to texts, composition, language, and languaging.
- Standard 3: Candidates apply and demonstrate knowledge of theories, research, and ELA to plan coherent, relevant, standards-aligned, differentiated, antiracist/antibias instruction and assessment.
- Standard 4: Candidates implement planned coherent, relevant, standards-aligned, differentiated, and antiracist/antibias ELA instruction and assessment to motivate and engage all learners.

Centering antiracism/antibias ELA instruction explicitly in four out of five core standards offers no wiggle room for new English teachers for the next decade: they will have to prepare for difficult conversations, teach in ways that acknowledge and pushback on whiteness, and move the field forward in terms of what it means to learn and teach English language arts. Forming a deeper understanding of others and constantly working to eradicate racism within the discipline and the school systems becomes a necessity for any future English language arts teacher.

In fact, future teachers must make progress on their own dispositions and beliefs in order to better serve all students in the classrooms of tomorrow. As teacher educators, Chris and Holly knew that changes to what students do in preparation to become teachers were necessary in light of the new standards, a perspective shared by the field following past adoptions of standards for the preparation of English teachers (see, for example, Searcy in this volume).

ENTER: THE ANTIRACISM IS A VERB PROJECT

Prior to describing this project and providing examples, it makes sense to acknowledge the fact that no one project, set of standards, or experience would move students or a program in the direction of antiracist pedagogy. Change must be coordinated and articulated through many experiences in coursework, internships, and critical self-reflection in order to make the value of antiracist pedagogy abundantly clear to PSTs.

That kind of change takes time but must start somewhere. For students at the UA, conversations about these topics happen primarily in three places:

a social justice/multicultural education course, methods one and two, and internships, which sometimes provide examples of racism and bias within the institution of education.

The "Antiracism Is a Verb" project was born to support PSTs' journeys into antiracist teaching. In developing the project, Chris asked preservice methods students to spend and record two hours self-directed learning that allowed them to focus on or critique racial and biased patterns that were highlighted through the mediums they chose. In describing this project to the class, Chris noted two "theories" of action that provided context for how this project works:

(1) This work is individualized and self-reflective, but we can all do the work better together as a community.
(2) Individuals often learn through continuums, moving fluidly between connections with the self to others to action.

As this chapter argues, antiracism is not something readily measurable within a person, and by extension, teachers and teacher educators should not approach the ARVP or related work in antiracist pedagogy prescriptively. In fact, pedagogies in classrooms that are often championed within the field of literacy lean heavily on the notions of student autonomy and choice (Gallagher, 2006), yet teacher education programs can feel antithetical to that.

For example, the Master of Arts in Teaching program at UA requires thirty-three graduate hours for licensure. Students follow a program designed by faculty (and school partners to a lesser extent) and approved by the state. In the corresponding Bachelor of Arts in Teaching program, students get to select six English hours of their choosing across a 120-hour degree program. Even so, the rigid structures of courses within colleges of education allow for spaces to implement conscious activities on antiracism, such as the "Antiracism Is a Verb" project.

Since the first iteration of this project in 2020, Chris made changes and assigned the project to his methods courses in 2021 and 2022, bringing Holly into the project as his teaching assistant in both years. In the most recent version, Chris contextualized for the ELA PST the concept of antiracism and established the assignment parameters.

First, Chris initiated the conversation around antiracism through a commonly used lens activity. In this activity, students draw a pair of glasses. Within the lenses, they write their pluralistic identities, such as *man*, *White*, *learner*, and so forth, that are both visible and invisible to others. The middle line between the lenses becomes the identity of which they are most aware. The two earpieces become the greatest hope and the greatest fear. Finally, outside of the lenses, they begin to brainstorm identities of which they are

Pre- and Corequisite Content Knowledge and Pedagogy Development   167

outside and with which their students might identify. This lens activity engenders thinking on exposure and intentional work that teachers and teacher educators must do to dismantle bias within their unconscious mind.

Once the lens activity concluded, Chris presented a definition of antiracism (Kendi, 2019) and reviewed the NCTE standards. Class discussions revolved around how power within educational systems is reified through racist policies and enactments. The lens activity and the discussion of antiracism and systems of power help contextualize and justify the "Antiracism is a Verb" project for PSTs.

Finally, Chris offered a potential "menu" of options for PSTs to begin the work of critical self-reflection and social reflection and critique (figure 13.1).

Chris made it clear to the PSTs that this menu is not a static entity but rather offers potential options for completing during one or two of the first weeks. The PSTs were encouraged to choose their own pathways toward

10 pts	15 pts	20 pts	20 pts
Watch a feature film or documentary that exposes you to a new culture.	Listen to two episodes of Nice White Parents or Thought Leader Podcast Series or RefleXions Podcast (NWA focused)	Curate a book list of novels for secondary English that can be used to support antiracist writing practices.	*Compose a summary and reflection in a format of your choice on your choices from the lists in the 10, 15, or 20 points column. Think about the following: How would you summarize what you learned? How will this impact your pedagogy? What are some activities or composition practices for the classroom that this activity generated in you?*
Visit the #DisruptTexts website and read the conversation around one of the disrupt texts CHATs about classic literature.	Find and read a journal article from your ELAD that takes up issues of social justice, equity, inclusion, diversity, etc.	Read a book connected to anti-racism and create an action to share your new knowledge.	
Go to the Learning For Justice website and read through lessons that support antiracist and culturally responsive teaching in secondary ELA.	Go to NCTE blogs, Edutopia, or another teacher practitioner website and read five posts about antiracist teaching practices in secondary ELA.	Curate a collection of antiracist social media posts/Tweets, such as #DisruptTexts, to share with your classmates.	

Figure 13.1 Menu Options for "Anti-Racism Is a Verb" Project.

their work in antiracism outside of the menu option. The only required option was the end-of-semester reflection in the last column, which has them pull together their work and reflect critically on their journeys into antiracism. Final parameters of the assignment are also offered through an assignment description.

Additionally, students are then asked to log their weekly accomplishments in their antiracism journeys. One student in the 2020 cohort, Caitlin Lane, took on a broad selection of activities throughout the semester, logging between two to four hours per week throughout the semester-long project (figure 13.2).

Throughout her project, Caitlin focused on the way race is presented in society through various media. However, she did not stop there. She used her research within her fieldwork internship, where she was teaching students in secondary ELA. In other words, she committed to the critical work and acted upon the work within her classroom spaces.

In another project, Cate Casey shared in her final reflection that an opportunity to read a book allowed her to not only learn about Indigenous populations but also to make connections to other cultures and ways of viewing the world:

> I read *Code Talkers* by Joseph Bruchac, a historical fiction that provides a culmination of real-life experiences of Navajo servicemen during World War II. Many of the tales he recounts come from the real experiences of marines in this position. With the Cherokee and Choctaw people being some of the first to engage in this practice in World War I, the Navajo stepped into this role as the two prior languages had been deciphered. What is interesting about this novel and the events it describes is that at the time we are working as a nation to destroy and eradicate the Native American culture and language, while conversely it is being sought after as an asset for the military and influential in our future victory in the war. It has to be an odd dichotomy to navigate as a member of the Indigenous nation to simultaneously have your culture destroyed while it is also viewed as a commodity and resource. I compared this to the idea of society continuing to oppress marginalized cultures and communities while also maintaining a fascination with the culture and seen as some foreign excitement. Take for example the obsession we have with Asia and its diverse cultures. Our country, especially with the recent pandemic, has targeted the Asian community with extreme hate, yet we are obsessed with their mainstream media and products such as k-pop, make up, or decor. We view these communities not as a group of people, but rather as a commodity or a product we can hang on our walls.

Within her reflection, Cate offered insights about one of her projects, the reading of *Code Talkers* by Joseph Bruchac. Once again, however, her reflection did not halt at merely analysis and reflection. Instead, she made

Pre- and Corequisite Content Knowledge and Pedagogy Development   169

Table 13.1   Example Log for "Antiracism Is a Verb" Project

Week	Caitlin Lane's "Antiracism is a Verb" Log
Week 1	• Watched documentary *13th* and discussed with a friend
Week 2	• Read *The New Yorker* "The Fight to Redefine Racism" • Watched Jane Elliot clip about Antiracism
Week 3	• Read the Teaching Tolerance "White Antiracism: Living the Legacy" and decided I wanted to implement some in the classroom • Watched so many Jane Elliot videos online (pretty sure I'm hooked on every word she says now) • Read the articles for class to be prepared for the speaker • Ordered the book called "White Fragility" from Amazon and patiently awaiting its arrival so I can dive into that • Listened to the 12-minute NPR segment on "White Guilt and the End of the Civil Rights Era"
Week 4	• Bought "How to be an Antiracist" by Ibram X. Kendi at TJ Maxx and have been reading a little bit everyday
Week 5	• Read a little more out of Ibram X. Kendi's book • Looked up some Teaching Tolerance lessons for my class to mix into our curriculum for more diversity and culturally dynamic aspects and content
Week 6	• Watched some Ted Talks about lesson and environment diversification and inclusive cultural ideologies in the classroom with students
Week 7	• Kept reading excerpts from the "How to be an Antiracist" by Ibram X. Kendi • Looked up some news media coverage about racism to incorporate in my internship classes
Week 8	• Watched some powerful YouTube videos about News Media Coverage of the Trayvon Martin and Breonna Taylor cases to include some school appropriate clips for my classes to watch and see how the media covers things like racism in society

Week 9	• Found two great website resources to show my classes about how to be an antiracist journalist in today's media
	• Still reading excerpts from Ibram X. Kendi's "How to be an Antiracist"
	• Links for the antiracist reporter websites I mentioned
	  ○ https://www.pressclubinstitute.org/how-to-be-antiracist-in-coronavirus-coverage/
	  ○ https://www.pressclubinstitute.org/event/what-would-antiracist-journalism-look-like/

(continued)

Table 13.1 Continued

Week	Caitlin Lane's "Antiracism is a Verb" Log
Week 9	• Read Vox's "What it means to be an antiracist" article • Listened to the *Today, Explained* podcast called "American Nightmare" • Read Refinery29's article titled "Your Black Colleagues May Look Like They're Okay—Chances Are They're Not"
Week 10	• Read the American Public Health Associations article titled, "Addressing Law Enforcement Violence as a Public Health Issue" • Read the Atlantic's article called, "The Case for Reparations" • Rewatched the movie "Get Out" for the second time • Watched the movie "12 Years a Slave" for the first time last weekend

Week 11	• Finished reading "How to be an Antiracist" by Ibram X. Kendi
	• Read "They Shoot Black People, Don't They?"
	• Watched a couple of YouTube videos about teaching antiracism in classrooms that I will put the links to in here:
	   ○ https://youtu.be/ufY-Hlc_mys
	   ○ https://youtu.be/r9DDE7NV1Nw
	   ○ https://youtu.be/4kvxtEmZN2Q

connections between Indigenous cultures and the societal treatment of Asian Americans during COVID-19. In her reflection, Cate illustrated the power of the project: becoming conscious of the injustices within society.

While this paper suggests that this project has helped students move forward in these terms, Chris and Holly are also quick to offer two caveats. First, students and faculty, in this case, take a *we're in this together* mentality with Chris and Holly dedicating the same amount of time to their own development along the way.

Second, alongside this work, and to a certain extent working in concert with the ARVP, is work that the program and the authors have undertaken with the Intercultural Development Inventory (IDI; Hammer 2008), a tool used to help people understand the extent to which they exhibit intercultural competence. PSTs who took the IDI demonstrated a willingness and openness to learning more about themselves and others (Riesco et al. under review).

CONCLUSION

The ARVP encouraged the mostly white PSTs to step outside their largely Eurocentric perspectives and engage with multimodal texts that centered BIPOC voices to "gain knowledge and perspective" (Goering, 2021, p. 69) from a myriad of perspectives. PSTs who engaged in this project actively sought media and art that focused on BIPOC perspectives and reflected on how they can include antiracist and antibias practices within their future secondary English classroom and as part of their professional identities.

By committing to working on this project for one hour a week throughout the semester, the PSTs had moments of ongoing learning during class dialogues on antiracism, which culminated in a final reflection that made them critically self-reflect on their own journeys into antiracist pedagogy. ARVP supported the expectation that PSTs should continue the work that builds antiracist practices within secondary English classrooms (Sensoy and DiAngelo, 2021) while illustrating the work needed to question their own knowledge and views toward unlearning racist structures and systems in their personal and professional lives.

REFERENCES

Finkel, S. (2021). New standards released for educators preparing to be English language arts teachers. National Council of Teachers of English. Accessed February 2, 2023. https://ncte.org/press-updates/new-standards-released/.

Gallagher, K. (2006). *Teaching adolescent writers*. Stenhouse.

Goering, C. Z. (2021). Setting the standard in anti-racist/bias instruction in English language arts and teacher education. *English Education, 54*(1), 65–71.

Hammer, M. R. (2008). The intercultural development inventory (IDI): An approach for assessing and building intercultural competence. In M. A. Moodian (Ed.), *Contemporary leadership and intercultural competence: Understanding and utilizing cultural diversity to build successful organizations*. Sage.

Kendi, I. X. (2019). *How to be an antiracist*. One world.

Moore, J., Manning, L., and Villanueva, V. (2018). Statement on antiracism to support teaching and learning. National Council of Teachers of English. Accessed February 2, 2023. https://ncte.org/statement/antiracisminteaching/.

NCTE Standards for the Initial Preparation of Teachers of English Language Arts 7–12 (2012). Accessed February 2, 2023. https://ncte.org/app/uploads/2018/07/ApprovedStandards_111212.pdf.

NCTE Standards for the Initial Preparation of Teachers of English Language Arts 7–12 (Initial Licensure). (2021). National Council of Teachers of English. Accessed September 6, 2022. https://ncte.org/wp-content/uploads/2021/11/2021_NCTE_Standards.pdf.

Rembert, K., Harris, P., and Hamilton, F. (2019, November 6). Being an anti-racist educator is a verb. NCTE Blog. https://ncte.org/blog/2019/11/being-an-anti-racist-educator-is-a-verb/.

Riesco, H. S., Wiersma-Mosley, J. D., Embry, C., Klein, T., and Goering, C. Z. (under review). "But I think it all kind of worked together": Intercultural competence development in preservice teachers. *Teachers College Record*.

Rutledge, L. (2021). Opinion No. 2021-042. Accessed February 2, 2023. https://content.govdelivery.com/attachments/ARAG/2021/08/16/file_attachments/1907584/2021-042%20%2808.16.21%29.pdf.

Sensoy, Ö., and DiAngelo, R. (2021). Understanding the structural nature of oppression through racism. In J. A. Banks (Ed.), *Transforming multicultural education policy and practice* (pp. 55–79). Teachers College Press.

Simmons, E. (1994). Sensitivity trainers and the race thing. *New Internationalist, 260*, 26–27.

Chapter 14

Beyond the Book

Expanding Critical Connective Literacies between Students and Authors on Social Media

Nora Peterman and Connor K. Warner

English Language Arts (ELA) teachers are consistently called upon to evolve and update their practice, as emerging technologies shift definitions of text and new skills are required to make meaning from those texts. As such, ELA methods classes and methods instructors must also continuously audit their practice to ensure they are preparing ELA teachers to be able to meet this challenge. The newly revised statement, "Beliefs about Methods Courses and Field Experiences in English Education" (Gallo et al., 2020), argues that, among others, two key principles of effective English methods courses are:

> Methods coursework should explore the nature of teaching and learning. Instructors can do this, in part, by supporting teacher candidates to understand that teaching and learning are social practices that impact and are impacted by the communities in which they are situated.
>
> Methods coursework should emphasize the diversity of literacies, texts, and learners that constitute our field and our work as English language arts teachers. To do this, coursework must support teacher candidates in attending to the cultural backgrounds of students and choosing texts and learning opportunities that nurture students' unique literacies.

This chapter explores the capability of reimagined social media-based author and illustrator encounters to contribute to meeting both these principles.

Whether in-person or online, bringing authors and illustrators into classrooms is a powerful practice for engaging students and developing their reading and writing identities (Moynihan, 2009; Gonzalez, 2020). The increasing prevalence of digital social media affords new opportunities for educators to reimagine the practice and purpose of author and illustrator encounters by creating spaces for students to engage in critical participatory dialogue about literature and the social contexts in which it is produced and received.

Drawing from research investigating how popular young adult authors use social media to engage with readers and the general public on issues of intellectual depth and societal importance, this chapter frames social media platforms as sites for reimagining author interactions by providing illustrative examples from the use of the approach in undergraduate English methods courses.

The approach described in this chapter inverts the traditional author encounter; rather than a single author or illustrator coming to a school once every few years, here ELA methods students virtually visited authors via close readings of Twitter feeds and interactions. The learning experiences described here did not require students to tweet or message authors directly (to avoid placing uncompensated labor burdens on authors). Nevertheless, ELA methods students who engaged in these experiences reported developing a sense of authentic connection with the authors. This connection influenced both students' own perceptions of young adult (YA) literature's complexity and of the possibilities for harnessing that complexity in their own future classrooms.

INVESTIGATING YOUNG ADULT LITERATURE AUTHORS AND SOCIAL MEDIA

This work stems from a larger ongoing study exploring the social media engagement of popular authors of children's and YA fiction. This research is grounded in critical, sociocultural perspectives of literacy (Vasquez et al., 2019), resource orientations toward youth culture (Alvermann, 2008; Moje and Luke, 2009; Morell, 2017), and scholarship examining evolving landscapes for digital media engagement (Jenkins, 2013; Lewis Ellison, 2017).

The learning experience described in this chapter focuses particularly on Twitter. Though YouTube and TikTok are, at the time of writing, the most popular platforms with youth (Vogels et al., 2022), the study's analysis of YA authors' social media use finds that the authors themselves were more active on Twitter, and their Twitter activity is likely to include public intellectual discourse alongside more ubiquitous marketing and branding campaigns (Warner and Peterman, 2022).

Using critical content analysis (Short, 2017), this study analyzes focal authors' Twitter practices, examining the topics, issues, and events they addressed and the positions taken. Telling cases of YA author engagement with public intellectual issues are derived from that analysis (Warner and Peterman, 2022). These cases are then used to develop the ELA methods learning experience described in this chapter.

VIRTUALLY ENCOUNTERING AUTHORS

There is no single "best" approach to designing critical, participatory learning across the multiple dimensions of authors' social media engagement. While a few broad recommendations for planning ethical and effective learning experiences have been derived from this work, specific pedagogical practices and expectations depend upon the purpose and context of each encounter.

What follows is an illustrative example of how to leverage Twitter in an ELA Methods course. In a relatively simple introductory assignment, teacher candidates were asked to select a YA fiction author from a list provided by the instructor (preferably someone whose work they have read and enjoyed). The candidates perused selected authors' Twitter feeds, making note of what issues and topics they were tweeting about. As they read, candidates were encouraged to consider the following: Who are they engaging with online? What topics, issues, and events are they tweeting about, and for what purposes? Who seems to be the intended audience?

Next, candidates read (or reread) at least one book by their selected authors. Drawing on specific examples from authors' Twitter feeds and books, each candidate shared an analytic commentary in which they identified the notable issues and topics their focal author addressed on Twitter and considers how similar issues or themes may be addressed in their book(s)—directly, allegorically, or tangentially.

Finally, candidates reflected on the pedagogical implications of their experience in a guided discussion, exploring questions with classmates such as:

- What insights about the author did you learn from their Twitter feed?
- Does having more firsthand knowledge about the author as a person change the perspective you bring to reading?
- How does reading about (and potentially engaging) with this author on social media influence your interpretation and response to their book?
- Based on this exercise, what are a few questions or responses that you would want to share with your author?

These questions and responses can later serve as a foundation for processing deeper and more sustained engagement with authors on social media over time.

Personal Connections via Twitter Feeds

Some might be skeptical that such a virtual encounter can lead toward the development of the same personal connections between self and text that are such a positive outcome of traditional author encounters. Yet traditional author encounters generally occur once each school year and require advance planning and coordination and potential speaker fees. In contrast, the accessibility and immediacy of social media allow educators to scaffold discursive engagement with authors over time—this example is only one introductory experience on which subsequent learning experiences can then build.

Students have the opportunity to regularly encounter authors through social media in a range of experiences with varying objectives and degrees of structure. Additional inquiry would be needed to more fully understand how developing meaningful and lasting connections through digital encounters compares with a traditional encounter, yet candidates who previously participated in this sample learning experience certainly did express deepened personal connections to authors and texts. For example, one ELA candidate chose to explore L. L. McKinney's feed, noting her appreciation for McKinney:

> talk[ing] about Youth and the importance of holding onto their own childlike wonder and writing to express their imagination + creativity. I also like them purely because they have the same personality as me, and are a bit unfiltered on their account. I think by learning about the author personally, it makes me even more intrigued to check out their books and look into them more. The more I learn about them and make connections to myself, the more I feel their books drawing me into a bond. (Amaya, Class Assignment)

Another candidate who chose to study John Green noted:

> Looking at John Green's online presence I see why I like his books. He seems like a real down to earth type of person and I think it reflects in his books. At least the one I read. "The Fault In Our Stars" [sic] was one of the first books I've read that made me cry. I felt the emotion of the characters and I think a lot of that is thanks to John Green being so real and being able to translate real feelings into his stories. (Justine, Class Assignment)

Yet another candidate who also chose John Green remarked that:

> It's nice to see authors replying and engaging with people about social issues and things that matter. It disconnects the author from their writing but also makes me, as a reader, feel more connected to them when reading the book.

Despite the fact that they neither got to meet authors, nor even exchange social media messages with them, candidates in this methods class felt that interacting with authors' Twitter feeds allowed them to get to know the authors in authentic ways, and, therefore, to enjoy and better understand their work.

One part of the Beliefs Statement quoted at the beginning of this chapter argues that good ELA methods instruction should help "supporting teacher candidates to understand that teaching and learning are social practices that impact and are impacted by the communities in which they are situated" (Gallo et al., 2020). This learning experience helps the ELA teacher candidates who undertook it to situate themselves within a community of authors, readers, and texts, gaining a greater understanding of all three in the process.

Intellectual Depths in YAL Twitter

By encountering the authors through their Twitter feeds, candidates also gained an appreciation for the intellectual depth of these authors' works and for the power and social impact they have in society. One candidate who chose Angie Thomas noted that

> She post[s] content that humanizes her. Thomas also balances this with tweets regarding social justice movements and educational initiatives . . . When she posts content she is aware of her social impact. (Jamie, Class Assignment)

Similarly, a candidate who read Laurie Halse Anderson's feed argued that "Anderson, unlike many other authors, realizes the power she possesses and utilizes it as an advantage to education the public" (Christopher, Class Assignment). Another candidate noted a thread of John Green's where he discusses his identity and beliefs as a Christian, observing:

> Anyone who is looking to get into a debate may enjoy John Green's twitter. John Green talks a lot about Christianity on his page making arguments as he is a Christian, but after scrolling through his page, not many have enjoyed the topics he has spoken about or have visibly disagreed with him. He expresses his concern for how Christians should share resources on reducing poverty and ill health, and believes in making theological arguments for his faith . . . Is there ever a held back feeling when putting beliefs out to social media in fear it may turn people away from reading his novels, or change their idea of the novels if they have already read them?

This led the candidate to return to Green's novel, *The Fault in Our Stars,* and reread it, discovering religious allegories and allusions that she had not seen before or expected.

TELLING CASES FROM YAL TWITTER

Research findings demonstrate how authors use social media to present their personal, political, and professional selves to the public (Warner and Peterman, 2022). These practices create opportunities for ELA methods students to facilitate critical, participatory readings across multiple dimensions of social engagement online: transactions around an author's own books/work, transactions around major topics and controversies in the field of children's literature, and transactions around current events and wider issues of social justice.

Re-storying Texts in Transaction with Authors

Many authors and illustrators actively engage with their readers on Twitter, as well as YouTube, TikTok, Instagram, and Facebook, in conversations explicitly inviting youth to question their characterizations and to propose or critique new plot developments in a given narrative. For example, Rick Riordan, the award-winning author of the Percy Jackson and the Olympians series, responded to a tweet questioning whether the protagonist, Percy, ever had a crush on Luke, another central character in the series. Although a romantic relationship between Percy and Luke is never directly stated in the text, Riordan's response invited multiple interpretations of the story—even if these interpretations diverged from his original intent:

> The only answer I can offer [to the question of whether Percy had a crush on Luke] is: Read the books and decide for yourself. Personally I see no evidence of that, but I am looking at it through my life perspective. What I intended isn't relevant once the books are published. The only "canon" is the text, which is for the readers. (Riordan, 2020)

Later in the thread, Riordan engaged with other readers who expressed concerns with "revisionist" readings of major characters by noting:

> Now a caveat: Big difference between saying "The only canon is the text" and saying "Your personal opinion is canon regardless of the text." Can you support your thesis? Where is your evidence? Yes, I was an English teacher; why do you ask? :-) (Riordan, 2020)

Digital interactions such as these destabilize pedagogical assumptions linking one's understanding of a text with interpretation of an author's intention, instead positioning young readers as possessing epistemic knowledge that affords multiple and potentially contradictory interpretations.

This perspective can be challenging for English teachers previously trained to prioritize the text-based evidence emphasized by standardized reading and literacy assessment. Yet, English education is a dynamic field in which methods coursework must continually evolve and adapt (Gallo et al., 2020). By posing questions such as those suggested in figure 14.1 (below) and introducing counternarratives, methods instructors support their students developing an agentic and critically reflective stance, productively disrupting static traditions and encouraging innovation.

Author's own books/work:
- What insights about the author did you learn from their twitter engagement? What are a few questions or responses that you would want to share with your author?
- How does reading about (and potentially engaging) with this author on social media influence your response to their book? Does having more first-hand knowledge about the author as a person change how you read their published work?
- Who decides how a story is read? Who does a story belong to once it's been published?

Major topics and controversies in the field of children's literature:
- Who/what determines whether a book is published?
- What makes an author "successful"? Why? Who gets to decide?
- How might industry expectations (established by publishers and corporations) influence this author's participation on social media be industry expectations implicated in the author's social media engagement?

Current events and wider issues of social justice:
- Who is the author engaging with online? What topics, issues, and events are they tweeting about, and for what purposes? Who seems to be the intended audience?
- Who can be considered a public intellectual in a digital age? Whose perspectives "count", and who decides?
- How are the perspectives of youth received and valued in these digital spaces?

Figure 14.1. Questions to Facilitate Critical Inquiry across Multiple Dimensions of Engagement on Social Media.

Authors' Twitter posts also invited further critique of singular textual readings by making the publishing process more transparent, including candid explanations and discussions about the market forces that influence texts and paratexts in children's literature. Reading across the data corpus, the most frequently occurring category of tweets was posts amplifying the ongoing development of authors' works-in-progress. Some of these tweets served a primarily commercial purpose, such as promoting new book cover "reveals" for upcoming novels.

Yet the promotional aspects of tweets were often entangled with complicated discussions about race and representation in the publishing and media industries. One rich example of this is found in series of threads shared by Angie Thomas in August of 2017, in which she responded to questions and comments about casting for the film adaptation of her award-winning novel, *The Hate You Give*. Addressing criticism that the actress cast for the lead role of Starr Carter (the novel's protagonist) has much lighter skin than the character's depiction in the book's cover art, Thomas noted that "For those asking when Amandla was cast—last year, before THUG even came out. Heck, BEFORE there was a cover. Be. Fore. Carry on" (Thomas, 2017).

With this timeline, Thomas allowed for the possibility of multiple and contradictory imaginings of Starr's character. Her tweet invited critical reflection on how students draw from both written narrative and visual imagery to develop a picture in their mind of a story. This also challenges readers to push back against the seemingly official characterizations inscribed through cover art and other promotional materials.

Transacting with Books as Socioculturally Situated Texts

The public platform and digital record afforded by Twitter allow ELA methods students to contextualize discrete transactions with authors within larger, ongoing topics and controversies in the field of children's literature. In the example above, Thomas repeatedly explained that she did not have any control over casting decisions for the film, going so far as to incorporate this information into her Twitter handle and biographical statement. Her initial tweets on this topic framed her experience as typical within the publishing industry, telling readers "Don't come into authors' mentions, going off on us about stuff we have no control over. I'm glad you're passionate, but check the bio" (Thomas, 2017).

As criticism mounted online (both on Twitter and elsewhere), Thomas shared a GIF depicting a Black woman yelling into a megaphone, which in turn is blaring into a microphone. Her original text accompanying this image revealed Thomas's mounting frustration, stating "STOP ATTACKING WOC AUTHORS OVER THINGS THEY DON'T CONTROL" (Thomas, 2017), and she extended her exhortation in a subsequent thread that further elucidated how systemic racism influenced this debate, comparing it discussions about other transmedia adaptations:

> And the "same five actors" comments are cute . . . except you were silent when it was the same five non-poc actors in YA movies . . .
> Let's not do this, YA community. Let's be better than this. Please. I love y'all. (Thomas, 2017)

Thomas also drew readers' attention to the ways in which stories by and about People of Color are systematically marginalized across the entertainment industry, sharing:

> For a book I thought wouldn't get published due to its subject matter, I am absolutely thrilled that THUG is even being made into a movie.
> I love the cast and the team behind it. I stand by it. I'd just ask that you support it. (Thomas, 2017)

In this thread, Thomas referred to industry-wide issues. She implied that the critiques over casting for the film were misplaced and that her fans should instead celebrate the cultural progress, however flawed or incomplete it may be, signified by Hollywood's recognition and adaptation of the book. As such, her tweets revealed how economic considerations in publishing influence whose stories are valued and how these stories are told.

Thomas's social media engagement thus extended a conversation with ELA methods students that began with analysis and discussion of a book and situated this work in its broader sociocultural context. Such transactions invite ELA teachers and their students to engage with major issues and controversies shaping the production and study of literature in real time.

Methods coursework and field experiences are spaces where these topics move from abstract theory to critical, concrete questions of practice as students interrogate how and why an author "matters" in a story, debate their parameters and definitions of cultural authenticity, and investigate how the (mis)representation of cultural identities and experiences and pervasive inequality in publishing and media entertainment impact learners.

Transactions around Current Events, Social Justice, and Equity

In addition to discussing their own work and other literature-related topics, some popular authors use Twitter and other social media to engage in critical civic discourse. As public intellectuals in a digital age, these authors facilitate discussions with their followers on current events, take ethical positions, and advocate for social change (Warner and Peterman, 2022). The issues that these authors discuss are critically salient to young people and their lived experiences, both in- and out-of-school contexts, tweeting about topics including racial justice, gender equality, climate change, and recent threats to democratic governance in the United States.

For example, a series of tweets by John Green addressed the passage of a Texas law that regulated the use of gendered pronouns, noting:

> I mean, if calling other people by their correct pronouns is one of the hundred biggest challenges in your life, I am super envious of your life. It sounds amazing. [. . .] Everyone uses pronouns to self-identify. I just did so. Twice. (Green, 2022)

Green's tweets on this political controversy generated passionate responses and debate among his followers and demonstrated the increasing porosity between authors' personal and professional identities in a digital age. The Texas law was one of many legislative actions enacted nationwide seeking to regulate and discursively erase transgender identities, purporting to protect children and youth through discriminatory law and policy. Inviting students into this digital forum challenged beliefs about the purpose of English education and where teaching and learning occur.

ELA teacher candidates often occupy a liminal space in these types of discussions. They draw from their own personal identities and professional experiences to wrestle with questions about how readers navigate digital intersections of the personal and political. By drawing from authors' social media to understand and interpret YA literature, readers can engage in more meaningful conversations about author power, positionality, and intent.

CONSIDERATIONS FOR PRACTITIONERS

Authors and illustrators are real people, unpredictable and with human flaws and foibles. When bringing social media-based learning experiences into the classroom, teachers must plan to address unexpected controversies, colorful language, or even logistical challenges such as an author unexpectedly taking a hiatus from social media. Moreover, teachers and students must navigate an often contentious political landscape in the work of this critical collaborative inquiry. Social media requires vigilance by teachers to help students productively navigate disagreements, block trolls and hate speech, and do what is necessary to ensure that the shared humanity of all students is honored and respected in ELA classroom discourse.

Finally, while the author's data collected on Twitter serves as representative examples, it is important to be mindful that digital technologies are always changing. As new media platforms gain popularity, the sites of critical engagement, as well as the norms of participation, will shift accordingly. Youth are often at the fore of digital innovations as their participation determines the success of social media startups. It is, therefore, incumbent upon teacher educators to proactively explore and become familiar with these various platforms (and to communicate this goal to future teachers) as the goal of this work must include authenticity and meaningful engagement.

CONCLUSION

The experiences of the ELA teacher candidates detailed in this chapter invite educators and researchers to consider individual and collective possibilities of amplifying student voices within the shifting interrelationships of readers and authors in a digital age, interrogating how meaning is formed and reformed by their own and others' social locations, and foregrounding youth agency in the production of knowledge. By transparently engaging in this work in ELA methods coursework, teacher educators can model the flexibility, improvisation, and willingness to dwell with uncertainty that is critical for successfully navigating the evolving landscape of English education.

Effective methods of instruction entail more than a recitation of established best practices in English education. Rather, it must promote ongoing professional growth and innovation, and always with an orientation toward building a more equitable and just field that honors the diversity of students' literacies and texts. Social media invites educators to consider individual and collective possibilities of amplifying student voices within the shifting interrelationships of readers and authors in a digital age, interrogating how meaning is formed and reformed by their own and others' social locations, and foregrounding youth agency in the production of knowledge.

REFERENCES

Alvermann, D. E. (2008). Why bother theorizing adolescents' online literacies for classroom practice and research? *Journal of Adolescent & Adult Literacy, 52*(1), 8–19.

Gallo, J., Hallman, H. L., Parsons, C., Pastore-Capuana, K., Pet, S. R., and Searcy, L. (2020). *Beliefs about methods courses and field experiences in English education.* Accessed February 14, 2023. https://ncte.org/statement/methodsinee/print/.

Gonzalez, D. (2020). "One day I want to be like you": The basics of a stellar author visit. *Michigan Reading Journal, 51*(2), 6. https://scholarworks.gvsu.edu/mrj/vol51/iss2/6.

Green, J. [@johngreen]. (2022, August 10). *I mean, if calling other people by their correct pronouns is one of the hundred biggest challenges in your life, I am super envious of your life. It sounds amazing . . . Everyone uses pronouns to self-identify. I just did so. Twice* [Tweet]. Twitter.

Jenkins, H. (2013). *Textual poachers: Television fans and participatory culture* (rev. ed.). Routledge.

Lewis Ellison, T. (2017). Digital participation, agency, and choice: An African American youth's digital storytelling about Minecraft. *Journal of Adolescent & Adult Literacy, 61*(1), 25–35.

Moje, E. B. and Luke, A. (2009). Literacy and identity: Examining the metaphors in history and contemporary research. *Reading Research Quarterly, 44*(4), 415–37.

Morrell, E. (2017). Toward equity and diversity in literacy research, policy, and practice: A critical, global approach. *Journal of Literacy Research, 49*(3), 454–63.

Moynihan, K. E. (2009). Local authors in the classroom: Bringing readers and writers together. *The English Journal, 98*(3), 34–38.

Riordan, R. [@rickriordan]. (2020, July 2). *The only answer I can offer [to the question of whether Percy had a crush on Luke] is: Read the books and decide for yourself. Personally I see no evidence of that, but I am looking at it through my life perspective. What I intended isn't relevant once the books are published. The only "canon" is the text, which is for the readers* [Tweet]. Twitter.

Riordan, R. [@rickriordan]. (2020, July 2). *Now a caveat: Big difference between saying "The only canon is the text" and saying "Your personal opinion is canon regardless of the text." Can you support your thesis? Where is your evidence? Yes, I was an English teacher; why do you ask? :-)* [Tweet]. Twitter.

Short, K. G. (2017). Critical content analysis as a research methodology. In H. Johnson, J. Mathis, and K. Short (Eds.), *Critical content analysis of children's and young adult literature: Reframing perspective* (pp. 1–15). Routledge.

Thomas, A. [@angiecthomas]. (2017, August 3). *For those asking when Amandla was cast - last year, before THUG even came out. Heck, BEFORE there was a cover. Be. Fore. Carry on* [Tweet]. Twitter.

Thomas, A. [@angiecthomas]. (2017, August 3). *Don't come into authors' mentions, going off on us about stuff we have no control over. I'm glad you're passionate, but check the bio* [Tweet]. Twitter.

Thomas, A. [@angiecthomas]. (2017, August 3). *STOP ATTACKING WOC AUTHORS OVER THINGS THEY DON'T CONTROL* [Tweet]. Twitter.

Thomas, A. [@angiecthomas]. (2017, August 3). *And the "same five actors" comments are cute...except you were silent when it was the same five non-poc actors in YA movies . . . Let's not do this, YA community. Let's be better than this. Please. I love y'all* [Tweet]. Twitter.

Thomas, A. [@angiecthomas]. (2017, August 3). *For a book I thought wouldn't get published due to it's subject matter, I am absolutely thrilled that THUG is even being made into a movie. I love the cast and the team behind it. I stand by it. I'd just ask that you support it* [Tweet]. Twitter.

Vasquez, V. M., Janks, H., and Comber, B. (2019). Critical literacy as a way of being and doing. *Language Arts, 96*(5), 300–11.

Vogels, E. A., Gelles-Watnick, R., and Massarat, N. (2022). Teens, social media and technology 2022. Pew Research Center. Accessed February 11, 2023. https://www.pewresearch.org/internet/2022/08/10/teens-social-media-and-technology-2022/.

Warner, C. K. and Peterman, N. (2022). Leveraging #YA Twitter for online ELA learning. *The English Journal, 111*(6), 22–29.

Chapter 15

Debating the Discourse of *Professionalism* with Preservice English Teachers

Heidi L. Hallman

Historically, teaching has been considered a semiprofessional due to teachers' lack of autonomy and limited decision-making powers (Samuels, 1970; Leiter, 1978). Ingersoll and Merrill (2011) assert that, still today, teaching remains a *semi-profession* because of its lack of a common body of knowledge, practices, and skills that constitute a basis for professional expertise. Despite this, teacher education has fought hard throughout the past thirty years to increase the status of the teaching profession.

In what is often referred to as the *professionalization agenda* (Shulman, 1986, 1987), education scholars have aimed to establish a research-base and formal knowledge base for professional educators. Doing this through working from a consistent set of standards for professional practice (Darling-Hammond et al., 1999; Darling-Hammond, 2000), the professionalization agenda has sought to articulate a common knowledge base.

Participation by the American Association of Colleges for Teacher Education in creating standards for teaching and teacher preparation that are unified across initial preparation, certification, and licensing, as well as the publication of *What Matters Most: Teaching for America's Future* (National Commission on Teaching & America's Future, 1996), have been key moments in pushing the professionalization agenda forward to today.

Teacher educators can trace these influences on the field and recognize that preservice teachers enter their classrooms expecting to become professionals. Despite not always understanding the history of the teaching profession, preservice teachers expect to learn how to become professionals through their teacher education coursework and field experiences in schools.

This chapter grapples with how teacher educators might address the concept of professionalism with preservice teachers in light of the current context. First, the chapter situates the concept of *professional* within the field itself, outlining how the definition of professional relates to how the role of "teacher" has changed over time. Next, the chapter articulates how teacher educators might situate the concept of professional within the current neoliberal, post-truth era.

And finally, themes from a discussion with preservice teachers are featured as a way to highlight tenets of novice teachers' understanding of professionalism. The chapter concludes by urging teacher educators to encourage novice teachers to consider the concept of professionalism from the viewpoint of a variety of stakeholders, thereby deepening the connotation of the term itself.

SITUATING THE TERM *PROFESSIONAL*

Hargreaves (2000) outlines the historical processes involved in the development of teacher professionalism across several different countries and identified four phases: the preprofessional age; the age of the autonomous professional; the age of the collegial professional; and the age of the postprofessional or postmodern professional. These ages are important to understand as they help delineate and locate the current moment.

One might think about the preprofessional era as one that was pedagogically and technically simple; the preprofessional era involved a novice teacher shadowing an experienced teacher as a way to learn the skills necessary to teach. This era also involved teaching content through transmission from teacher to students.

It is worth noting that teaching at this time was commonly described by some as a *vocation*, or a calling. The term vocation, associated oftentimes with a religious vocation as well as with the act of serving others, still has resonance with the work of teaching. However, the description of teaching as vocation has largely been left out of the discourse of teacher professionalism since the preprofessional age.

With the use of the term vocation, an assumption might be made that teaching as vocation may undermine the idea that teaching can be "taught" and is, instead, something innate that just must be animated. Yet, teaching as vocation, though now largely absent from discussions in the field, could contribute to the conversation about teaching (Hallman, 2022).

After the preprofessional era, Hargreaves locates the beginning of the age of the autonomous professional in the 1960s. In this era, teachers' salaries increased and teacher education was largely moved to university courses. As a result, pedagogy became a site of debate and inquiry.

During the age of the collegial professional, beginning in the 1980s, teachers became part of professional communities and teacher education was fully integrated into universities. At the same time, however, education reform increased the complexity in the governance and regulation of teaching, and such reform mandates became part of the education landscape. As a result, teachers had to shift in how they considered themselves to be autonomous professionals, for now they were also learning how to respond to reform mandates.

In the postprofessional age, Hargreaves argues that economics, globalization and digital communication brought further changes to teachers' professionalism. New patterns of international economic organization led to new forms of interconnectedness. Hargreaves (2000) argues that up to the collegial professional era, changes in teaching had led increasingly to greater teacher autonomy. This, in turn, had led to greater teacher professionalism. However, since then, educational reforms, complex governance structures, and the digital revolution in communication have continued to undermine teachers' autonomy, resulting in increased de-professionalization of the work of teachers and teaching.

Assaults on teacher professionalism have only intensified throughout the COVID-19 era and beyond. It should be noted that the post-COVID reality of mass teacher attrition may continue to affect teacher professionalism in ways that are still unknown. Public conversations about teaching as a profession are currently dominated by a narrative of negativity (Hargreaves, 2021). Characterized through portrayals of the complex realities, challenges, and successes of work in classrooms, such conversations have highlighted the field's struggle with teacher retention. In a recent paper, Kraft and Lyon (2022) write:

> It would be a mistake to assume that the teaching profession has held a relatively static position in the public's eyes or the labor market. The state of the teaching profession has changed dynamically over time in response to a host of influences including macro-economic trends, shifting political narratives, evolving labor movements, and persistent reform efforts. (p. 25)

Teacher attrition has also recently received a large amount of public attention. Many news outlets featured the U.S. Labor Department's data outline that public educators quit at an average of 83 per 10,000 a month during the first 10 months of 2018; such statistics have prompted renewed interest in perpetuating a narrative of a profession in crisis. 2018 marked the highest rate of exit for public educators since 2001 (Hackman and Morath, 2018).

The pandemic era, however, ushered in a new wave of discussion about teacher resignations. An October 18, 2021, Washington Post article highlighted untenable work environments, teachers' desires to provide for students and families in ways that extend beyond teaching, and the great emotional toll that teaching takes on teachers themselves (Streeter, 2021).

A very recent study (Kush et al., 2022) found that teachers were 40 percent more likely than health care workers to report anxiety symptoms. Indeed, teachers' work has become an incredibly complex enterprise over the course of the pandemic era; providing lessons via remote learning during times of school closures was just one challenge that nearly every teacher faced in the past two years.

THE NEOLIBERAL TURN AND THE TEACHING PROFESSION

It is important to note that the discourse of teacher professionalism hinges on both "from within" and "from without" mandates. In other words, the term *professional* has been used to reference both externally imposed mandates on teachers, such as a neoliberal adherence to accountability measures and learning standards that govern school subjects, as well as practices that are internally enacted by teachers themselves, such as the preservation of autonomy. Teachers have worked to continue to professionalize themselves through actions that promote increased teacher autonomy and the professionalization of the field.

In addition to taking stock of how the field has conceptualized teaching, teacher educators must recognize the ways in which education has been heavily influenced throughout the last twenty years by neoliberalism and postindustrialism. These changes have been characterized as effects of neoliberal policies, and scholars in education (e.g., Apple, 2000, 2006; Au, 2007; Ball, 2007, 2012; Loh and Hu, 2014) have emphasized that these policies have stressed market-based solutions, individualism, and privatization across global contexts.

Though neoliberalism cannot be generalized across contexts, Harvey (2007) notes that neoliberalism has become "ingrained in popular consciousness as a kind of common-sense" (p. 3), stressing a functional and economically oriented view of education above all else.

Savage (2013), Lingard et al. (2014), and Hallman (2018) have noted that, for example, the social, personal, and emotional purposes of schooling have been touched by neoliberalism in ways that have reoriented education to be in line with economic imperatives. Schooling, therefore, is now viewed as primarily important from an economic standpoint, and young people are pushed to engage with it in this manner.

Foucault (2008) called this phenomenon the "economization of the social" and Rose (1996) coined the term "neosocial"; both terms underscore the reality that institutions like schools—that have historically been organized for the promotion of the social good—have been realigned to be in consonance with the promotion of economic prosperity, stressing ideals of performativity, consumer choice, deliverable products, measurable outputs, and employment-related skills.

The neoliberal worldview is one that posits a transactional view of the teacher—a vision in which the teacher is viewed as an educational service provider, with the child and family positioned as customers. Such a transactional model, aligned with market-based principles, disrupts the view of teaching as connected with others and places it squarely in the marketplace. With this model, we have traversed a long distance from the era of the autonomous professional.

Now, teachers as professionals are touched by the neoliberal agenda by participating in educational reform in the United States that has been increasingly reliant on narrow accountability measures, standardized tests, and "teacher-proof" curricula (Ball, 2007). And, such school reform efforts frequently position teachers as the implementers of educational change, rather than as contributors or experts. Loh and Hu (2014) write that education, as a whole, has been reoriented so as to "provide human capital so as to 'service' and 'compete' in the global economy" (p. 14).

Particular practices, such as the implementation of benchmarking and academic standards (Au, 2007), have become the norm in most schools, and teachers in U.S. school contexts must sift through how such practices affect their orientation toward teaching and learning. A shift to the neoliberal agenda in U.S. schools—one driven by markets, standardized testing, and school effectiveness—has become the dominant force in defining "successful" schools. Rizvi and Lingard (2010) argue that neoliberalism has become the common sense of education and education policy, producing what they refer to as a "neoliberal imaginary."

An important facet of how neoliberalism has affected teachers' everyday lives is through the turn to the technical. Smyth (2011) notes that teachers have felt the ways that neoliberalism has touched them through experiencing the "technical turn" in teaching—one akin to promoting discourses of technocratic professionalism—teachers have been forced to become complicit in the myth of "skills formation" (p. 15).

Teachers, even those early in their careers, may be concerned with building resumes that convey such skills to future employers. Though not professionalism in the way the field considers it—a professionalism built upon autonomy, choice, and knowledge—a new type of professionalism now must co-exist within the teacher, one driven by this technical turn.

A Discussion with Novice Teachers about the Discourse of *Professionalism*

Teacher educators are tasked with making sense of this trajectory of professionalism while also guiding preservice teachers toward inhabiting the role of a professional. After the completion of their teacher education program, a focus group was conducted with ten novice teachers that asked them to consider the concepts of *professional* and *professionalism*. This focus group discussion is drawn upon as a way to invite a conversation between the theoretical aspects of professionalism and the actual experiences and perceptions of novice teachers.

The ten novice teachers who participated in the focus group discussion had just completed their semester-long student teaching experience and had graduated from the secondary English education program at a midwestern public university. Seven of the ten teachers were preparing to begin their first year of in-service teaching at a middle or high school in the area, two of the teachers were preparing to begin graduate school, and one teacher was undecided about future plans.

The focus group discussion elicited a number of participant stories and these stories were analyzed both inductively and deductively (Miles and Huberman, 1994). The analysis of data was inductive in the way it first sought to find recurring themes in preservice teachers' stories of self about professionalism. The analysis process also used deductive coding constructs as a way of triangulating the findings that were gleaned through the inductive analysis.

In following this deductive process, themes that were expected to be present about professionalism were sought. For example, several teachers spoke about the desire for autonomy within their classrooms as a marker of professionalism. This theme resonates with the literature (Hargreaves, 2000) in ways that reference the eras of teacher professionalism. Next, three themes from the focus group are featured about teacher professionalism today.

The first theme entitled "Teaching is more complex now" presents some of the challenges that novice teachers assume were ushered in by the pandemic era. In some cases, this was true. In other cases, the pandemic era became the context of the challenge, but may not have solely contributed to how the challenge was manifested. The second theme "Compliance, not Critique" outlines a tension that novice teachers feel in deciding whether to align themselves with a utilitarian, compliant view of teaching or one rooted in critique. Finally, the third theme "The Technocratic Professional" links the views of novice teachers to the current era, one shaped by neoliberal standards of accountability.

Teaching Is More Complex Now

During the focus group discussion, novice teacher Marisol started speaking with her peers in the focus group by recounting a story of being in a field experience during the pandemic era. She had been assigned to work with an English teacher at a local high school and the teacher was teaching sophomore English via Zoom. Marisol told her peers that she was uncomfortable seeing the students in a sea of black Zoom boxes, but as a guest in this classroom, she felt helpless to change some of the decisions that had already been put in motion. She said:

> The teacher kept us in the large Zoom group and almost no one put their camera on. The teacher didn't seem to even mind and just kept going with her lesson. I wondered if I was in her place as the teacher what I would do. I wondered if she had tried break-out rooms. I wondered if she had tried getting the students to turn on their cameras. But when I thought about it, I realized that maybe even if she had tried those things, maybe they didn't work. Maybe it was just hard to get anyone to talk.

After Marisol reflected on the possibility that even good plans in the classroom (or virtual classroom) might yield ineffective change, it was obvious that her hope in such interventions was in question. Her colleague, Rebecca, responded to her, and said:

> I think the same thing. I mean . . . I think that I could try different things, but even those things may not get students to talk. Zoom made things complex because sometimes I would expect that a student was just a black box and was not listening, but then I would be surprised when I discovered that the student was listening and I had underestimated their engagement in class.

In the conversation above, Marisol and Rebecca both negotiate their thoughts about the role of the teacher in the present era versus what they believe it used to be before the pandemic altered this. Both novice teachers experienced changed perceptions of how students might be excited and engaged in their classes. The era of Zoom prompted both Marisol and Rebecca to question students' presence when they felt they were unable to accurately assess students' presence.

Novice teacher Kelly expanded on this theme by saying, "teaching is more complex now." When Kelly was asked what she meant by that, she had a lengthy description of all of her thoughts about teaching and how it was tied to teachers as professionals:

> The complexity relates to both the environment and the students. So now [during the pandemic era] we have introduced all these different ways to teach–hybrid, in-person, and online. We did not have all of these options before. Students were in front of us. But now they are in front of us, but they are also absent. Marisol couldn't tell if her students were multitasking, engaged in her lesson, or just absent. Teachers are supposed to respond to students, but it's almost impossible to respond when you don't know what you are responding to.
> I just said teaching is more complex now, but that also relates to how teaching used to be. Teaching used to be about teaching content and the teacher was the presenter of that content. But now, even our students are online all the time. They can get content about anything easily. So, it is making me ask the question, "What is my job now as a teacher?"

Kelly introduces the issue of a teacher's role and how it continues to shift away from content expert and toward interpreter of content. And, the role of an interpreter is, indeed, more complex. The role of interpreter brings critique and nuance to content. But, with every critique comes the need to situate the critique within a context.

Novice teachers might note that teachers were transmitters of content before content was readily available online, but teachers have always had to be interpreters of content. This is the job of teaching. However, novice teachers often lament the aspects of teaching that they find more complex today, though this may be an imagined reality. They are pointing to the challenge they see as the need for compliance, while at the same time, grounding their pedagogy in critique.

COMPLIANCE, NOT CRITIQUE

Building on the concept of compliance versus critique, Marta said, "We have to adhere to the standards, so we might as well accept them." After hearing that statement, Marta's colleague, Jack, interrupted her and said, "But we owe it to ourselves and our students to understand *why* a particular standard exists." Jack's push to Marta was to encourage her to adopt a critical stance toward standards.

Shaunna, a preservice teacher, echoed the theme of compliance that Marta introduced by saying, "There's just a lot I can't change [in my classroom], so I make peace with these limits." Shaunna seemed to see such compliance as realistic and the only way forward. Like his response to Marta, Jack responded to Shaunna's assertion about limitations and said, even directly referencing the term *professional:*

> I hear you about accepting the limits that teachers themselves can't always change things. But, I just think we, as teachers, need to always question the things we're asked to do. We aren't robots, we're professionals. We have a lot of knowledge and need to be able to use it.

Jack's insistence of teachers as professionals consistently prompted the view of teacher as agent. Though he was often the single voice in the group in this regard, Jack wanted to endorse a view that resonated with the era of the autonomous professional, an era where teachers were valued for their unique contributions to student learning in their classrooms and an era that fostered a collegial professionalism.

Marta and Shaunna's stance was skeptical that this was a likely reality for teachers, and their stance read more like a coping strategy toward recognizing that some loss of teacher autonomy might be inevitable. Marta and Shaunna may, to us, look jaded from the outset; however, this was their narrative about professionalism. They envisioned themselves as adherents to a project of utilitarianism in teaching, one that took orders from above and acted them out in the classroom.

Austin did not see utilitarianism as a compromise. Instead, he referenced the very practical nature of teaching:

We can offer critique, but we still operate as practitioners. This means that we must put things into a very practical reality. We're responsible for teaching students to read and write proficiently, so some of that work is just very practical.

Austin's view tries to urge teachers not to dichotomize practice and critique and instead recognize that all practices must hone in on interpretation.

THE TECHNOCRATIC PROFESSIONAL

How do we, as teacher educators, make sense of the stance that Marta and Shaunna take? How do we also maintain the enthusiasm for professionalism that Jack seems to convey? What has changed in the profession that has led each of the novice teachers to adopt the views that they hold? As we consider the ways that novice teachers discuss professionalism, an absence of a recognition of larger change seems apparent. Instead of drawing on some larger narrative of professionalism, novice teachers seem to grapple with the definition that they feel best suits their worldview. Perhaps teacher educators need to provide more guidance.

The shift from autonomous professional to one of technocratic professional is linked to larger societal change. Instead of critiquing a vision of skills formation and compliance to external mandates, preservice teachers like Marta and Shaunna frequently take these aspects of teaching as a "given." In essence, they place the technocratic professional in a realm where "teacher" is linked to a utilitarian function.

Teacher educators must always be sensitive to the idea that utilitarianism in teaching is not a bad; it is a given. As teachers, we know we must be practical. Austin's drive for the practical is not incorrect. It is important, for example, alongside critique, work to move forward and apply concepts to practice when teaching children. This theory–practice tension for teachers and teacher educators alike can become a site for frustration; however, it is important to stress that a choice between critique and utility is not an either/or choice.

Though the choice between critique and utility is false, novice teachers must know that utility and critique will always have a tension that exist between them. While a critical stance in teacher education might promote not merely an "acceptance" of standards but also a deconstruction of them, utility strips the deconstruction away. As one of the teachers, Marta, said, "We have to adhere to the standards, so we might as well accept them." Marta's colleague, Jack, interrupted her and demanded critique. Jack's push to continue to adopt a critical stance while also recognizing how teachers must act in the classroom holds onto a view of teaching as one that can be animated by both critique and utility.

When speaking about what it means to work between critique and utility, preservice teachers chalk up difficulties as "just part of the landscape of education today." Shaunna, a preservice teacher, iterated that she was removed from the decision-making, saying, "There's just a lot I can't change [in my classroom] so I make peace with these limits." As a result of this compromise, novice teachers often adopt coping stances that help them recognize that some loss of teacher autonomy might shape who they are as teachers. Consequently, they envision themselves as adherents to a greater project of utilitarianism in teaching.

In addition to an ambivalence expressed by novice teachers about being boxed into technocratic professionalism, novice teachers may cling to the technical turn in teaching (Smyth, 2011) as a way to legitimate teaching practices. Through locating "good teaching" within skills, routines, and practices, teaching becomes technical and planned—a safe space in a climate of lack of autonomy. Yet, with the loss of the human element and a lack of autonomy about larger issues that affect schools and classrooms, teaching can easily be reduced to a profession that prioritizes nonhuman activity. Skills and routines ultimately cannot substitute for the relational aspects of teaching.

CONCLUSION

What might teacher educators stress with novice teachers about professionalism's arc in the domain of teaching? First, it is important that novice teachers have some understanding of the field's history; the movement from teachers being prepared in normal schools at the start of the twentieth century (Labaree 2004) to the establishment of teacher education at four-year institutions of higher learning is an important facet of their understanding of teaching as a profession. Hargreaves (2000) work outlining the eras of the teacher professional can illuminate what aspects of professionalism are maintained by teachers themselves and what aspects are prompted by the ways education is now managed and promoted (Apple 2006).

Second, the discourse of professionalism must be put in conversation with multiple stakeholders' views. There is an understanding that professionalism involves not just the teacher, but parents, students, faculty, staff, administration, and community members. Communicating with a wider audience about what it means to be a teacher today can help novice teachers understand multiple, and sometimes conflicting, messages about professionalism.

Finally, novice teachers may benefit from conversation about the multiple meanings of the term *professionalism* itself. Dodillet (2019) refers to two contrasting views of professionalism as *science-based professionalism* and *pedagogic professionalism*. A concept of *science-based professionalism* is founded on a belief in the effectiveness and outcomes of how education research is translated into practice. In contrast, a *pedagogic professionalism* places agency within the teacher and urges the teacher to make sense of the contradictions or contradictory claims that may be present in education research. This research about professionalism grapples with the myriad ways that novice teachers may conceptualize professionalism.

Teacher educators must strive to debate the discourse of professionalism with novice teachers, urging them to locate themselves within the debate. As novice teachers enter the profession and begin to find themselves in a very practical way within this debate, understanding professionalism will help them gain clarity about how their agency intersects with the structures of schooling.

REFERENCES

Apple, M. (2000). *Official knowledge: Democratic education in a conservative age.* New York, NY: Routledge.

Apple, M. (2006). *Educating the "right" way: Markets, standards, God, and inequality* (2nd ed.). New York, NY: Routledge.

Au, W. (2007). High-stakes testing and curricular control: A qualitative metasynthesis. *Educational Researcher, 36*, 258–67.

Ball, S. J. (2007). *Education plc: Understanding private sector participation in public sector education*. London: Routledge.

Ball, S. J. (2012). Performativity, commodification and commitment: An I-spy guide to the neoliberal university. *British Journal of Educational Studies, 60*, 17–28.

Darling-Hammond, L. (2000). Teacher quality and students' achievement: A review of state policy evidence. *Education Policy Analysis Archives (EPAA)*, 8. http://dx.doi.org/10.14507/epaa.v8n1.2000.

Darling-Hammond, L., Wise, A. E., and Klein, S. P. (1999). *A license to teach: Raising standards for teaching*. San Francisco, CA: Jossey-Bass.

Dodillet, S. (2019). Constructing professionalism in teacher education: Analytical tools from a comparative study. *Education Inquiry, 10*(3), 208–25.

Foucault, M. (2008). *The birth of Biopolitics: Lectures at the College de France, 1978–1979*. New York: Palgrave Macmillan.

Hackman, M. and Morath, E. (2018, December 28). Teachers quit jobs at highest rate on record. *Wall Street Journal*. Accessed January 11, 2023. Retrieved from https://www.wsj.com/articles/teachers-quit-jobs-at-highest-rate-on-record-11545993052.

Hallman, H. L. (2018). Personalized learning through 1:1 technology initiatives: Implications for teachers and teaching in neoliberal times. *Teaching Education*. http://doi.org/10.1080/10476210.2018.1455874.

Hallman, H. L. (2022). At the crux of vocation and profession: Teachers' work in Catholic schools. *International Studies in Catholic Education, 14*(1), 1–16. https://doi.org/10.1080/19422539.2022.2035977.

Hargreaves, A. (2000). Four ages of professionalism and professional learning. *Teachers and Teaching: History and Practice, 6*(2), 151–82.

Hargreaves, A. (2021). What the COVID-19 pandemic has taught us about teachers and teaching. *Facets, 6*, 1835–1863. https://doi.org/10.1139/facets-2021-0084.

Harvey, D. (2007). *A brief history of neoliberalism*. Oxford: Oxford University Press.

Ingersoll, R. M., and Merrill, E. (2011). The status of teaching as a profession. In J. Ballantine and J. Spade (Eds.), *Schools and society: A sociological approach to education* (4th ed., pp. 185–189). Pine Forge, PA. Press/Sage Publications.

Kush, J. M., Badillo-Goicoechea, E., Musci, R. J., and Stuart, E. A. (2022). Teachers' mental health during the COVID-19 pandemic. *Educational Researcher, 51*(9), 593–97.

Kraft, M. A., and Lyon, M. A. (2022). The rise and fall of the teaching profession: Prestige, interest, preparation, and satisfaction over the last half century (EdWorkingPaper: 22-679). Retrieved from Annenberg Institute at Brown University; Accessed January 10, 2023. https://doi.org/10.26300/7b1a-vk92.

Labaree, D. (2004). *The Trouble with Ed Schools*. Yale University Press.

Leiter, J. (1978). The effects of school control structures on teacher perceptions of autonomy. Paper presented at the annual meeting of the American Educational Research Association, Toronto, January 11, 2023.

Lingard, B., Sellar, S., and Savage, G. C. (2014). Test-based accountabilities and data infrastructures: Re-articulations of social justice as equity in education policy. *British Journal of Sociology of Education, 35*(5), 710–30.

Loh, J. and Hu, G. (2014). Subdued by the system: Neoliberalism and the beginning teacher. *Teaching and Teacher Education, 41,* 14–21.

Miles, M. B. and Huberman, A. M. (1994). *Qualitative data analysis: An expanded sourcebook.* Thousand Oaks, CA: Sage Publications.

National Commission on Teaching and America's Future. (1996). *What matters most: Teaching for America s future.* Washington, DC: Government Printing Office.

Rizvi, F. and Lingard, B. (2010). *Globalizing education policy.* New York: Routledge.

Rose, N. (1996). Governing "advanced" liberal democracies. In A. Barry, T. Osborne, and N. Rose (Eds.), *Foucault and political reason: Liberalism, neo-liberalism and rationalities of government* (pp. 37–64). Chicago, IL: The University of Chicago Press.

Samuels, J. J. (1970). Impingements on teacher autonomy. *Urban Education, 5,* 152–71.

Savage, G. C. (2013). Governmentality in practice: Governing the self and others in a marketized education system. In D. Gillies (Ed.), *Educational leadership and Michel Foucault* (pp. 66–84). London: Routledge.

Shulman, L. (1986). Those who understand: Knowledge growth in teaching. *Educational Researcher, 15*(2), 4–14.

Shulman, L. S. (1987). Knowledge and teaching: Foundations of the new reform. *Harvard Educational Review, 57,* 1–22. http://dx.doi.org/10.17763/haer.57.1.j463w79r56455411.

Smyth, J. 2011. *Critical pedagogy for social justice.* New York: Continuum.

Streeter, Leslie. 2021. Why so many teachers are thinking of quitting? *Washington Post Magazine,* October 18, 2021.

Index

The Absolutely True Diary of a Part-Time Indian, 104
adaptive instruction, 152
Alford, Katie, 13
Alston, Chandra L., 131
Alsup, Janet, 7, 13, 22, 42, 129
Amari and the Night Brothers, 40–42, 44
American Progress (painting), 93
Anderson, Laurie Halse, 177
antiracism, 27, 30, 61–62, 64, 67, 70–71, 128–29, 131–33, 161–71
Apple, Michael W., 188, 195
Appleman, Deborah, 79, 87
approximations of practice, 90–91, 97
argument writing, 49–60, 80, 120; Toulmin's model of argumentation, 52
assessment, 27, 39, 56–57, 76–77, 80, 90, 105–10, 117, 120, 127–34, 143–44
attrition of teacher candidates, 155–56
Au, Wayne, 188, 189
awareness to application, 116, 123–24

Baker-Bell, April, 61, 65, 142
Ball, Stephen J., 188, 189
Barker, Lisa M., 111, 112
Beach, Richard, 141
Bell, Julie, 75

Berry, Amanda, 38, 45
Beyond Katrina: A Meditation on the Mississippi Gulf Coast, 44
Bomer, Katherine, 119
Bomer, Randy, 122
book challenges, 41–42, 101–2
Boyer Commission Report, 144
Brass, Jory, 26, 27, 31
Buchmann, Margret, 26, 70, 124
Burke, Brianna R., 101, 103, 109, 113

canonical texts, 40, 75, 77–78, 84, 89, 107–9, 111, 161, 178
Caughlan, Samantha, 6, 8, 12, 28, 65, 116, 124, 141
Cercone, James, 29
Chase, Natalie, 110
Chisholm, James S., 75, 82
The Circuit, 111
classroom context, 20–21, 32–33, 37–45, 61–68
Code Talkers, 168
Collier, Nicole, 12
community of practice, 29, 38–39, 140
"competing centers of gravity," 13, 14, 21, 26–28
complexity of teaching, 190–92
compliance *versus* critique stance, 192–93

Compton, Christa, 75, 90, 97
Compton-Lilly, Catherine, 143
Conklin, Hilary, 8, 119
Consalvo, Annamary, 110, 118
content area literacy, 141
content area methods course, 26, 76, 145
contested space, 61–72
continuous learning, 163
Cook, Mike P., 75, 82
cooperating teacher, 124
COVID-29 pandemic, 101, 116, 154, 168, 171, 187–88, 190–92
Covino, Katharine, 101, 110
craft conscience, 154–55
Critical Media Literacy and Popular Culture in ELA Classrooms, 130
critical race theory (anti-) legislation, 163–64
The Crucible, 78
culturally relevant, or culturally sustaining, 40–45, 61–71, 80
curriculum revision, 61–67, 70–71

Daniels, Harvey, 75, 78, 81
Darling-Hammond, Linda, 185
David, Ann D., 118
descriptive linguistics, 34, 67
dialogism, 12–13; dialogic reflection, 11–22; dialogic teaching, 67–68, 75, 111–12
digital conferences, 117
digital media, 15, 16, 18, 141, 143, 173–74, 176, 178, 180–83, 187
dispositions: teacher candidate professional, 165
dissonance, 25–35. *See also* tension
The Distance Between Us, 94
diversity, 6–8, 15, 20, 40, 53, 65, 77, 103, 106, 109, 129, 130, 132–33, 142, 145, 152, 164, 169, 173, 183; linguistic, 3, 4, 6, 61, 63–72, 107, 132, 141–43, 145; and texts, 4, 39–42, 75–76, 92–98, 106–12, 142
Drama, 107

Ebarvia, Tricia, 101–5, 109, 111
Elbow, Peter, 51, 58
Ellison, Tisha L., 143, 174
Emig, Janet, 7, 129
Endacott, Jason L., 128, 129
Engel, Steven, J., 26
English coursework, 161
Ervin, Jennifer, 105, 106, 110, 112

Falter, Michelle M., 13, 131
Fassbender, William J., 87, 98
Fecho, Bob, 12, 89
Feiman-Nemser, Sharon, 26, 70, 124
field-based teaching and learning, 18–20, 25–35, 37–46, 57, 63–65, 69–70, 116, 141–42, 152
financial hardship, 3, 5, 149–59
first year composition classes (FYC), 116–18, 122
five-paragraph essay, 4, 49–53; alternatives to, 53–59
Fowler-Amato, Michelle, 115, 118, 122
Fredricksen, James E., 26, 83
Freedom Summer, 40, 41
Freire, Paulo, 67, 142
Friese, Elizabeth E. G., 12

Gallagher, Kelly, 11, 51, 127, 166
Gallo, Jessica R., 1, 11, 15, 25, 32, 37, 38, 40, 41, 45, 46, 49, 65, 76, 77, 80, 81, 87–89, 94, 95, 98, 101, 103, 106, 115, 123, 129, 137, 141, 145, 149, 173, 177, 178
Garcia, Antero, 42, 75
García, Ofelia, 143
George, Marshall, 128, 130, 163
Germán, Lorena, 40, 41, 102, 109, 111
The Giver, 78
Glazer, Jeremy, 149
Goering, Christian Z., 127–32, 134, 161, 163, 171
Goldhaber, Dan, 29
grammar and language instruction, 18–19, 31–34, 65
Green, John, 176–77, 181

Greenfield, Kristina, 101, 103, 109, 113
Grossman, Pam, 75, 90, 91, 97, 98
Guise, Megan, 75, 79, 82–84

Haddix, Marcelle, 42
Hallman, Heidi L., 6, 8, 11, 13, 15, 25, 28, 32, 37, 38, 40, 41, 45, 46, 49, 65, 76, 77, 80, 81, 87–89, 94, 95, 98, 101, 103, 106, 115, 116, 123, 124, 129, 137, 141, 145, 149, 173, 177, 178, 185, 186, 188
Hamlet, 78
Hargreaves, Andy, 186, 187, 190, 195
Harkness discussions, 89
Hatchet, 92
Haviland, Victoria S., 26
Hillocks, George, 51
historical teacher preparation, 186–87
How the Garcia Girls Lost Their Accent, 107
How to Be an Antiracist, 162

identity: authors, 177, 180–81; professional, 4, 7, 13–15, 20–21, 94–95, 103–6, 119, 129, 155, 157, 163, 166–67, 185–95; students, 13, 16–17, 19–21, 67–69, 102–3, 105, 166–67
Igra, Danielle, 75, 90, 97
inquiry-based teaching, 49–52, 59, 67–68, 122, 144
Intercultural Development Inventory, 171
interdisciplinary, 43–45, 93–94
International Literacy Association, 137
interpretivist methods, 141
Into Thin Air, 92

Jensen, Amber, 11, 13
Johnson, Lamar, 62, 63, 142
Juzwik, Mary M., 12

Kendi, Ibram X., 131, 162, 167, 169, 170
Kerns, William, 137, 138
King and the Dragonflies, 40

Kittle, Penny, 11, 51
Klein, Stephen P., 185
Krieg, John M., 29

Lamott, Anne, 58
Lave, Jean, 140
Lee, Crystal C., 131
Leiva, Camila, 143
lens activity, 167–68
lesson planning, 87–88, 97, 132, 175; model, 88–90
Lewis, William, 87, 89, 90, 92
LGBTQ+ texts, 107–8
Lillge, Danielle M., 26, 31
Lingard, Bob, 188, 189
Listen, Slowly, 40
Liston, Daniel P., 13, 38
literature circles, 4, 34, 39, 43, 75–84
Lochte, Hilary, 61
Long, Danette, 98
Long Sloan, DeAnn, 75, 79, 82–84
Long Way Down, 40
Lord of the Flies, 110
Luke, Allan, 142, 174
Lupo, Sarah M., 87, 89, 90, 92
Lyiscott, Jamila, 130

Malcahy, Cara, 110
Manning, Logan, 162
Marcus Vega Doesn't Speak Spanish, 40
McKenna, Michael C., 87, 89, 90, 92
metacognition, 51, 57–58
Metz, Mike, 49
Mirra, Nicole, 130
A Monster Calls, 40
Moore, Cynthia P., 11, 13, 26
Moore, Jazmen, 162
Moore, Michael, 42
Morrell, Ernest, 42, 102, 103, 112, 143, 144
Muhammad, Gholdy, 67, 70
multilingual students, 142–43, 162
multimodality, 39, 42–43, 45, 69, 92, 97, 162, 171

narrative writing, 54–57
National Reading Panel, 140
navigating genres, 122
NCTE Beliefs about Methods Courses and Field Experiences in English Education, 11, 15, 25, 32, 37, 38, 40, 41, 45, 46, 49, 59, 60, 65, 76, 77, 80, 81, 87–89, 94, 95, 98, 101, 103, 106, 115, 123, 129, 137, 141, 145, 149, 173, 177, 178
NCTE James R. Squire Office of Policy Research in ELA, 130
NCTE position statement: Educators' Right and Responsibilities to Engage in Antiracist Teaching, 133
NCTE Standards for Initial Preparation of English Language Arts Teachers, Grades, 17–22, 163
Newell, George E., 90, 97
New Kid, 40, 41, 45
Nyachae, Tiffany, M., 101, 107, 111, 112

O'Brien, David, 141
O'Donnell-Allen, Cindy, 75
Olan, Elsie L., 26, 83
Olsen, Kristofer, 98
Ordinary Girls, 107
Orzulak, Melinda J. M., 26
Other Words for Home, 40–42, 45
The Outsiders, 77

Palace, Crystal, 75, 78, 81, 83
Parker, Kimberly N., 40, 102, 109, 111
Parsons, Christopher M., 1, 11, 15, 25, 28, 32, 37, 38, 40, 41, 45, 46, 49, 65, 76, 77, 80, 81, 87–89, 94, 95, 98, 101, 103, 106, 115, 123, 129, 137, 141, 145, 149, 173, 177, 178
Pasternak, D. L., 6, 8, 28, 65, 116, 124, 128, 130, 141, 163
Pastore-Capuana, Kristen, 11, 15, 25, 29, 32, 37, 38, 40, 41, 45, 46, 49, 61, 65, 76, 77, 80, 81, 87–89, 94, 95, 98, 101, 103, 106, 115, 123, 129, 137, 141, 145, 149, 173, 177, 178

pedagogical content knowledge, 4, 37–46, 142
pedagogic professionalism, 195
Pell Grants, 150
Perry, Kristen H., 143
Pet, 40, 42, 44
Peterman, Nora, 173, 174, 177, 181
political context, 7, 21, 27, 30, 45, 49, 61–62, 65, 71, 91, 101–3, 129, 139–40, 150–51, 163–64, 177–78, 181–82, 187
positivist models, 140
Pradl, Gordon, 7, 129
prescriptive linguistics, 32–33, 50–51, 59, 64, 67, 68
priority setting, 155
professional community, 2, 7, 11–14, 20–21, 62, 89, 152, 158–59; and anti-racism, 131, 162–65
professionalism, 185–95
program advising, 158
program redesign, 63–66, 103, 113, 130
public view of teachers, 61, 101–2; and neoliberalism, 188–89

questionnaires, 156–57

Ragland, Jeff, 75, 78, 81, 83
rationale for teaching, 4, 7, 30–31, 34, 37–46, 49–59, 76–84, 87, 91–95, 109, 129, 133, 137, 157
reading instruction: interactive models of, 139; science of, 137–38; social practice, 140–41, 152; top down *versus* bottom up models, 138–39
reflection, 4, 5, 8, 11–22, 26, 32–35, 38–39, 43, 57–58, 65–68, 81–83, 102–4, 115–25, 132–33, 152, 157, 165–71, 175; critical reflection, 12–13, 34, 167, 179–80
Reinking, David, 137
Renzi, Laura, 6, 8, 28, 65, 116, 124, 141
research writing, 49–52, 144
retention of teachers, 63–64, 155–56, 187–88

Rhym, Darren, 13, 26
Riesco, Holly S., 161, 171
Ringler Pet, Sue, 11, 15, 25, 32, 37, 38, 40, 41, 45, 46, 49, 65, 76, 77, 80, 81, 87–89, 94, 95, 98, 101, 103, 106, 115, 123, 129, 137, 141, 145, 149, 173, 177, 178
Riordan, Rick, 178
Rizvi, Fazal, 189
Roberts, Kate, 87, 90, 94
Ronfeldt, Matthew, 75, 90, 97
Rush, Leslie S., 6, 8, 28, 65, 116, 124, 141

Savage, Glenn C., 188
Scarborough's Reading Rope, 139–40
Schaafsma, David, 42
Scherff, Lisa, 143
Schutz, Kristine M., 91, 98
science-based professionalism, 195
Searcy, Lara, 11, 15, 25, 32, 37, 38, 40, 41, 45, 46, 49, 65, 76, 77, 80, 81, 87–89, 94, 95, 98, 101, 103, 106, 115, 123, 127, 129, 137, 141, 145, 149, 165, 173, 177, 178
Sellar, Sam, 188
Semingson, Peggy, 138
Shahan, Emily, 75, 90, 97
Shaughnessy, Meghan M., 91, 98
Shea, Brooke, 111, 112
Shelton, Stephanie A., 11
Shipp, Lyschel, 102, 110
Shoffner, Melanie, 37, 42, 131
Show Me a Sign, 40
Shulman, Lee S., 12, 37, 38, 142, 185
Simple View of Reading, 138–40
Smagorinsky, Peter, 6, 11, 13, 26, 75, 76, 79, 80, 83, 137, 143
social justice in teacher education, 4, 16–17, 31, 41, 61–72, 98, 101–2, 110–12, 125, 130–34, 143, 149–59, 161–71, 177, 181–82; linguistic justice, 31, 61–72
social media, 173–83

socratic seminars, 89
Specialized Professional Association (SPA) program, 127–29
standardized tests, 52–53, 63–64, 102, 143–44, 178, 189
standards, 127–34, 161–71, 185, 188; accreditation, 6, 127, 128, 130; Common Core, 92, 128; ELA and content standards, 6, 39, 41, 59, 64, 67, 80, 87, 94, 98, 141, 145, 189; NCTE Standards for Initial Preparation of English Language Arts Teachers, Grades, 5, 17–22, 30, 64, 127–34, 163–65, 167; resistance *versus* acceptance, 191–95
Strom, Kathryn J., 115, 123
Strong, John Z., 87, 89, 90, 92
structured literacy, 139
student voice, 66–67, 182–83

Teachers, Profs, Parents, Writers Who Care blog, 118
teachers as agents of change, 31, 61–62, 71, 102–3
teachers as critical pedagogues, 102–3, 169, 194
technocratic professional, 193–94
Tensen, Tracy, 111, 112
tension, 13, 16–19, 21–22, 25–35, 62–66, 69–70, 95–96, 150, 153–59, 190–91, 194
text sets, 4, 39–40, 43, 75–77, 80, 87–98, 107
Thein, Amanda H., 75, 79, 82–84
Theobald, Roddy, 29
There There, 92
Thomas, Angie, 177, 179–81
To Kill a Mockingbird, 78
Torres, Julia, 40, 102, 109, 111
Tovani, Cris, 77, 80
Tremmel, Robert, 7, 129
Twitter: authors' use of, 175–85
"two-worlds pitfall," 9, 26, 70, 124, 154, 194

The Underground Railroad, 93
unit planning, 4, 27, 40, 43–45, 75–84
university-school partnerships, 8, 25–35, 116, 124
university writing center, 118–19

VanDerHeide, Jennifer, 90, 97
Van Driel, Jan H., 38, 45
Viesca, Kara M., 115, 123
Villanueva, Victor, 162
visual texts, 14, 42–43, 79, 87, 93, 179–80
vocation, 187

Walpole, Sharon, 87, 89, 90, 92
Warner, Connor K., 173, 174, 177, 181
Wender, Emily, 149
Wenger, Etienne, 38, 140
What Matters Most: Teaching for America's Future, 185
Whiting, Melissa E., 6
Whitney, Anne E., 26, 83

Williamson, Peter W., 75, 90, 97
Wilson, Amy A., 12
Wise, Arthur E., 185
Wolf Hollow, 40
work hours: for teachers, 153; for teacher candidates, 154–55
working class colleges, 150–51
A Wrinkle in Time, 77
writing conferences, 117–25
writing instruction, 49–60
writing structure, 49–54; alternatives, 53–57
Wynhoff Olsen, Allison, 87, 90, 97, 98

Yaden, David, B., 137
Yagelski, Robert P., 7, 129
young adult literature, 4, 5, 39–45, 104, 161, 174–83; and authors' social media, 175

Zeichner, Kenneth M., 8, 12, 13, 38, 119
Zuidema, Leah, 42

About the Authors

JULIE BELL

Julie Bell is an associate professor of Teacher Education and the Secondary Education Graduate program chair at the University of Nebraska at Omaha. She teaches undergraduate courses in content area reading and English language arts methods and graduate courses in young adult literature and the secondary capstone. Bell's research interests include English education and the mentoring of preservice and in-service teachers.

KATHARINE COVINO

Katharine Covino is an associate professor of English Studies, who teaches writing, literature, and teacher-preparation classes at Fitchburg State University. Current scholarship explores (a) critical pedagogy, (b) applying indigenous lenses to cultural myths, and (c) action research with English teachers. Covino has recently published *Teaching/Writing: The Journal of Writing Teacher Education* (2021), *English Journal* (2020), and in the edited collection *Young Adult and Canonical Literature: Pairing and Teaching* (2021). Before university teaching, she taught middle school and high school in Austin, Texas.

WILLIAM J. FASSBENDER

William J. Fassbender is an assistant professor of English Education at Montana State University. He teaches undergraduate and graduate courses on reading, planning, instruction, and assessment, digital literacies, and qualitative research methods. His current research focuses on media literacy and the impact of technology on secondary English classrooms.

MICHELLE FOWLER-AMATO

Michelle Fowler-Amato is an associate professor of English education and the director of English teacher education in Old Dominion University's English department. She teaches undergraduate and graduate courses in composition and English methods. Michelle's research interests include adolescent literacy, critical and culturally sustaining approaches to English education, and the use of design-based research and teacher inquiry groups to work toward equity, access, and justice in classrooms and school communities.

JESSICA R. GALLO

Jessica R. Gallo is an associate professor of English Education at the University of Nevada, Reno. Her research focuses on English teacher preparation, middle and secondary writing pedagogy, and rural education. Gallo has served as co-chair of the English Language Arts Teacher Educators (ELATE) Commission on Methods Teaching and Learning (2019–2023). She has also been a National Writing Project Teacher Leader since 2008 and is a former co-director for the Rural Wisconsin Writing Institute, a site of the Fox Valley Writing Project.

JEREMY GLAZER

Jeremy Glazer is a former high school teacher and is currently an assistant professor in English Education at the Rowan University College of Education. He teaches undergraduate and graduate courses in English methods as well as educational foundations. His research interests include the lives of teachers and classroom discussion.

CHRISTIAN Z. GOERING

Christian Z. Goering is a professor of curriculum and instruction at the University of Arkansas where he prepares future English teachers, teachers of English teachers, and educational researchers to interpret and act on the world for good. He serves as coordinator of secondary education, director of the Northwest Arkansas Writing Project, and as vice-chair of faculty senate. From 2018 to 2020, he chaired the English Language Arts Teacher Educators.

HEIDI L. HALLMAN

Heidi L. Hallman is a professor and chair in the Department of Curriculum and Teaching at the University of Kansas. Her research interests include studying how prospective teachers are prepared to teach in diverse school contexts. Hallman's published work includes a coauthored book *Secondary English Teacher Education in the United States: Responding to a Changing Context* (Bloomsbury 2017), a national study of how English teachers are prepared.

AMBER JENSEN

Amber Jensen is an assistant professor of English at Brigham Young University, where she teaches methods, writing pedagogy, and digital literacies courses to undergraduate preservice English teachers and directs the Central Utah Writing Project. Jensen's research interests include teacher development, agency and advocacy, writing instruction across modes and genres, and secondary school writing centers. She is the founding editor of *The Journal of Peer Tutoring in Secondary Schools*.

WILLIAM KERNS

William Kerns is an assistant professor in the School of Education for the University of Arkansas at Little Rock. He teaches undergraduate and graduate courses in methods of instruction, literature, content area reading, and literacy. His research interests include historical and current trends in discourse on the science of reading, and critical literacy in the teaching of literature.

HILARY LOCHTE

Hilary Lochte is an assistant professor at Buffalo State University, in the English Department. Her research, teaching, and service focus on the needs of students and teachers in urban schools, as she provides support for new and practicing teachers to utilize diverse literature in service of culturally sustaining literacy. She teaches courses in children's literature, young adult literature and language, literacy, and culture in teaching. She also supervises student teachers.

MIKE METZ

Mike Metz is an assistant professor of English Education and the director of Teacher Education at the University of Missouri. He teaches undergraduate and graduate courses in language and literacy education. His research examines teaching practices that promote Critical Language Awareness in secondary schools with publications across the fields of English Education, Linguistics, and Teacher Education.

CHRISTOPHER M. PARSONS

Christopher M. Parsons is associate professor of English Education and Coordinator of Secondary English Education at Keene State College, New Hampshire. He teaches courses on English grammar and language ideologies and methods of teaching secondary English. He also works as a college field instructor for ELA teacher candidates. His scholarship on methods courses and field instruction has been published in the journal *English Education* and the edited collection *Methods into Practice: New Visions in Teaching the English Language Arts Methods Course*. Parsons served as co-chair of the English Language Arts Teacher Educators (ELATE) Commission on Methods Teaching and Learning (2019–2023).

KRISTEN PASTORE-CAPUANA

Kristen Pastore-Capuana is an assistant professor of English at Buffalo State University, where she teaches undergraduate and graduate English education courses. She is also the co-coordinator of field experiences and community partnerships. Her research interests include critical literacy practices, secondary English language arts teacher development, and teacher agency. Prior to becoming a teacher educator, Kristen taught high school English language arts at Cheektowaga Central. She is also the assistant director of the Western New York Network of English Teachers (WNYNET).

NORA PETERMAN

Nora Peterman is an assistant professor of Language and Literacy and Urban Teacher Education at the University of Missouri–Kansas City. She teaches undergraduate and graduate courses in children's literature and literacy methods. Her research interests include children's and young adult literatures, digital literacies, and the cultural, political, and intergenerational dimensions of youth literacy and language learning.

LARA SEARCY

Lara Searcy is an associate professor, English Education Specialist at Northeastern State University in Tahlequah, Oklahoma, where she teaches and advises English teacher candidates. She is a former high school English teacher and middle school Literacy Resource Specialist and is Nationally Board Certified in AYA-ELA. Her research interests include teacher efficacy, standards-based reforms, social justice literacies, and teacher professional development. She is a proud member of the National Council of Teachers of English (NCTE) and is the former President of the Oklahoma affiliate (OKCTE).

HOLLY SHEPPARD RIESCO

Holly Sheppard Riesco is currently a third-year doctoral student at the University of Arkansas in the Curriculum and Instruction program in English Education. Prior to entering the doctoral program, she taught secondary ELA for fifteen years. Her research interests center critical literacy, new literacies, young adult literature, and the valuation of students' lived literacies. She has coauthored the book *Adolescent Realities: Engaging Students in SEL through Young Adult Literature* (Rowman & Littlefield 2020).

MELANIE SHOFFNER

Melanie Shoffner is a professor of education in the College of Education at James Madison University, Virginia, where she regularly teaches courses in ELA methods, curriculum theory, and literature. Her scholarship focuses on dispositional development and reflective practice in teacher education; recent publications include the coedited book *Reconstructing Care in Teacher Education after COVID-19: Caring Enough to Change* (Routledge 2022). She is a former chair of ELATE, former Fulbright Scholar to Romania, and current editor of *English Education*.

CONNOR K. WARNER

Connor K. Warner is an associate professor in the University of Utah Urban Institute for Teacher Education. Dr. Warner's primary scholarly agenda centers on the development and design of preservice teacher preparation programs, while his secondary research interests include representation of minoritized groups in K-12 English and Social Studies curricula and the role of social media in shaping reader interactions with young adult literature. He is the coauthor of *Rethinking Teacher Preparation Program Design* (Routledge 2021).

EMILY WENDER

Emily Wender is a professor of English at Indiana University of Pennsylvania. A former middle and high school English teacher, she teaches methods courses and supervises field experiences. Her current research interests include developing teacher and reader identities and diversifying the teacher workforce.

ALLISON WYNHOFF OLSEN

Allison Wynhoff Olsen is an assistant professor of English education at Montana State University and director of the Yellowstone Writing Project. A former high school English teacher, Wynhoff Olsen examines the relational processes of writing in classrooms, curricular moves that promote a *listening argument*, and how a rural sense of belonging mediates teachers' experiences with curriculum as well as their schools and local communities. Her published work includes a coauthored book *Teaching English in Rural Communities: Toward a Critical Rural English Pedagogy* (Rowman & Littlefield 2021).

www.ingramcontent.com/pod-product-compliance
Lightning Source LLC
Chambersburg PA
CBHW031833230426
43669CB00009B/1335